IMAGES
of America

KNOXVILLE'S 1982 WORLD'S FAIR

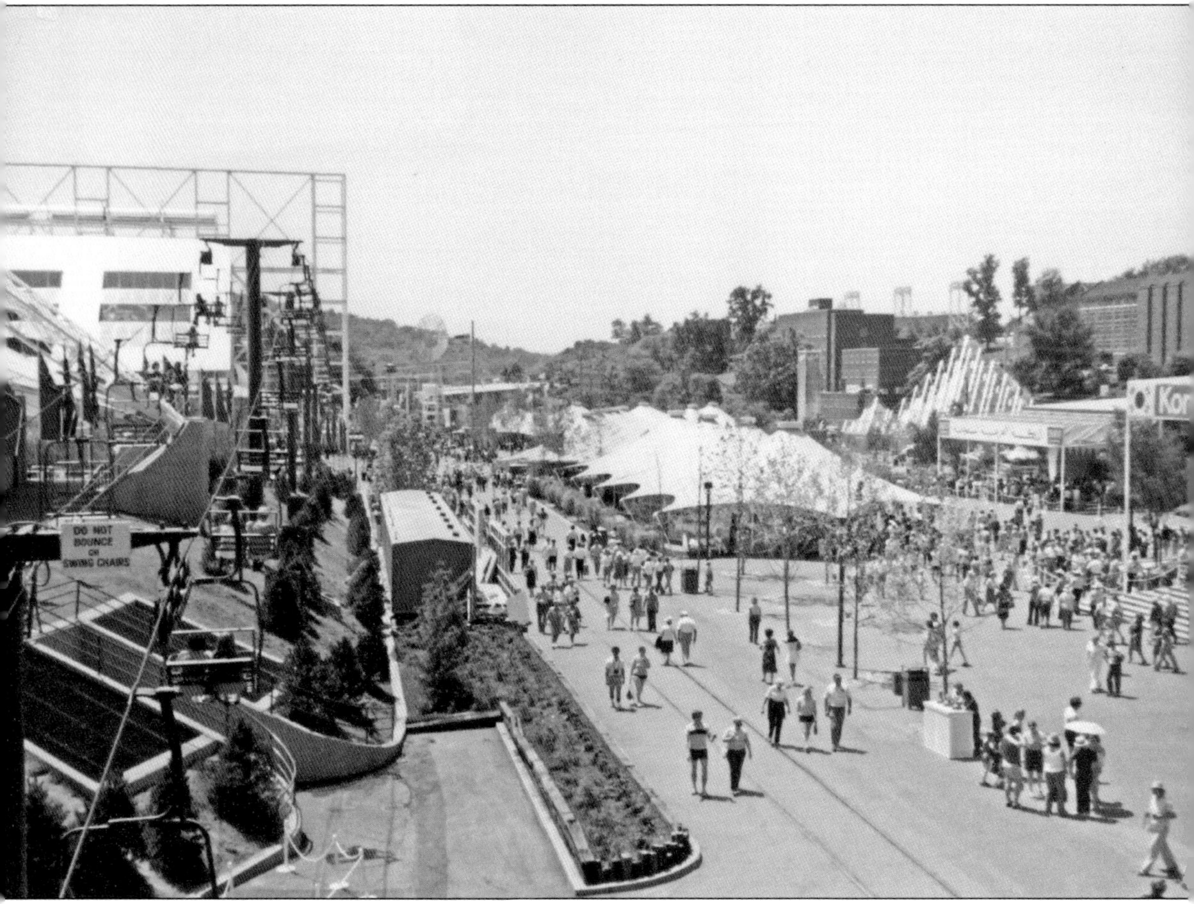

On the Cover: From May 1, 1982, until October 31, 1982, the city of Knoxville, Tennessee, invited the world to visit, as 22 countries participated in the first world's fair to be located in the southeastern part of the United States. The theme , "Energy Turns the World," was appropriate and provided a rallying point for the participating countries, vendors, and citizens of Knoxville as they prepared for the big event. Visitors arrived by the thousands to see the exhibits, enjoy the entertainment, ride the rides, buy souvenirs, meet new people, and sample foods from around the world. The International Energy Exposition was called Expo '82 and "one big party" by the media, who also claimed, "You've got to be there."

IMAGES
of America

KNOXVILLE'S 1982 WORLD'S FAIR

Martha Rose Woodward

ARCADIA
PUBLISHING

ISBN 978-0-7385-6835-5

Published by Arcadia Publishing
Charleston, South Carolina

Printed in the United States of America

Library of Congress Catalog Card Number: 2008937403

For all general information contact Arcadia Publishing at:
Telephone 843-853-2070
Fax 843-853-0044
E-mail sales@arcadiapublishing.com
For customer service and orders:
Toll-Free 1-888-313-2665

Visit us on the Internet at www.arcadiapublishing.com

Contents

ACKNOWLEDGMENTS

Writing history is a tedious endeavor that requires help from many resources and numerous people.

First I want to thank my fine son, Barrett, who kept my household running, which freed my time for writing. He was also sent on many trips to get paper, ink, fresh fruit, and other supplies, which he did in good spirits. He frequently helped me to laugh at the problems instead of yielding to the frustrations.

I also want to thank my two wonderful daughters, Erin Akroush and Ashley Danzey, and their kind husbands, Sam Akroush and Gordon Danzey, for their encouragement and humor. They cheered me on and kept me laughing.

Once again, as with my first book, I relied heavily on three men—former mayor Randy Tyree, Jesse Barr, and William Denton—for information and photographs. I appreciate them for the kindnesses they have shown me and their wisdom and help on research.

Mark Rowlett, who works at Thompson Photos, became a real source of help as he pointed me toward the Frank H. McClung Museum, which led me to director J. Chapman, who helped greatly, and to computer wizard, Laura Starrett, who converted slides to TIF files.

Mendy Prather Hyde, who responded to my plea through an e-mail to a mutual friend, provided me with excellent photographs made by her dad, Jim Prather, which allowed us to get a great view of a typical visit to the fair. I am pleased Jim's photograph was selected as the cover image.

Many thanks as well to photographers Charlie Brookes and Miles Roberts, who gave permission to use the hundreds of slides they made during the fair. I could not have completed the book without their beautiful photographs.

INTRODUCTION

Although gold dust is precious, when it gets in your eyes it obstructs your vision.

—His-tang Chih Tsang, Zen master (735–814)

Before there was a World's Fair in Knoxville, a group known as the Downtown Businessman's Association (DBA) met every Friday at noon to discuss business possibilities for the city of Knoxville. They often discussed two major problems: l. lack of jobs and 2. the need to do something about an unsightly plot of 70 acres of land that adjoined the campus of the University of Tennessee to the downtown district of the city. Not much was going on at that site except for rats, rubbish, rabbits, and deserted railroad cars.

These city leaders wanted to clean up the eyesore and provide jobs. They needed a big idea, and hosting a World's Fair began to be tossed around as a possibility after Stewart Evans, a member of the DBA, visited Oklahoma and heard a presentation by a man named King Cole.

Cole set a fire in Evans with a glowing review of the 1974 World's Fair hosted by Spokane, Washington. Although the 1982 World's Fair was often called "Jake's Fair," after the president of the United American Bank who was instrumental in securing the loans needed to make the fair a reality, Stewart Evans was the first man with the plan.

Jake Butcher and his older brother C. H. Butcher Jr. were heavily involved in every financial deal for the fair, but there were hundreds of businessmen and women involved in the day-to-day work of the production of this massive undertaking.

Since Knoxvillians had lived through the recession of the 1970s by wearing WIN, or "Whip Inflation Now," buttons suggested by Pres. Gerald Ford and had suffered in long lines at the pump because of the gas rationing under Pres. Jimmy Carter, people were searching for something to feel good about. They were also seeking jobs that might put some money into their pockets.

As Mayor Kyle Testerman began the process of leading the city into the future with the idea of hosting a World's Fair, he created a committee he named Knoxville's International Energy Exposition. However, a younger man, Randy Tyree, who had movie-star good looks, amazed the city by declaring himself as a candidate for the office of mayor and shocked them by winning the election by 350 votes in a memorable upset. He came into office at age 34 as the youngest man ever to be elected to the office of mayor in Knoxville, Tennessee. He brought along his wife, Mary Pat, a former beauty queen, and quickly took up the matter of the 1982 World's Fair Project. The handsome mayor and his glamorous wife made such a stir in social circles they were dubbed by the press as "Ken and Barbie," a nickname that brings a smile to their faces to this date.

Mayor Tyree took up the work on the World's Fair by working closely with the Knoxville International Energy Exposition (KIEE). He relied heavily on Jake Butcher as the chairman of the KIEE and Bo Roberts as the president. Tyree also named numerous other individuals into key positions. Roger Hibbs was treasurer, Thomas Sudman was secretary, King Cole was executive consultant, James Drinnon was general manager, Charles Fraser was U.S. commissioner general,

Thomas Bell was chairman of the Management Committee, and as commissioner general, Dortch Oldham was the senior official for the U.S. government. Hundreds of others worked on the fair; it was a group effort that would see the fair to its completion.

Mayor Tyree and KIEE faced daily opposition as a local group, known simply as "Citizens Against the Fair," held them to the fire and pushed for the issue of hosting a fair to be placed on a ballot so citizens could simply vote it up or down. This never happened, leaving many bitter against the mayor, city council, and the Butchers.

The success or failure of the fair was interwoven in the financial dealings of the Butcher brothers, the flamboyant bankers who were spreading money around town like water out of a sprinkler. Another key player in the mix was Jesse Barr, who worked for Jake in his bank in downtown Knoxville. Many say Jake was the man with the golden personality who was out front getting all the attention, while Jesse was the workhorse doing the day-to-day deals. As public and private money was mixed, the city, and just about anyone who wanted a loan, was able to secure the multimillions of dollars needed for an effort as massive as that of a World's Fair. Architects, attorneys, engineers, carpenters, painters, cashiers, ride attendants, entrepreneurs, and many others worked tirelessly for over two years on "all things World's Fair." The fairgrounds resembled a busy beehive as each worker did his/her part. On April 30, 1982, as final touches were placed on the exposition, there was a lot of celebrating and hand clapping as everything was ready for the event to open on schedule on May 1, 1982.

After a festive opening ceremony full of colorful pageantry, which included introductions of the Knoxville International Energy Exposition committee members as well as dignitaries, politicians, dancers, and singers, U.S. jets flew over the fair site. Everyone settled in for performances by choirs, bands, and a presentation by the military.

Pres. Ronald Reagan gave the keynote address at noon on May 1, 1982, on the subject of energy to fit with the fair's theme, "Energy Turns the World." As he spoke from the Court of Flags, an estimated 87,000 people cheered wildly.

On the scorching hot days from May 1 until October 31 in 1982, huge crowds poured through the gates as "the world came to Knoxville." Attendance the first week reached over 387,000. The daily average was 60,000, and the overall number of visitors reached 11,141,00.

There were some disagreements about the total attendance for the fair. The daily average was said to be 60,000, while the grand total was 11,141,000; however, it was not known how many who went through the turnstiles were actually paying customers. Many who attended the fair were employees, while some held season passes and should have been counted only once. Some were vendors and delivery personnel, and others won or were given free tickets. There were discounts given for group tours. Once at the fair, many visitors left the fairgrounds and returned during one visit. Record keeping was not precise; therefore, it is estimated that approximately six million actually paid the full price to get into the fair.

Twenty-two countries from around the world shared their artifacts, fashions, dances, music, and more. Over 200 entertainers performed, including Bob Hope, Charlie Pride, Jerry Lee Lewis, Dinah Shore, Glen Campbell, June and Johnny Cash, Loretto Lynn, gospel quartets, cloggers, ballet dancers, high school and college bands, and many, many more.

Knoxville's 1982 World's Fair was called "one big party" as the people, the fashions, the food, the fun, and the memories all came together for the "scruffy little city by the river" as it turned the corner on technology and faced its future.

One

Before the Fair

You got to be careful if you don't know where you're going, because you might not get there.

—Yogi Berra

The April 1970 description in the *Wall Street Journal* referring to Knoxville, Tennessee, as "the scruffy little city by the Tennessee River" became the rallying call for the Knoxville International Energy Exposition, or KIEE, who felt they had a lot to prove to those smart guys up in New York City.

In August 1976, Stewart Evans and his group of downtown businessmen, who first came up with the idea of hosting a fair, applied to the Bureau of International Expositions (BIE) in Paris, France, for permission to host a fair in Knoxville and began buying the required amount of land and setting the finances into place. An official announcement of approval came in December 1978 as Pres. Jimmy Carter sent a letter to KIEE.

"Expo '82" was made possible by a five-step financial ladder built on a 43-bank foundation. The fair's planners sought grants and public funding to reduce the city's cost for financing the fair and the redevelopment of the 70 acres in the Lower Second Creek Valley. Pres. Jimmy Carter also helped with financing by working to secure the approval of $12.45 million in various federal grants, while the Knoxville City Council pledged $11.6 million in tax-increment bonds. Other public funding included $20 million for a federal pavilion and $10 million for a state pavilion. City council also added $12 million in bonds to be paid by the buildings' revenues after the fair. The grants and bond money totaled $66 million.

In order to secure the cash flow that was going to be needed for the daily operations of the fair, a five-tier plan was created. Tier One was $2 million from six Knoxville banks. Much of this money had already been loaned and was to be repaid last. Tier Two was $2 million from six Knoxville banks backed by corporate guarantees. This would be the second of the moneys drawn on for use and the fourth repaid. Tier Three was $6 million from First National Bank of St. Louis, Missouri. This was the third of the moneys used and the third to be repaid. Tier Four was $3 million from First National Bank of St. Louis. This was the fourth drawn on for use and the second repaid. Tier Five was $12 million, which was made up of $5 million from Chemical Bank of New York; $3.5 million from American Security Bank of Washington, D.C.; $1 million each from Commerce Union Bank in Nashville, Barclays International Bank of London, and First National Bank of Atlanta, Georgia; and $500,000 from the National Bank in Charlotte, North Carolina. This would be the last money used and the first repaid.

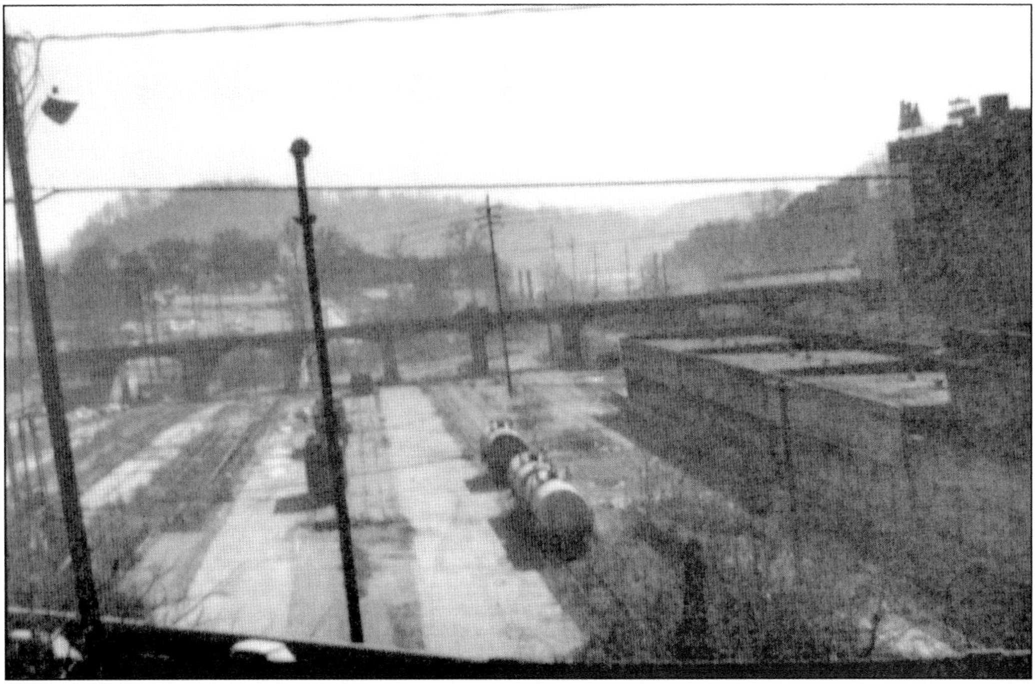

In 1974, Knoxville, Tennessee, faced the problem of urban blight with the 70 acres of land adjoining the University of Tennessee and the city's business district. Something needed to be done to clean up the land and build something on it that would bring in more tax revenues. (Courtesy of Randy Tyree.)

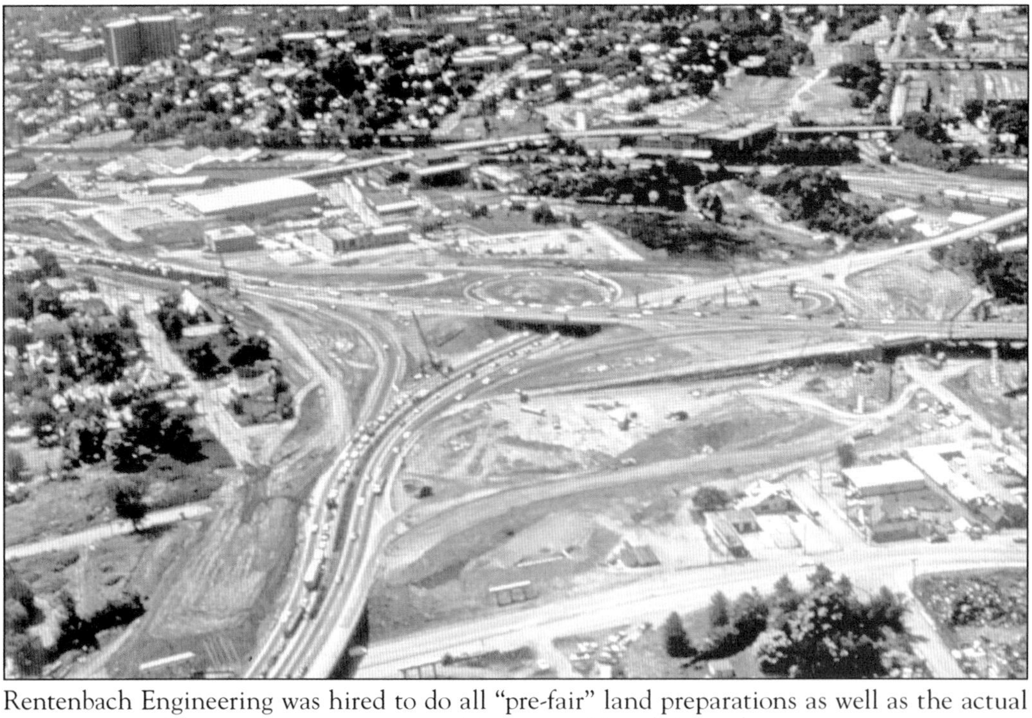

Rentenbach Engineering was hired to do all "pre-fair" land preparations as well as the actual construction of the permanent structures. (Courtesy of Randy Tyree.)

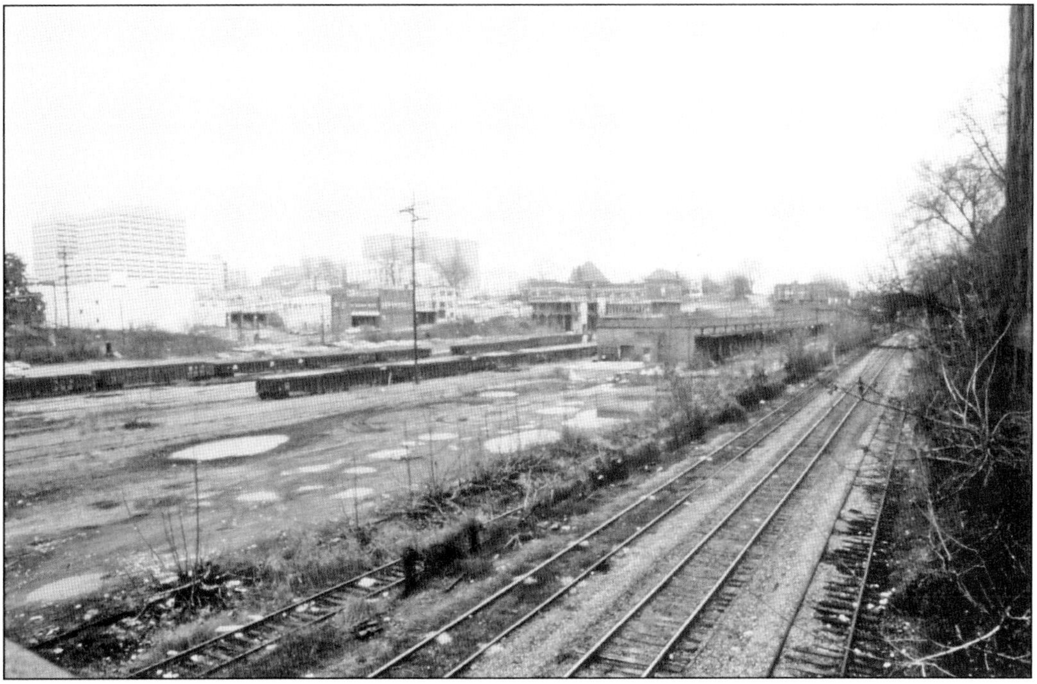

The railroad yard had once been a busy and important center for commerce. However, changes in the way goods were delivered and time had taken its toll on the area. Of the 13 railroad tracks that covered the acreage, 12 were removed. (Courtesy of Randy Tyree.)

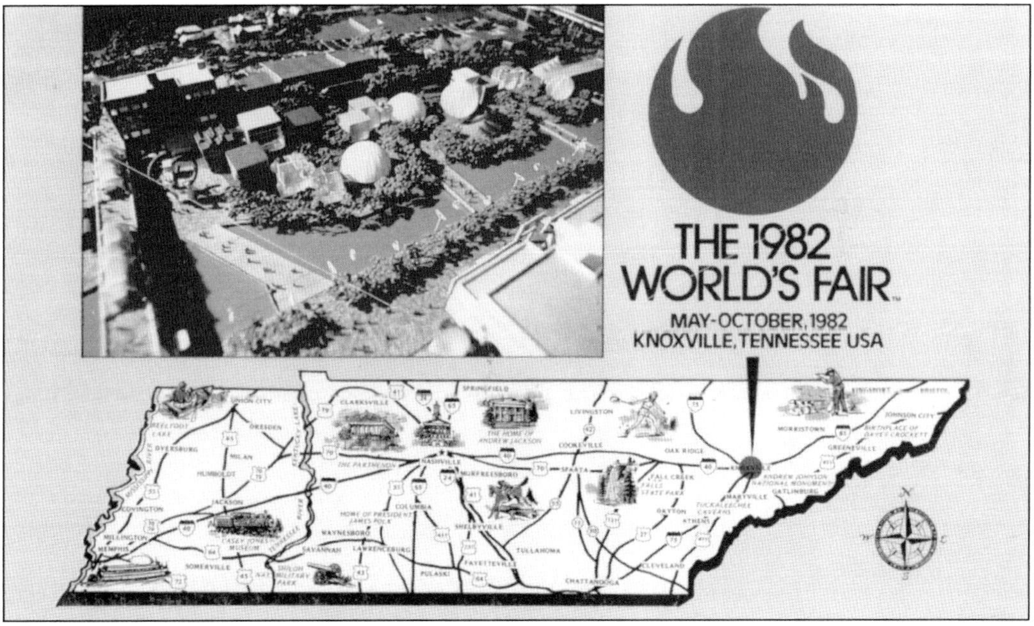

This postcard helped visitors by providing a map of the state of Tennessee, as all roads are shown leading to Knoxville. The red "circular flame" logo became popular during the fair; it was painted and printed on everything. The fair site is shown on this card in a pre-planning artist rendition done for the KIEE. It would change dramatically as buildings and pavilions became a reality. (Courtesy of KIEE.)

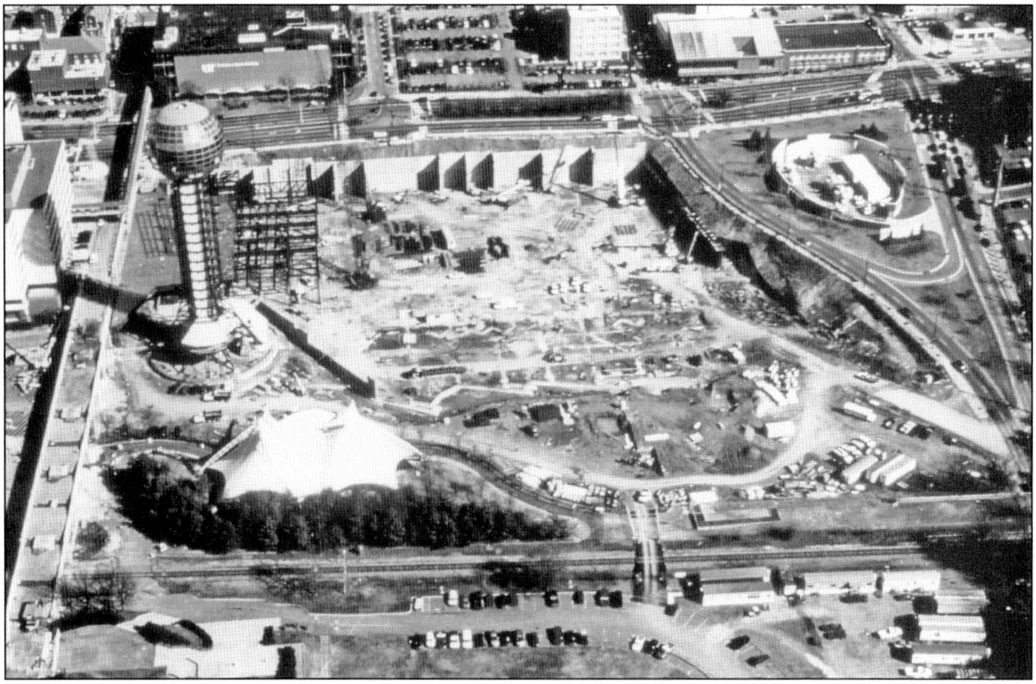

Members of KIEE point to the facts that the fair opened on time, hosted 11 million plus visitors, and generated enough money to pay off some loans. (Courtesy of Randy Tyree.)

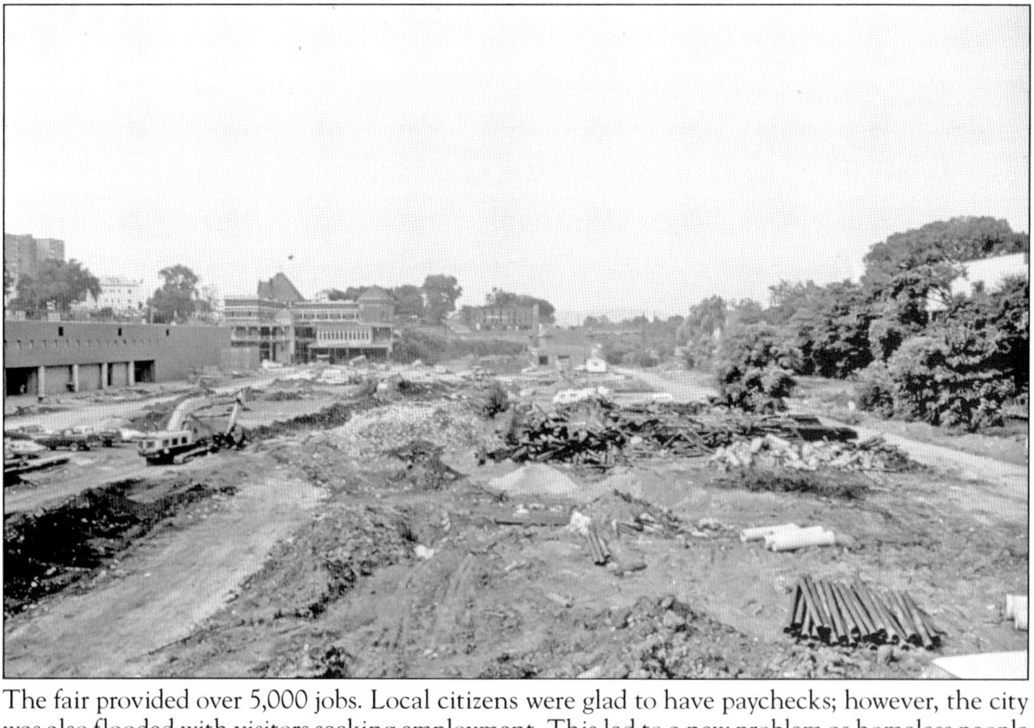

The fair provided over 5,000 jobs. Local citizens were glad to have paychecks; however, the city was also flooded with visitors seeking employment. This led to a new problem as homeless people wandered the downtown area in search of food and shelter. (Courtesy of Randy Tyree.)

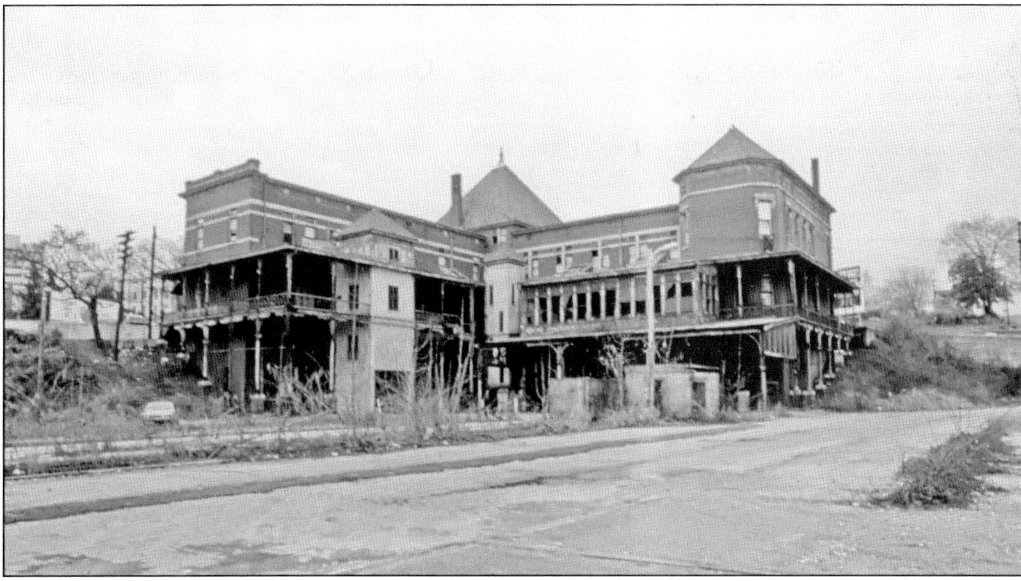

One of the buildings that remained on the fair site was the L&N train station, built in 1917. Much care was taken to restore the building to its grandeur. The stained-glass windows set back into place cost over $1,750 per window, a huge sum of money at the time. The building became the site for office space, an upscale restaurant, and public restrooms. It was used by fairgoers as a place to find some relief from heat as temperatures soared to 90-plus. (Courtesy of Randy Tyree.)

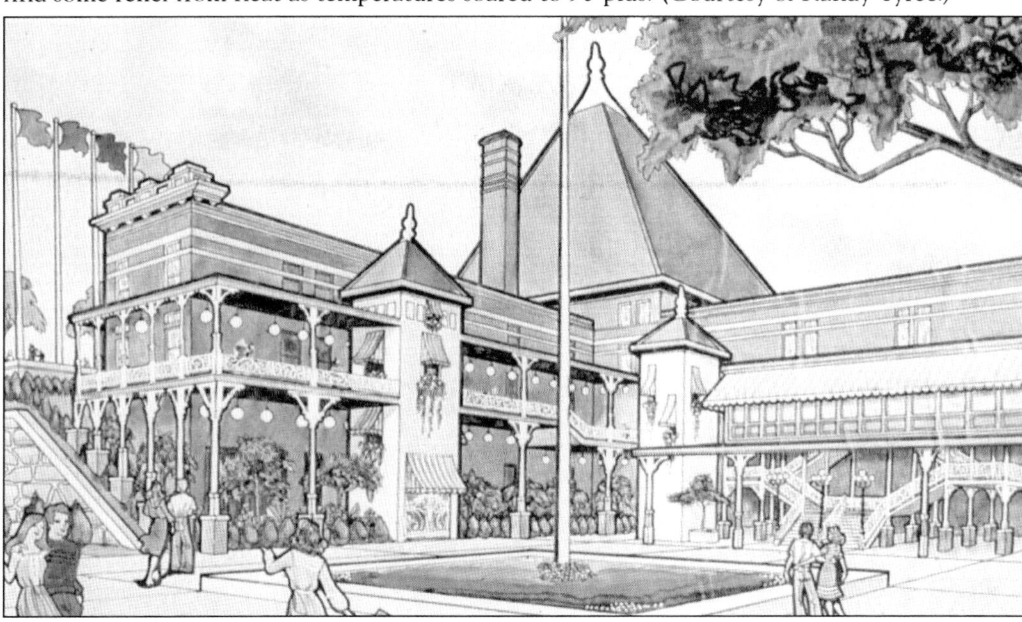

This postcard demonstrates the vision of the KIEE for the restoration of the L&N train station. Private money was mixed with public funds to bring the building back up to standards. Much care was taken to stick to the original designs and patterns inside and outside the massive building, once an epicenter of travel in the community. The 100-plus-year-old Louisville and Nashville Passenger Station was added to the National Register of Historic Places in 1982. The style of architecture is Renaissance while its areas of significance are architecture, commerce, and transportation. It is privately owned and continues to be a multiuse building. (Courtesy of KIEE.)

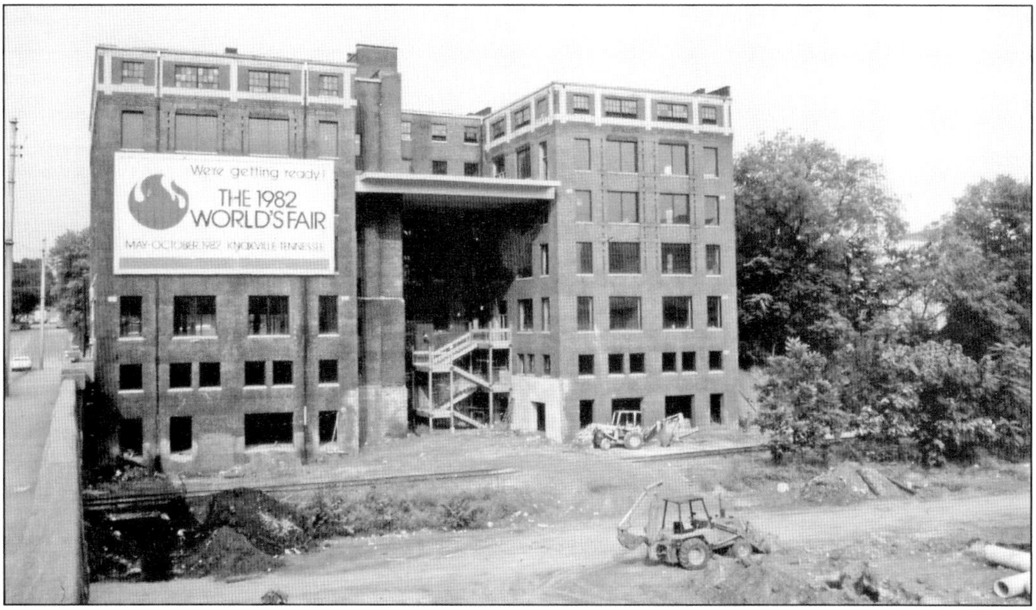

The Candy Factory was one of the major eyesores located in the blighted area that became the fair site. KIEE often discussed the merits of saving the building, which was in terrible shape. Pressure from a group who sought historic preservation saved the red brick structure. The building was used as the Folk Art Center, a place in which handmade crafts and other items were sold. The building had once been used by a candy-making company and was used for that same purpose during the fair, which made it a popular spot. (Courtesy of Randy Tyree.)

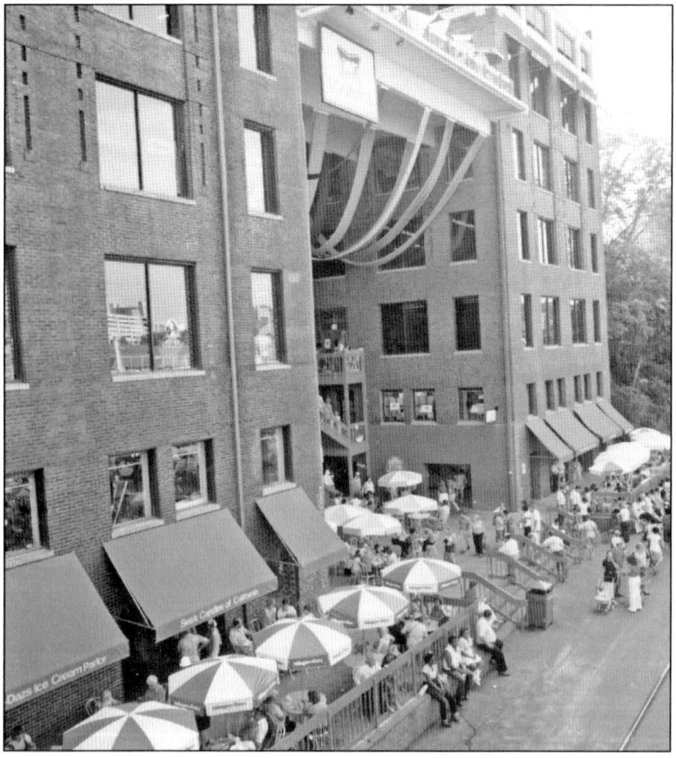

A VIP Lounge was located on the third flood of the Candy Factory. It became the site for "members only," as only those with clearance passes, namely the KIEE members and city officials, were given access to the exclusive setting. Jake Butcher's offices were located high atop the building. He was frequently seen standing inside the floor-to-ceiling clear-glass windows looking out over the fairgrounds. Butcher, ever the showman, held keys to every door of everything in the entire fair. After hours, he used his access to the behind-the-scenes workings of the fair to escort his private guests into exhibits, pavilions, and the Sunsphere as if the fair was his personal empire. (Courtesy of Randy Tyree.)

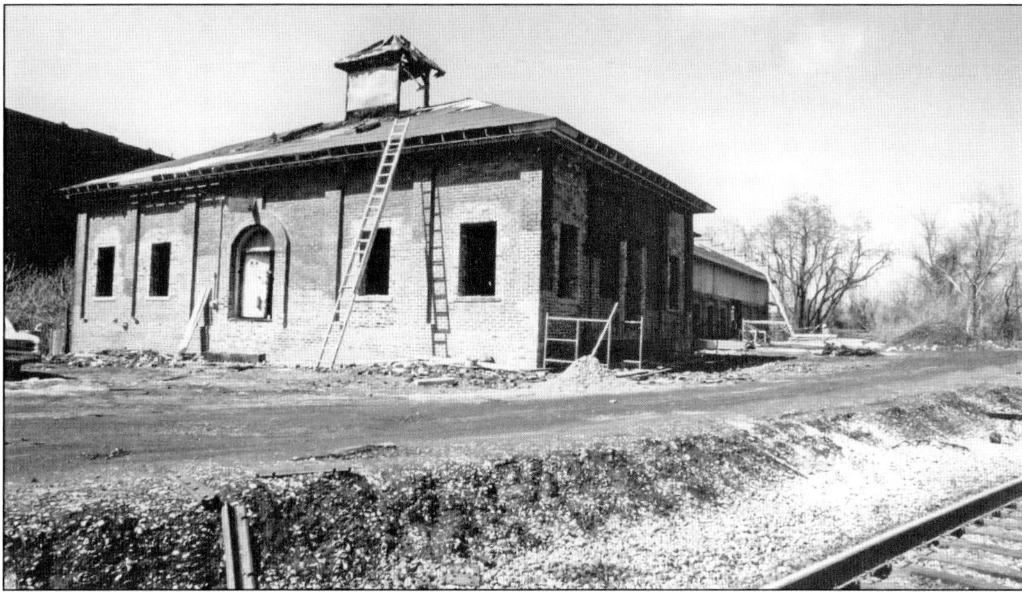

Another historic building in need of restoration was the Foundry, built in 1865 for casting railroad spikes and flathead nails from cannonballs left over from the War Between the States. It had burned in the past and over the years fell into disuse. It was saved and renovated for use as the Strohaus during the fair by a group who pushed for restoration of historic structures. (Courtesy of Randy Tyree.)

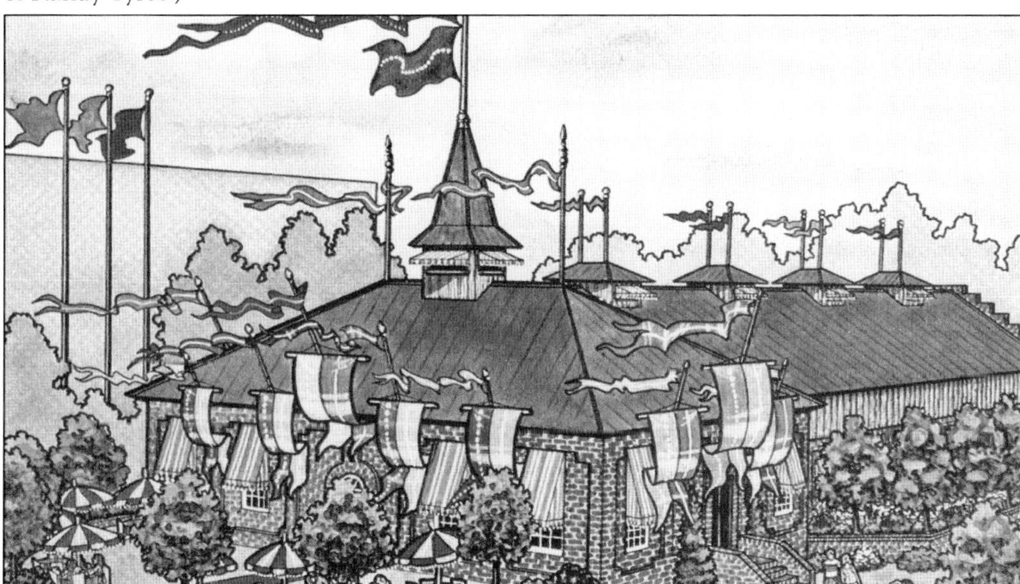

The Foundry is pictured here, around 1860, as it was imagined by an artist before the construction crews worked their magic on the historic building. The remodeled and revitalized structure looks almost exactly the same as it was imagined. It was named the Strohaus during the fair and became a favorite watering hole for thirsty fairgoers who also loved beer and polka music. Many people have fond memories of dancing on the tables amid the festive atmosphere. The partying began at some point in the early afternoons and became more joyous and rowdy after dark. (Courtesy of KIEE.)

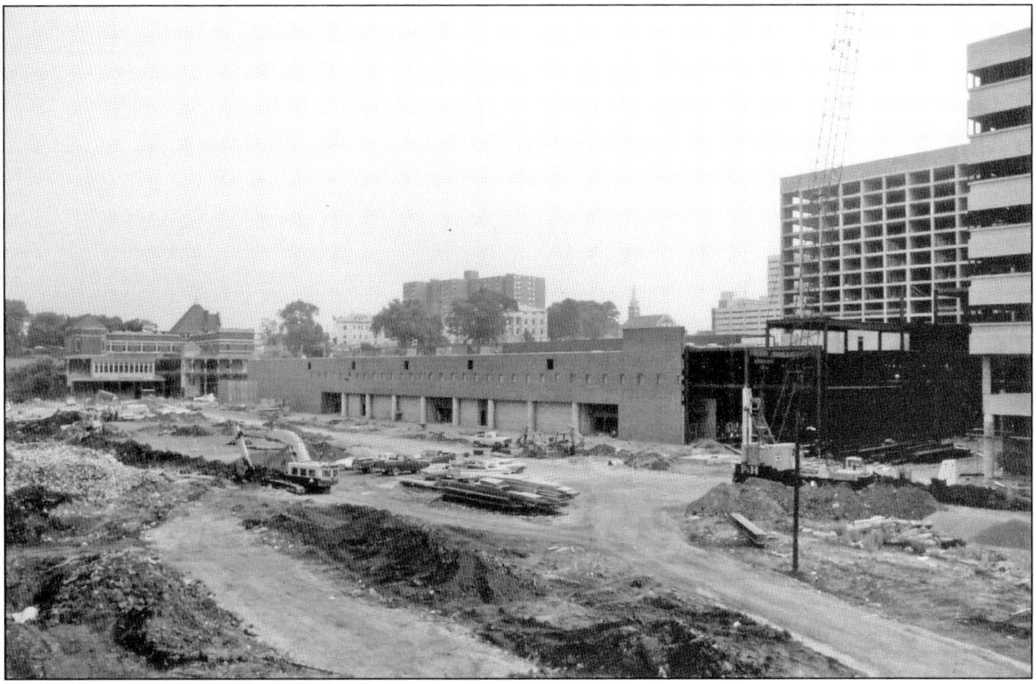

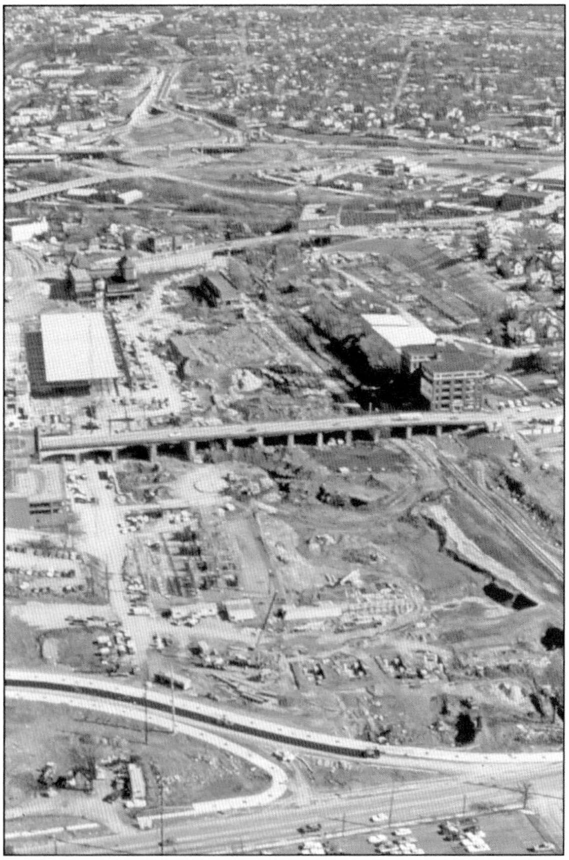

Once the site was prepared for the beginning of the building phase, there was still more work to be done. Former mayor Randy Tyree wrote in 1991, "What if today we were sitting on our duffs, still hosts to a 72 acre, weed-filled gulch of railroad tracks and dilapidated buildings in the heart of this downtown area and suffering from the daily agony of inching our way through Malfunction Junction? I doubt that our community would now be enjoying the economic benefits derived from a wide range of post-fair developments such as the Whittle complex, revitalization of the Old City or the numerous corporate commitments that have been made in our downtown area." (Courtesy of Randy Tyree.)

Construction on the 70 acres that would become the 1982 World's Fair continued around the clock from January 3, 1980, until the wee hours of the morning on May 1, 1982. It was often difficult to envision how the bleak area could be given a rebirth. "We went a lot on faith," said former mayor Randy Tyree. (Courtesy of Randy Tyree.)

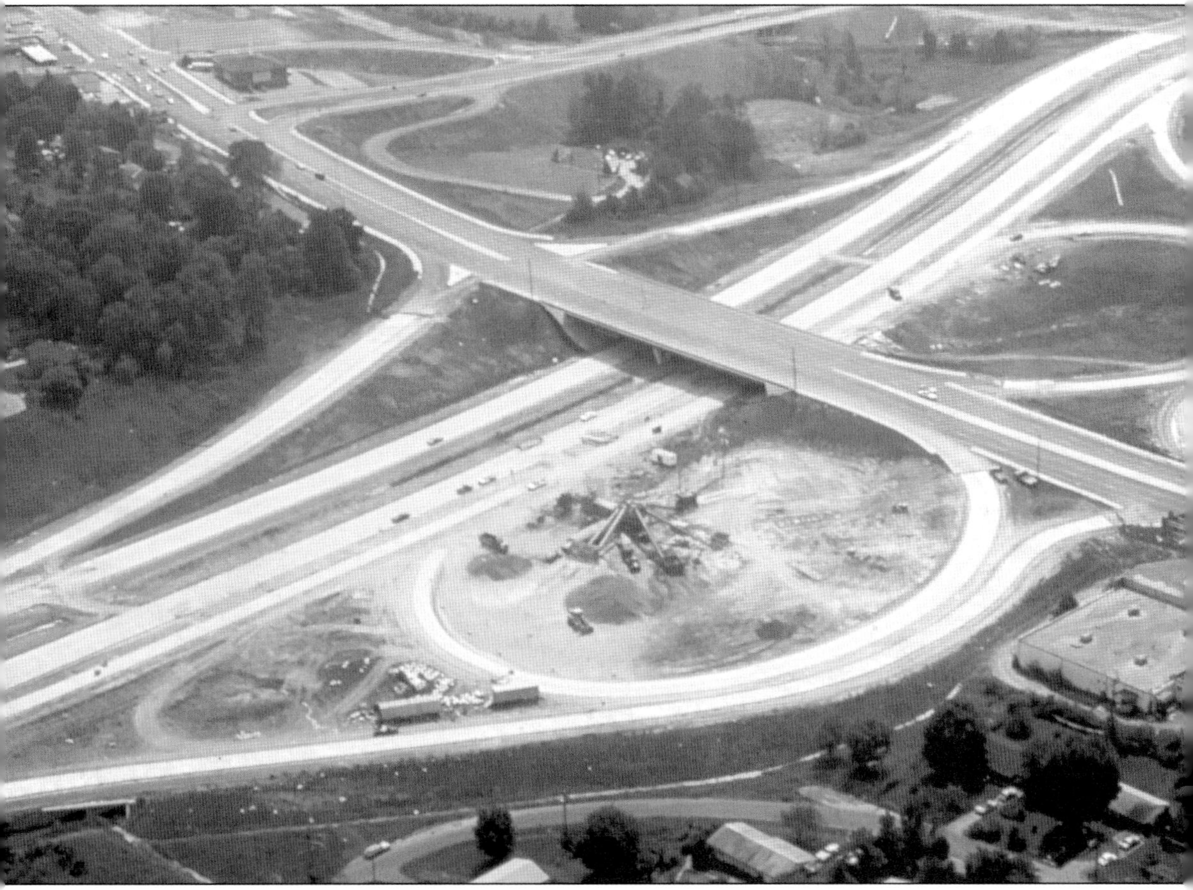

As governor of the state of Tennessee, Lamar Alexander played an integral part in the pre-fair planning and production for the fair. In July 2007, he wrote the following statement about his involvement: "Everyone had a part to play during the lead up to the 1982 World's Fair in Knoxville. My part as Tennessee's governor was making sure that the road work was finished. When I became governor in 1979, Knoxville was famous for an interchange called 'Malfunction junction.' The president of the Knoxville Chamber of Commerce told me 'Malfunction junction' needed to be solved before the fair opened. Well, when I asked him how he would do that, the Chamber president replied, 'I would recruit the best possible person I could find to be the Commissioner of Highways, give him an objective and meet with him once a month to make sure the job got done.' So, after I was elected I recruited the president of the Knoxville Chamber of Commerce and told him to be the Commissioner of Highways. We set an objective of finishing the road work before the fair opened, and Bill Samson got the job done." (Courtesy of Randy Tyree.)

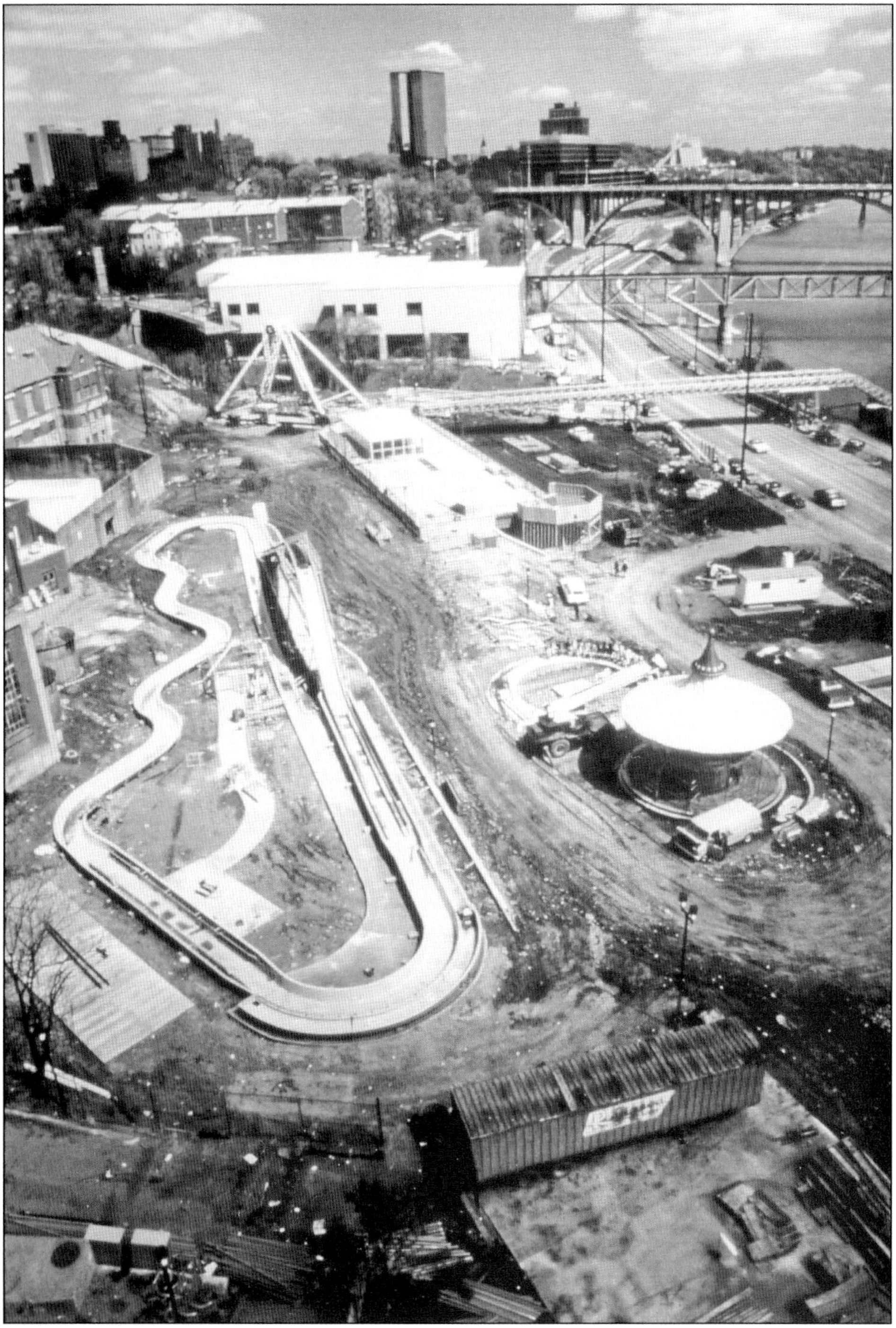

The midway is an integral part of any fair. Preparing the acreage for the various rides to be installed took planning, engineering, and time. As preparations got underway to install the log flume, pictured here as the large blue circular structure, and the numerous other rides that provided joy to fairgoers, excitement began to build in the community, especially among the children. (Courtesy of Randy Tyree.)

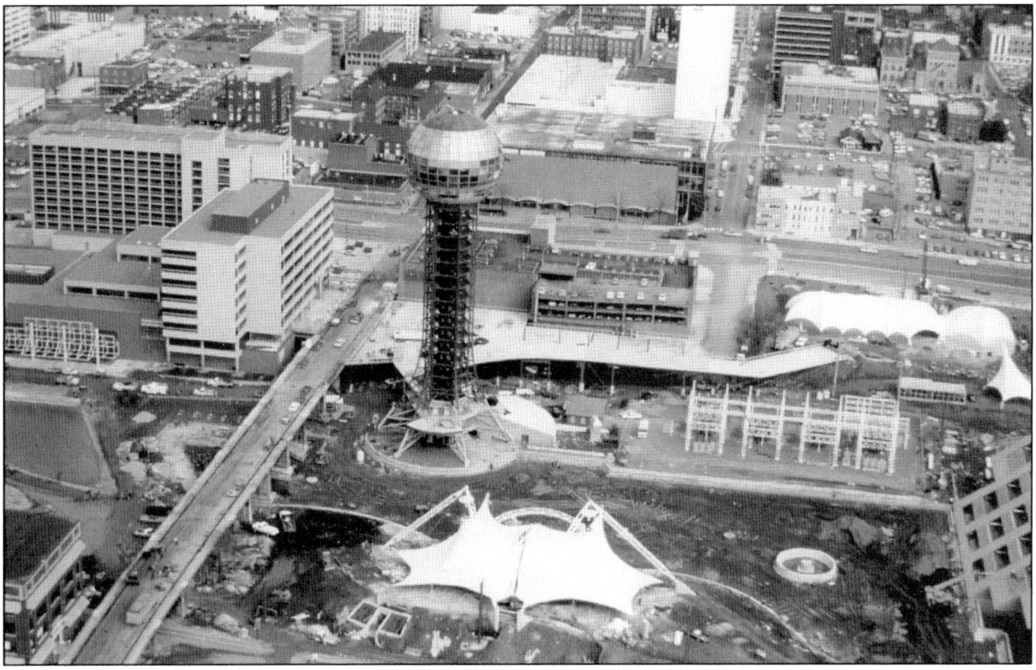

After January 1981, an unusual structure began to rise up like a phoenix rising from the ashes as the Sunsphere was being constructed. Once in place, the strangely shaped building would become a memorable part of the Knoxville skyline. (Courtesy of Randy Tyree.)

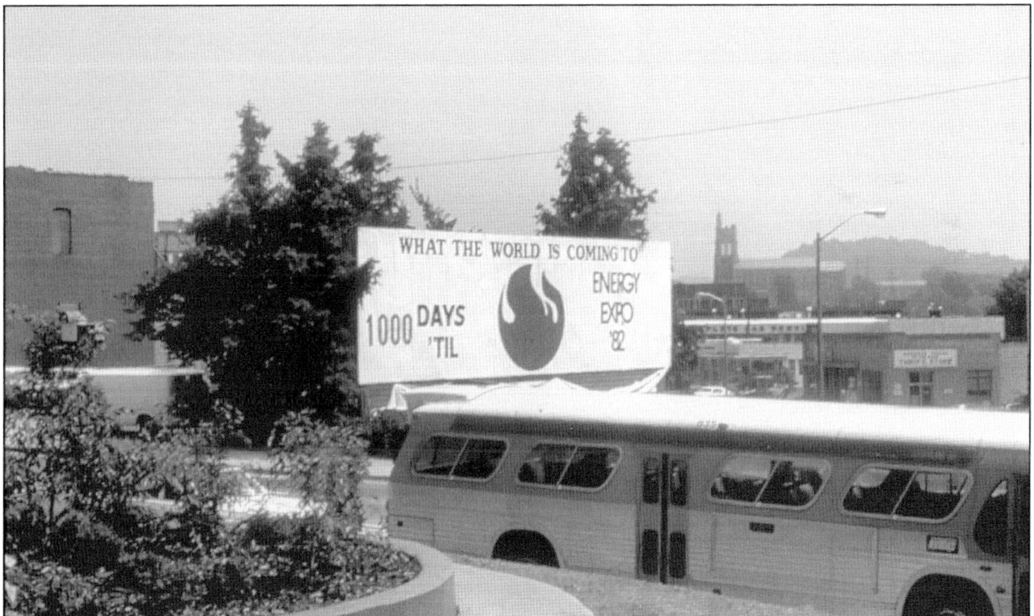

Part of the job of the KIEE was to prepare local citizens for the fair and to market it to the entire southeastern United States. Billboards went up on all roads leading into Knoxville 1,000 days before the opening of the fair. The countdown had begun, and excitement grew daily. The red circular flame made its debut and became one of the most widely used logos in World's Fair history. (Courtesy of Randy Tyree.)

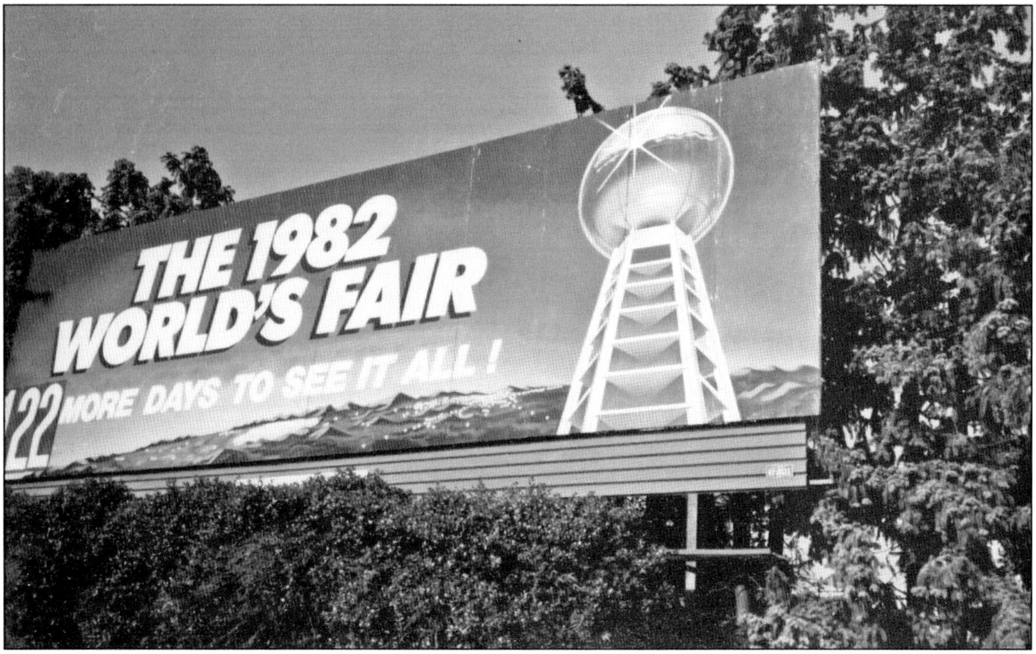

As the billboard shows, 122 days and counting were left before the fair would open. The Prather family, from Norcross, Georgia, became interested in the 1982 World's Fair by reading about it in the newspapers. They were entranced by reports of the golden ball sitting on a large tower shown on this billboard. They would like the real Sunsphere even better. (Courtesy of Jim Prather.)

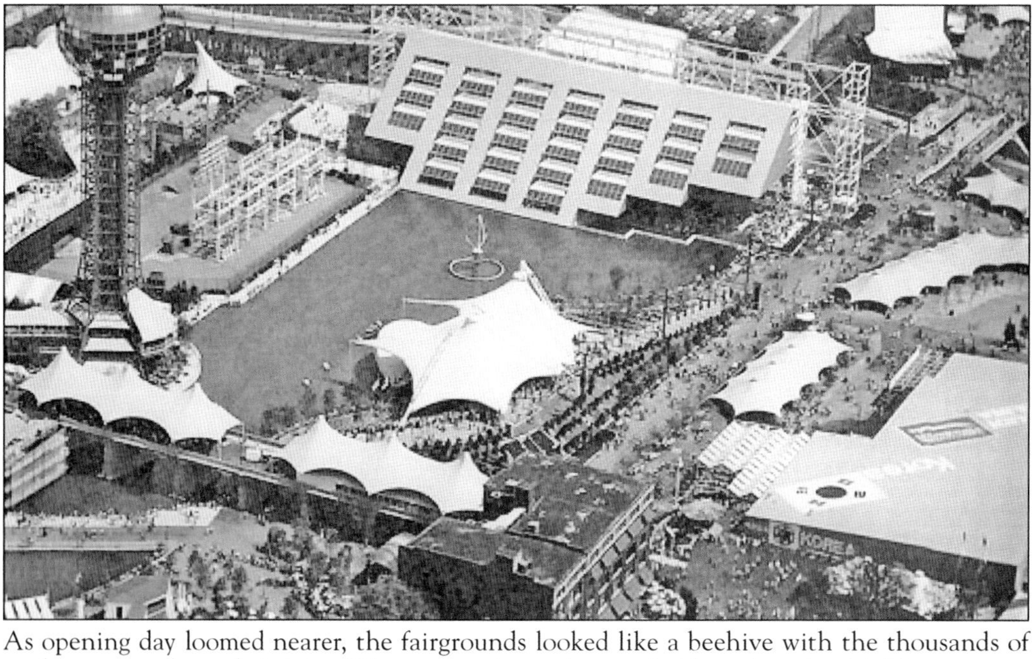

As opening day loomed nearer, the fairgrounds looked like a beehive with the thousands of workers going about their jobs. "There were times when we held our breaths thinking we were not going to have it ready by opening day," said Jesse Barr, who worked on much of the financing for the fair. "But thanks to excellent weather and hard work by thousands of people, we made it." (Courtesy of Randy Tyree.)

Two

OPENING DAY

I don't know the key to success but the key to failure is to try to please everyone.

—Bill Cosby

Looking back at the 1982 World's Fair, it is possible to see the many successes. However, on May 1, 1982, as the opening ceremonies were underway, it was not clear if all the planning and dreaming were going to bring good results. In an extravaganza that involved hundreds of performers, the fair was kicked off as over 87,659 people gathered to see the fair site and to hear Pres. Ronald Reagan give the keynote address.

In most of the ways that count, the fair was a success. There were 11,127,786 visitors. The debt of $30 million in loans was paid off to 43 banks. Twenty-two countries participated, which was more than had participated in the fairs in Seattle, San Antonio, or Spokane. A blighted downtown area of Knoxville was completely revitalized. As $225 million in highway improvements were completed, 5,000 jobs were created, many of them permanent, at a time of high unemployment throughout the United States. Several historic buildings were saved from the wrecking ball. Some businessmen made small fortunes—and people had fun.

If money was a problem, it was not apparent during opening day as "the world came to Knoxville." Gates were open by 8:30 a.m., and exhibits opened at 10:00 a.m. as the crowd began to pour in. The first day saw 140 tour buses hauling thousands of curious visitors. Music, balloons, marching bands, dancers, singers, famous people, politicians, representatives from foreign countries, and fireworks rounded out the big day as the newspaper proclaimed, "We are there!"

In an effort to include everyone who had worked on the fair, introductions on opening day went on for nearly an hour, making the ceremony far too long for people who were forced to stand in the hot sun.

Jake Butcher was described in Joe Dodd's book, *World Class Politics*, as a person who had it all: "The helicopter-hopping banker was worth a self-proclaimed $40 million. He had been a guest in the White House of President Jimmy Carter. He knew the high and the mighty of Tennessee and the surrounding states. To be sure, failures had slipped in. Butcher had run for governor twice and lost, in the Democratic primary in 1974 and in the General Election against Lamar Alexander in 1978."

Jake's reason for success was described by author Jerry DeLaughter as "savvy." "I have seen very few people with as much savvy," explained the writer. "Savvy has a lot to do with instincts, personality, judgment. I guess you can develop savvy, but it helps to be born with it."

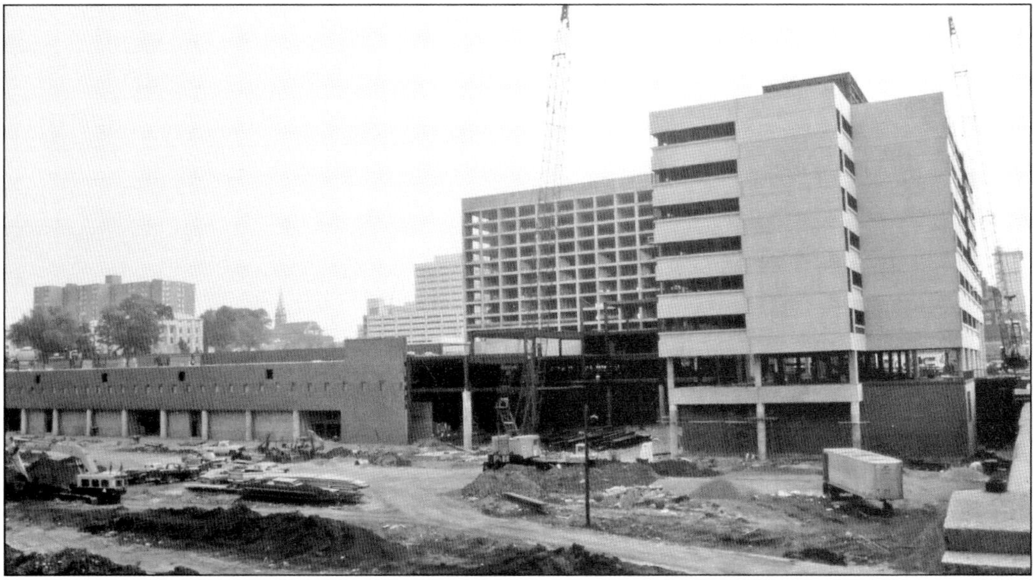

One hotel and a building used as the Lifestyle and Technology Center were built on land seized by the city from several longtime business owners. This action was the beginning of much of the bad feelings caused by the way the fair was implemented. As Don Ault, fair historian, explained, "Once Knoxville International Energy Exposition was formed by Mayor Kyle Testerman; the fair was a done deal." (Courtesy of Charlie Brookes.)

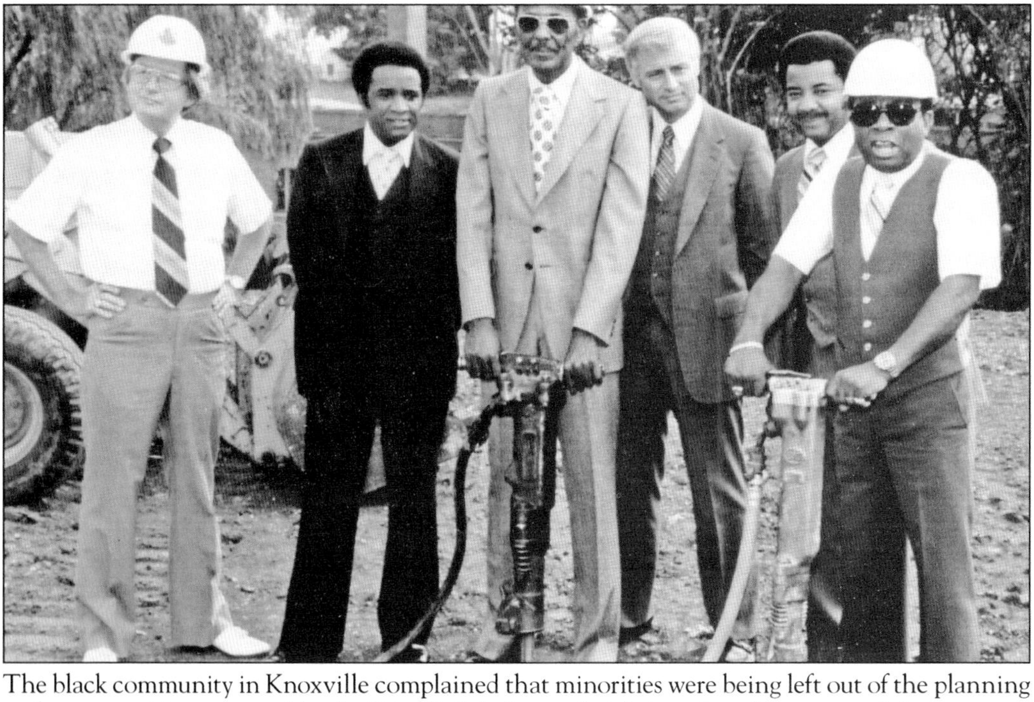

The black community in Knoxville complained that minorities were being left out of the planning and opportunities presented by the World's Fair. It was decided to allow 16 percent of the contracts made for the fair to be given to blacks. Mayor Randy Tyree is seen here with leaders from the black community. From left to right are unidentified man in hard hat, Casey Jones, Felix Gaiter Sr., Mayor Randy Tyree, Theotis Robinson Jr., and Tommy Moore. (Courtesy of Randy Tyree.)

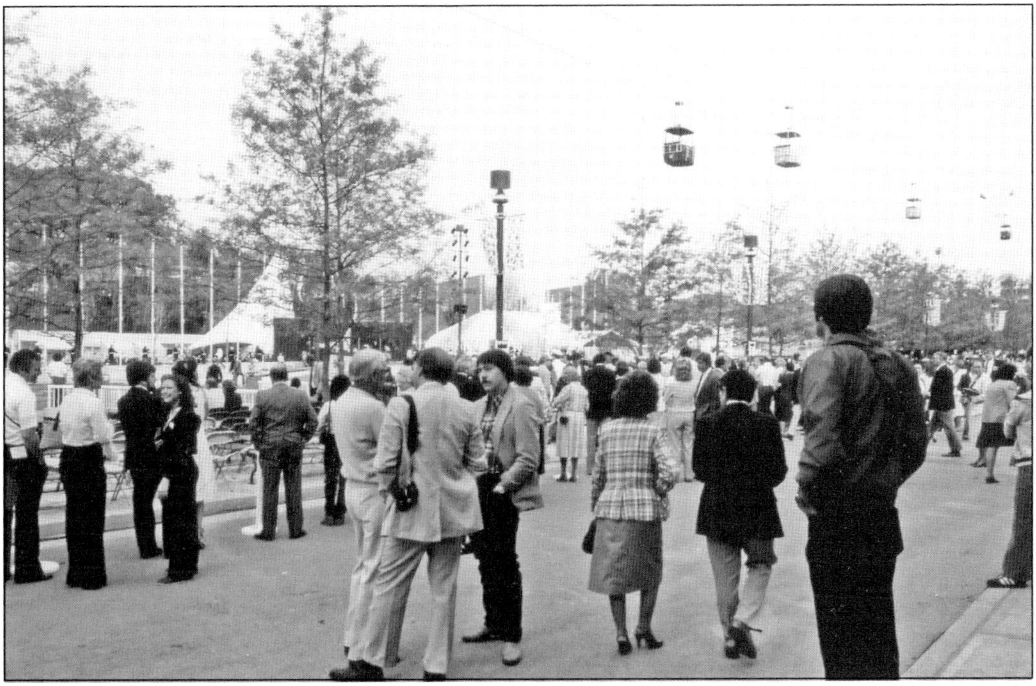

Tickets cost $9.95 for one adult, $8.25 for one child. There were 324,000 visitors the first week, while the average daily attendance was 60,000. (Courtesy of Charlie Brookes.)

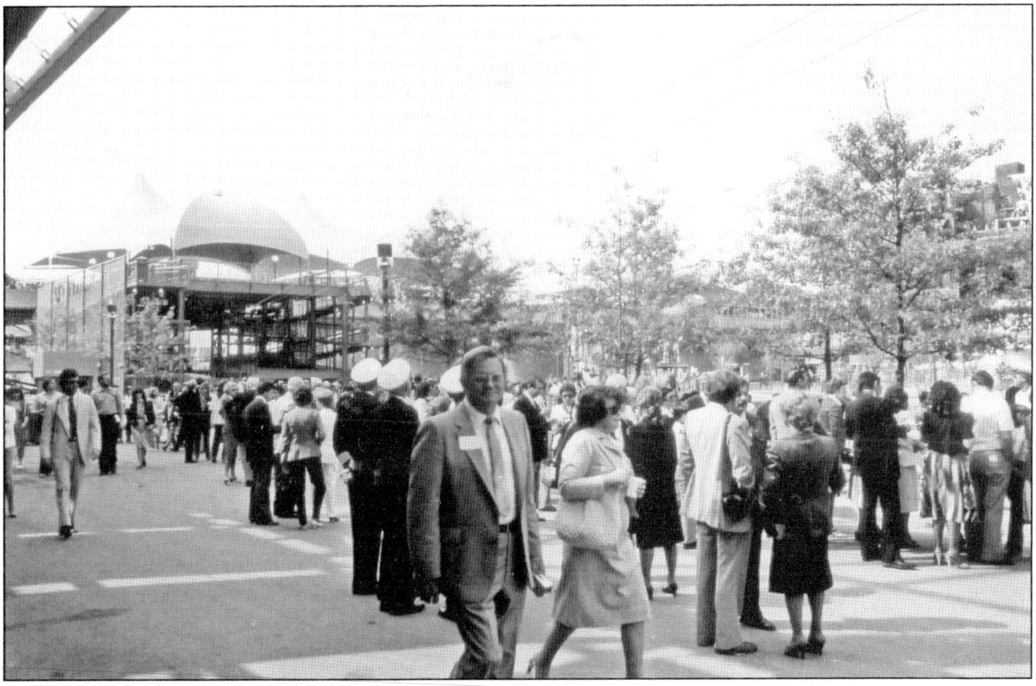

Local citizens dressed in their finest "church" clothes out of respect for the biggest event to ever hit Knoxville. After all, the president of the United States and the First Lady were in town. (Courtesy of Charlie Brookes.)

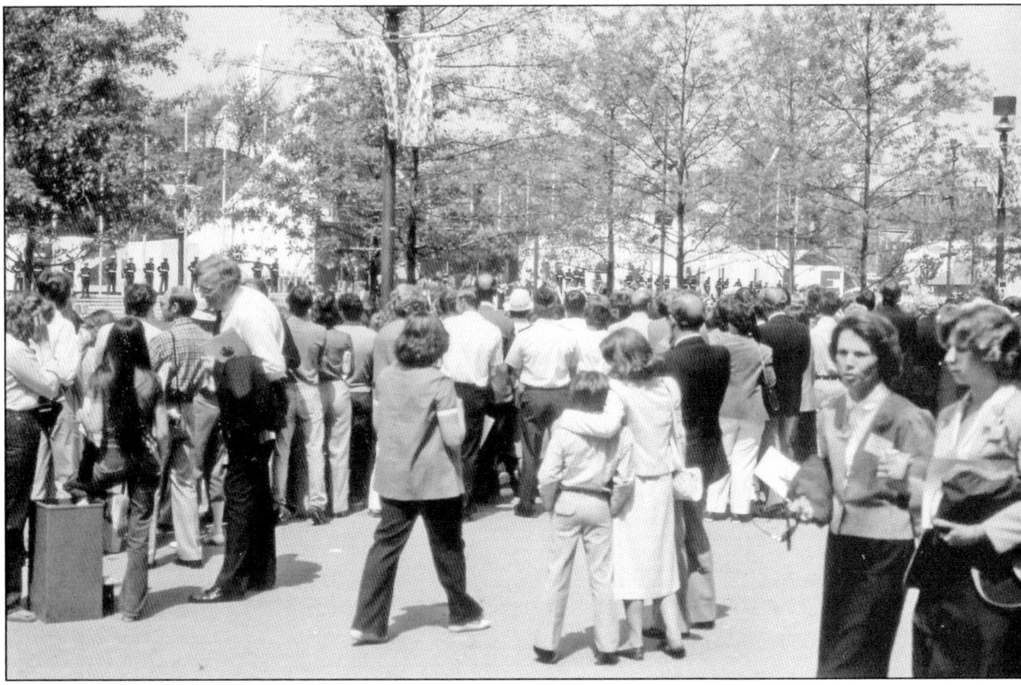

Eager parents brought their children for the once-in-a-lifetime opportunity to see a sitting president. (Courtesy of Charlie Brookes.)

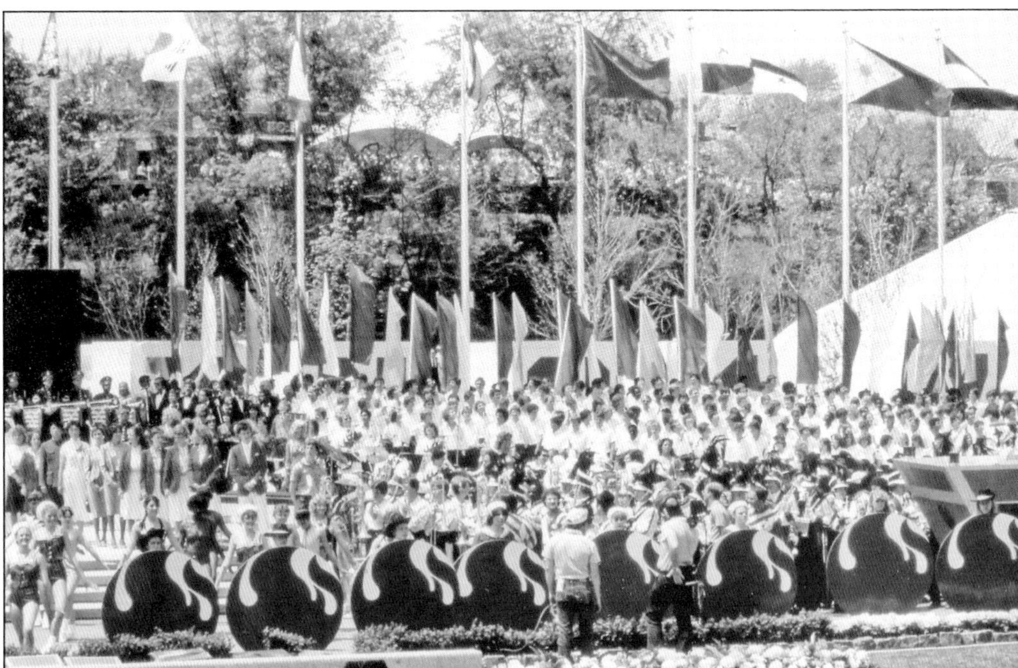

In an extravagant two-and-a-half-hour ceremony, the 1982 World's Fair opened on May 1, 1982. The event was televised and broadcast live on radio. (Courtesy of Charlie Brookes.)

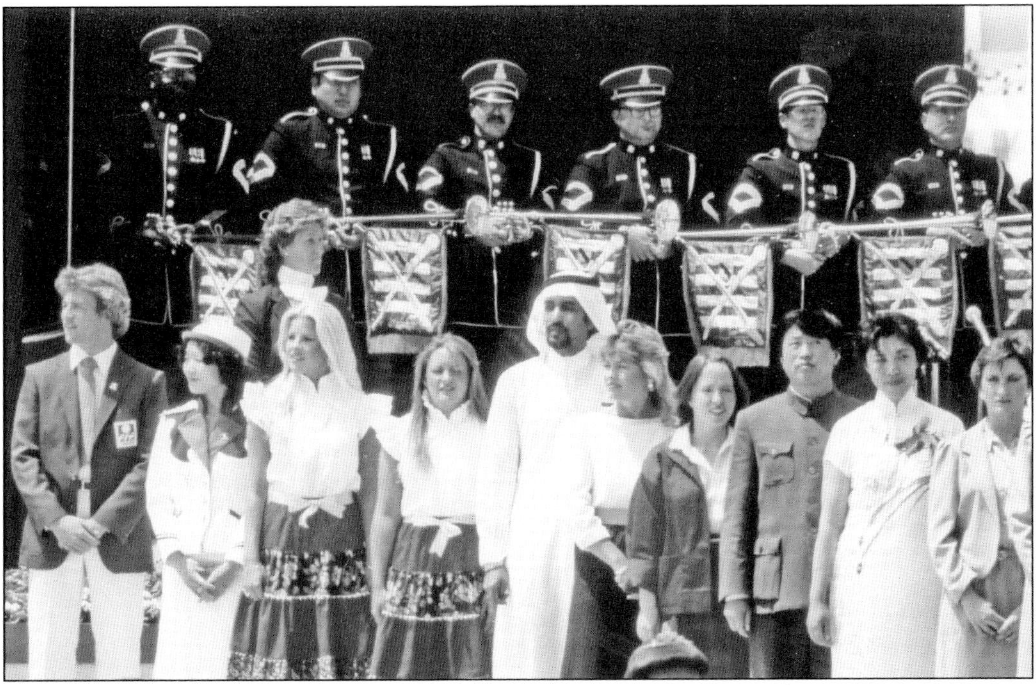

Each country sent representatives as ambassadors to the World's Fair. For the opening ceremonies, the guests were asked to dress in clothing typical of their native countries. (Courtesy of Charlie Brookes.)

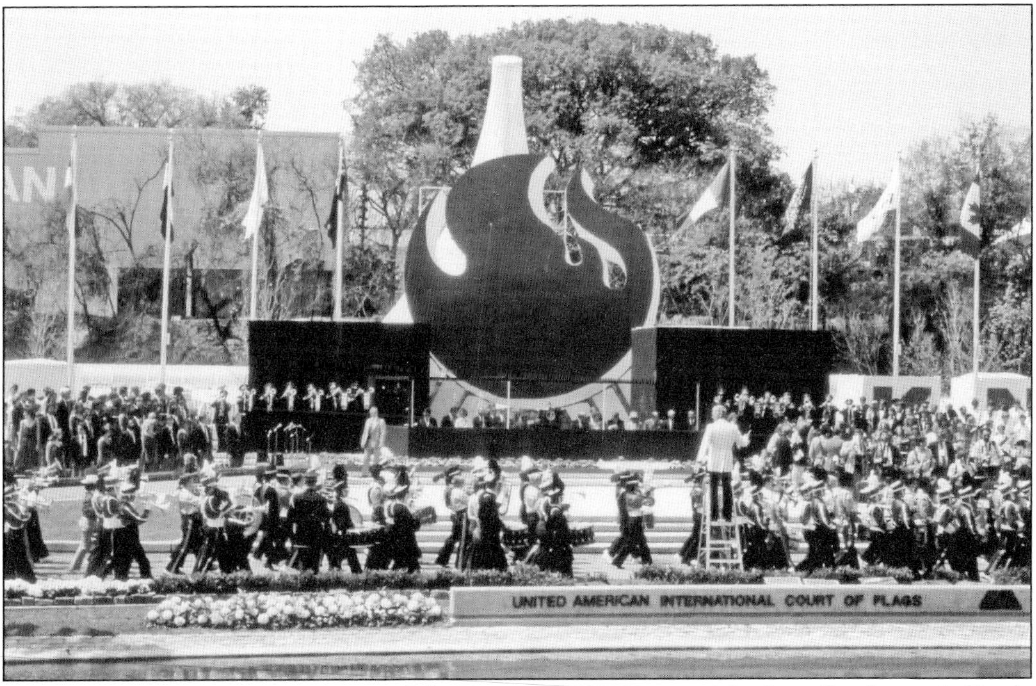

The University of Tennessee Choir and the University of Tennessee Marching Band provided lively music for the grand event. Hundreds of other singers and musicians were part of the entertainment for the event as well. (Courtesy of Charlie Brookes.)

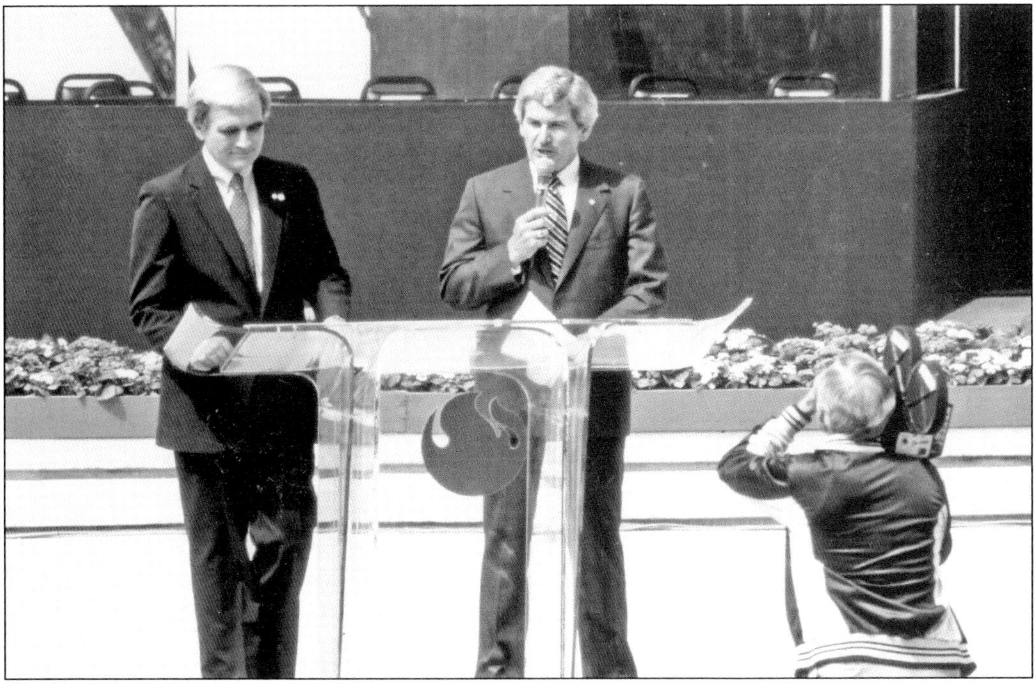

Jake Butcher (right) and S. H. Roberts were in charge of the ceremony as well as much of the fair. The red logo known as the circular flame was nicknamed "Sparky." (Courtesy of Charlie Brookes.)

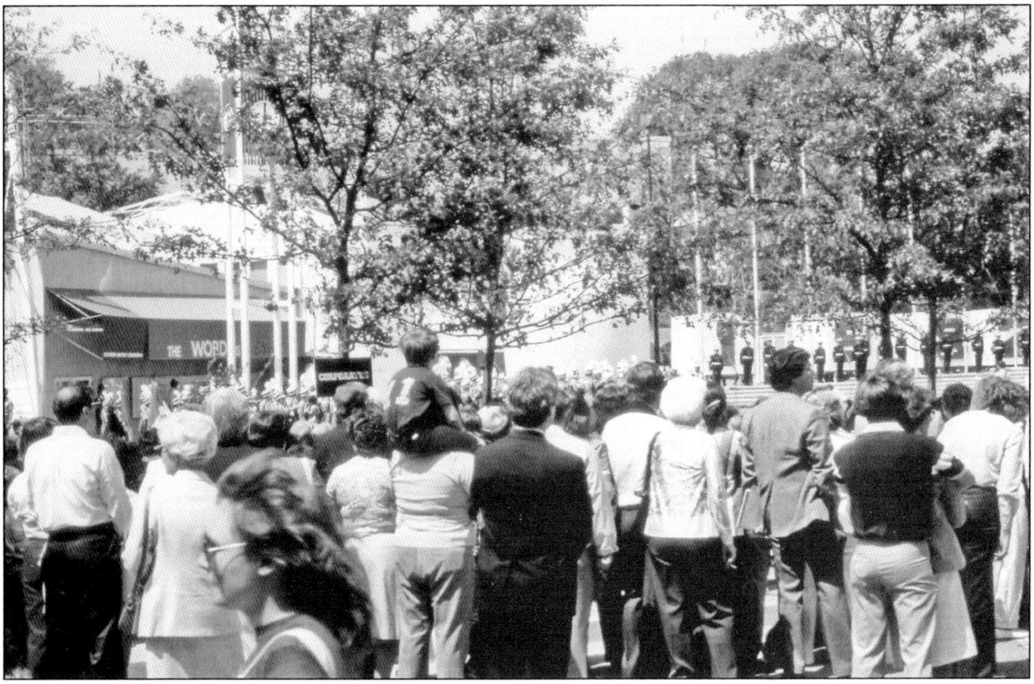

Although the temperatures soared and there were not enough seats, the crowd listened respectfully and cheered wildly for Pres. Ronald Reagan. (Courtesy of Charlie Brookes.)

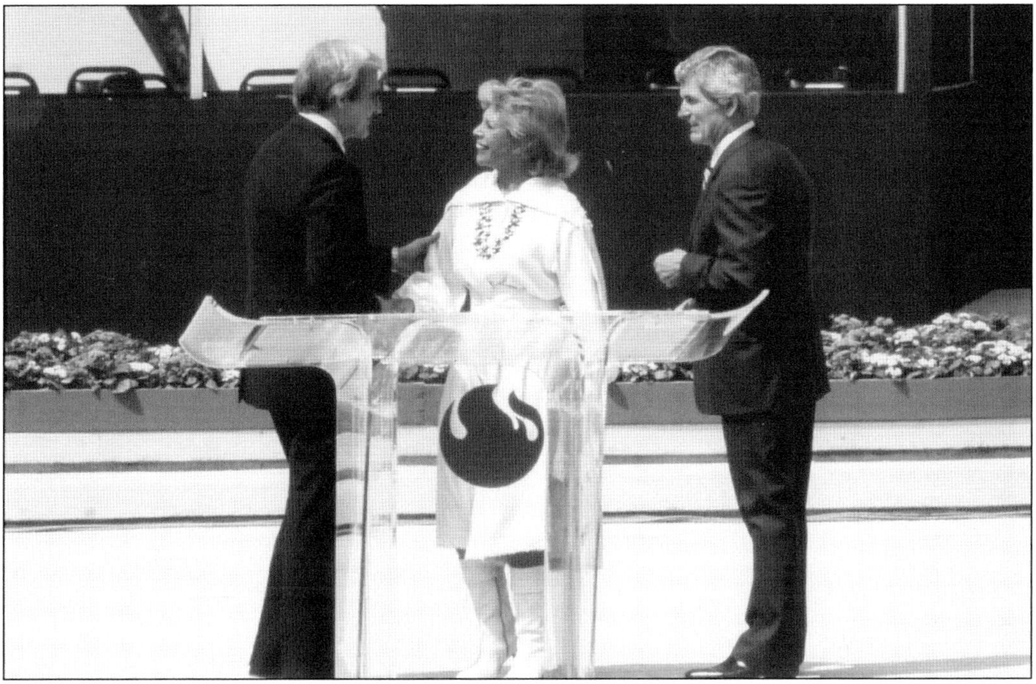

Dinah Shore, a singer and television star who was born in Winchester, Tennessee, was a crowd favorite as she provided introductions for the opening ceremonies. (Courtesy of Charlie Brookes.)

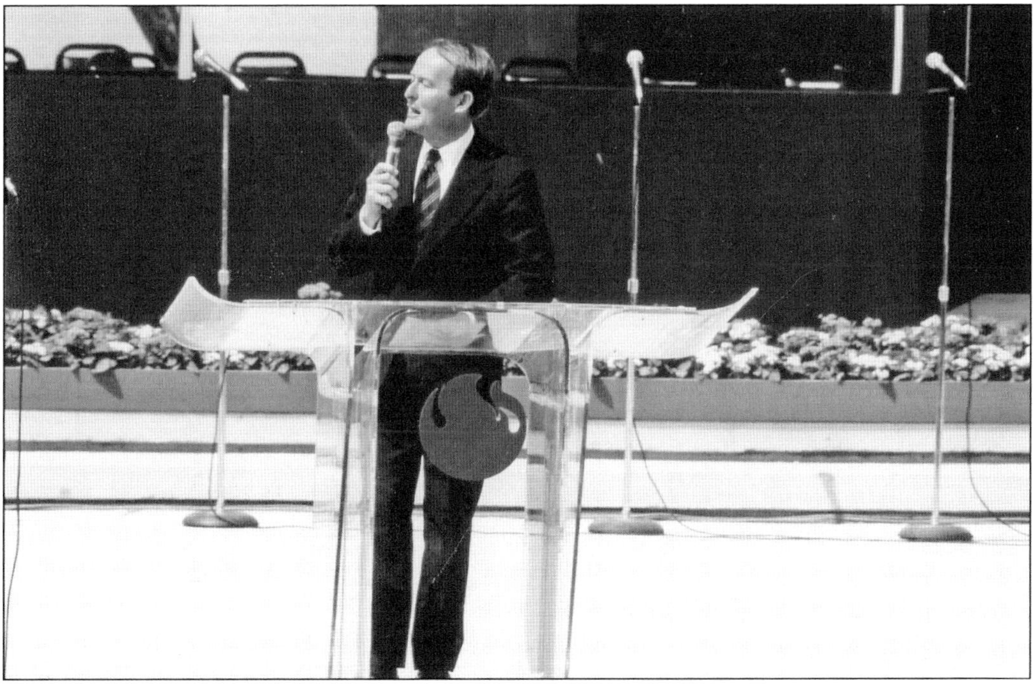

Lamar Alexander, who was born in Maryville, Tennessee, welcomed the crowd to the historic event. He was the governor of Tennessee in 1982 and is currently a U.S. senator representing Tennessee. (Courtesy of Charlie Brookes.)

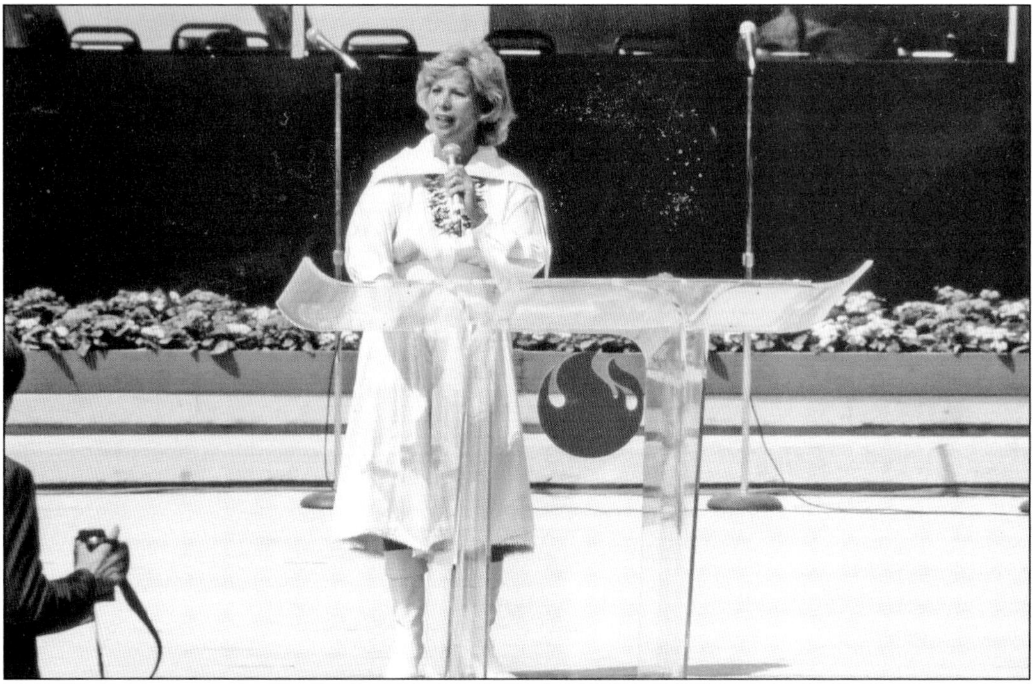

Dinah Shore, singer and television star, was known for a commercial she sang about cars. "See the USA from your Chevrolet, America is waiting for you to call" are some of the words from the song she sang weekly on the variety show she hosted. Shore told the crowd she also loved the song "The Tennessee Waltz." (Courtesy of Charlie Brookes.)

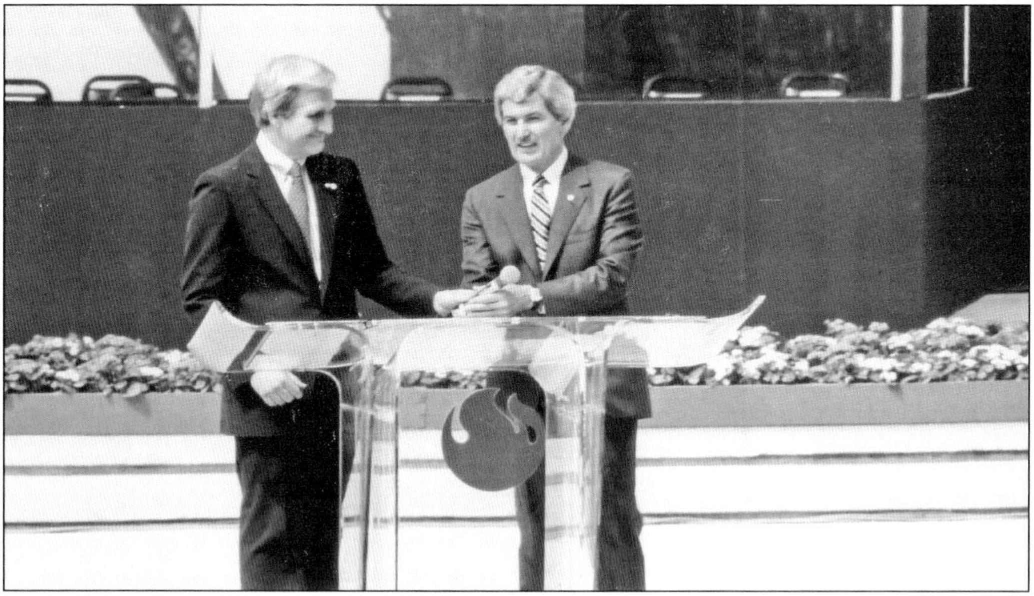

It must have been a heady day for Jake Butcher to see his dream of the World's Fair as it became a reality. Many people referred to the fair as "Jake's Fair." Another phrase often heard in those days was "Jake IS KIEE." However, his dreams would be short-lived. The day after the fair closed, the 17 banks under his control were visited by federal regulators who were looking for irregularities; they found plenty. (Courtesy of Charlie Brookes.)

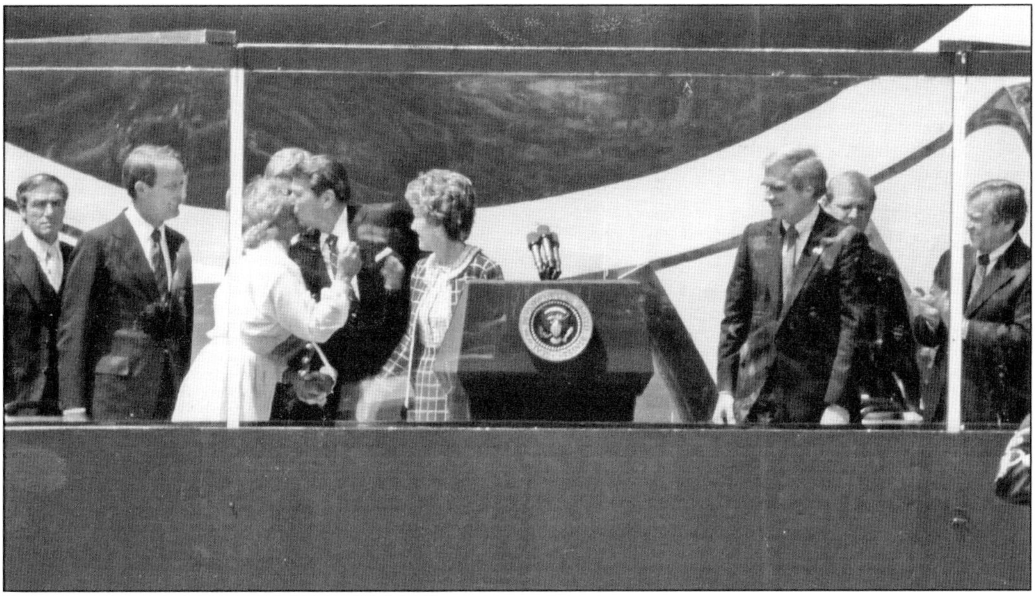

According to information provided by Ed Russell, retired U.S. Secret Service, Pres. Ronald Reagan arrived on time accompanied by First Lady Nancy Reagan. Others seated near the president were, from left to right, agent Bob Deprospero of the U.S. Secret Service with the president, Gov. Lamar Alexander, Dinah Shore, Nancy Reagan, S. H. Roberts, agent Joe Sullivan of the U.S. Secret Service with the First Lady, and Sen. Howard Baker. (Courtesy of Charlie Brookes.)

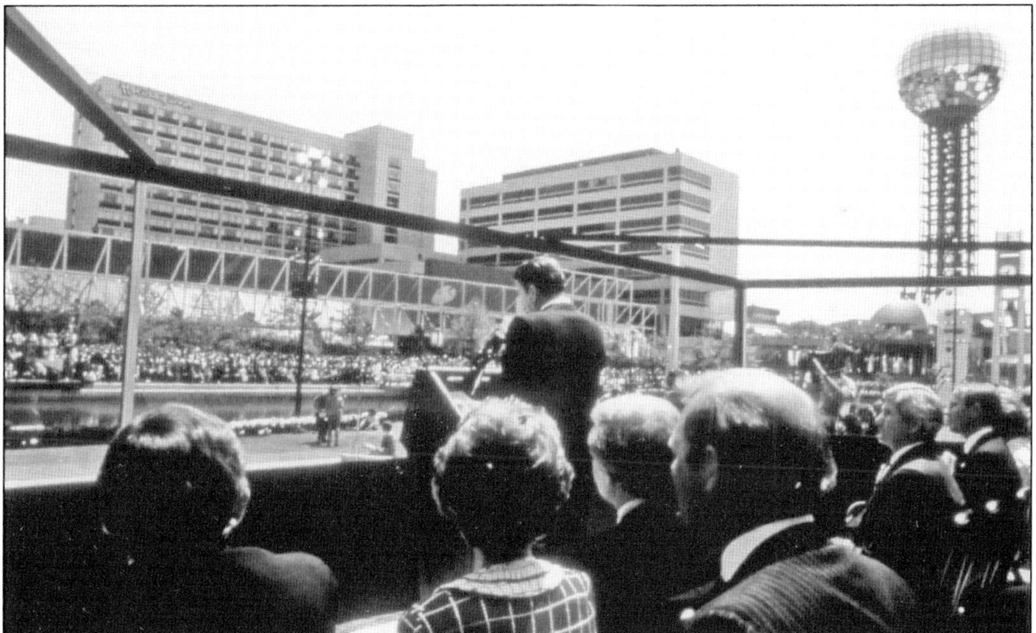

Pres. Ronald Reagan, who spoke from behind lexan (bulletproof) glass, began, "Ladies and gentlemen, your Governor, Senator Baker, your Congressman, members of our Cabinet, and a good friend and loyal Tennessean, Dinah Shore: It's a pleasure for me to be here this afternoon in the shadow of the Sunsphere, a symbol of energy potential, near the banks of the Tennessee River, whose force we have tapped for centuries." (Courtesy of Charlie Brookes.)

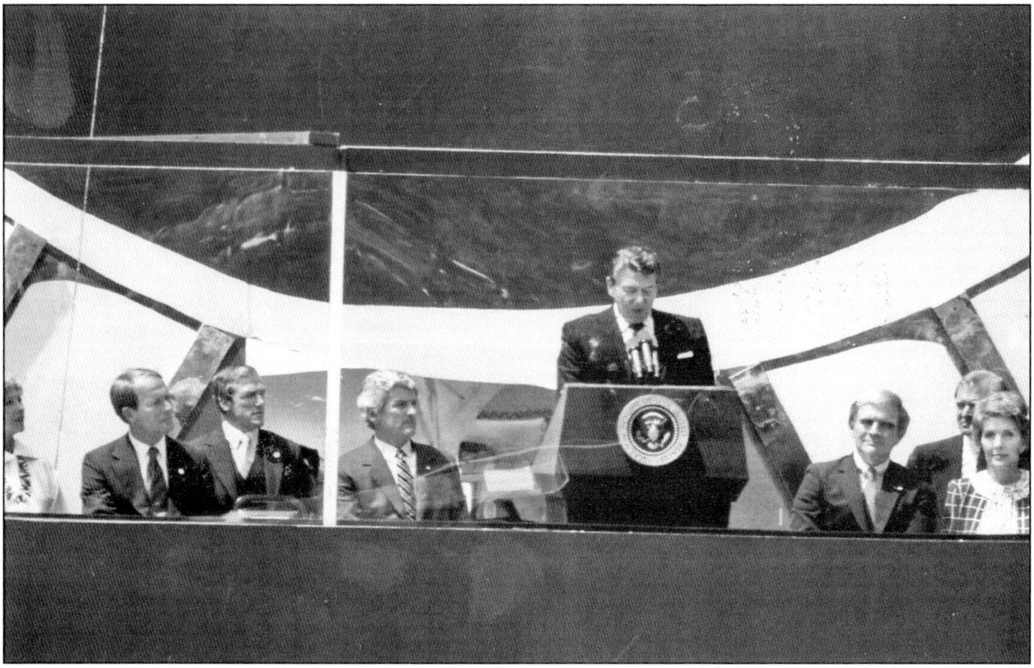

President Reagan said, "I believe the challenge of this generation of Americans is to turn our country to a different path, to restore it to the principles that made it great, because the free world—indeed, western civilization—needs a strong United States." (Courtesy of Charlie Brookes.)

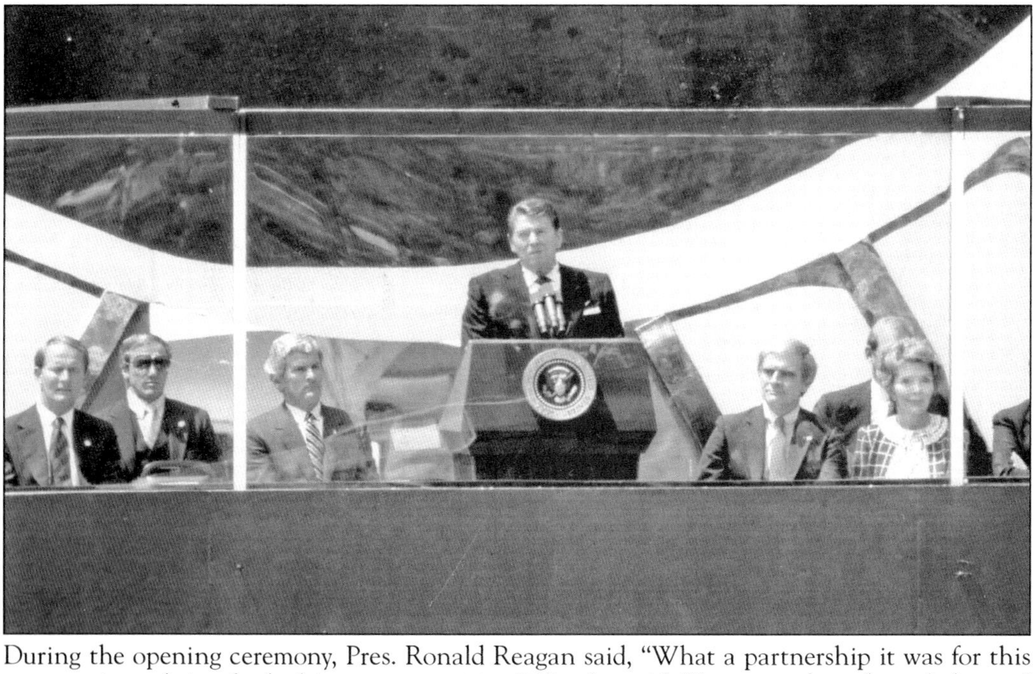

During the opening ceremony, Pres. Ronald Reagan said, "What a partnership it was for this community to bring forth this great exposition." He also said, "As we pool our knowledge and resources here in Knoxville, our cooperation will become the keystone of a more peaceful and stable world. And now, I am looking forward to seeing something of this exposition. Thank you all. Have a good time, and God bless you. (Courtesy of Charlie Brookes.)

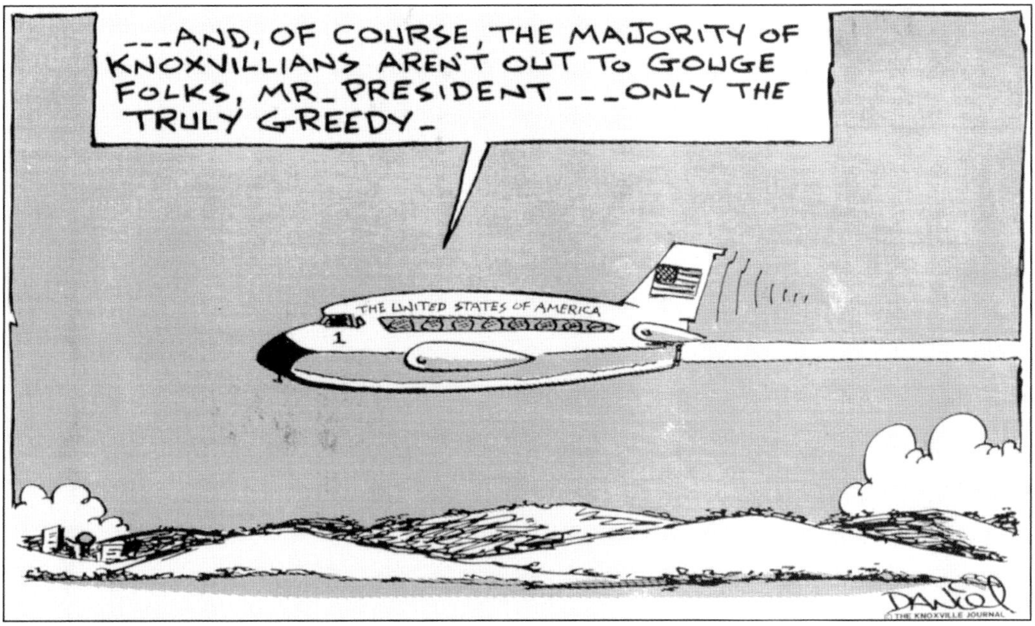

Cartoonist Charlie Daniels gave the community a preview of the behind-the-scenes rumors about the greed with this cartoon, which pokes fun at the presidential visit. (Used by permission of the artist.)

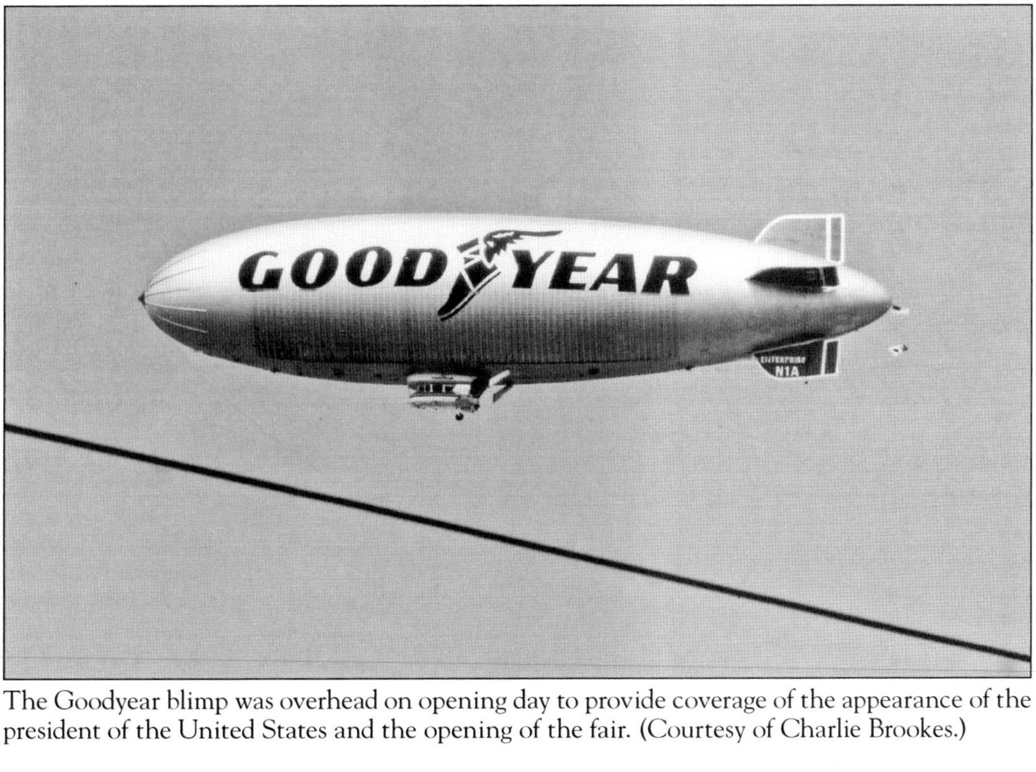

The Goodyear blimp was overhead on opening day to provide coverage of the appearance of the president of the United States and the opening of the fair. (Courtesy of Charlie Brookes.)

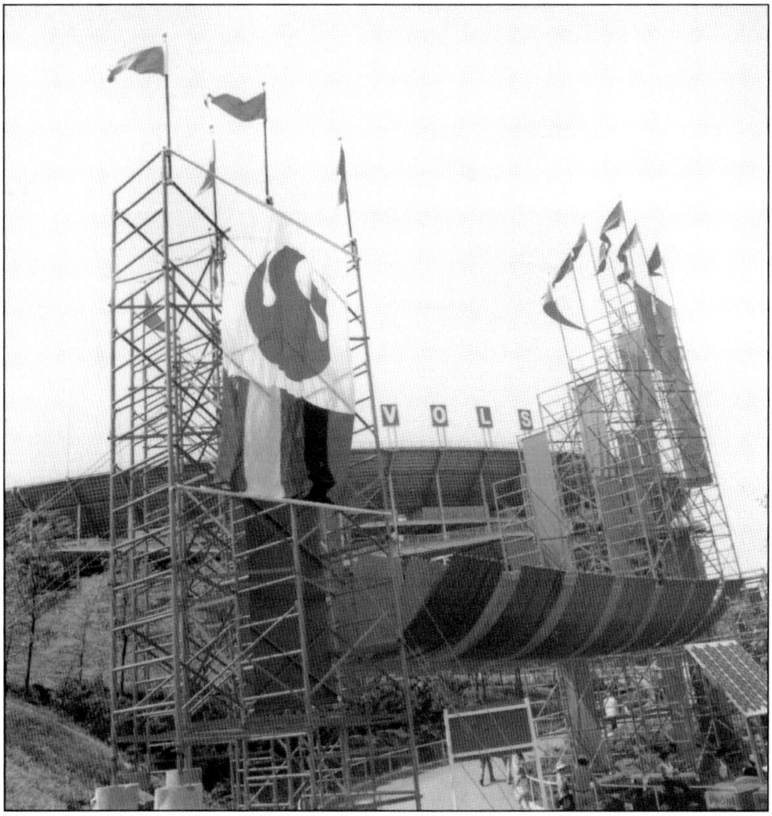

The large, metal structure shown here is one of the actual entrances to the fair as photographed by Don Ault. Ault and his family operated an exhibit about automobiles located inside the Technology and Lifestyle Center. Although Ault's exhibit began with an automotive focus, he soon began selling lapel pins, which he ordered from Taiwan. He remembers the pickle pins as being all the rage as well as the "deely boppers," a kind of headband with two stars on top that were swinging on springs. (Courtesy of KIEE.)

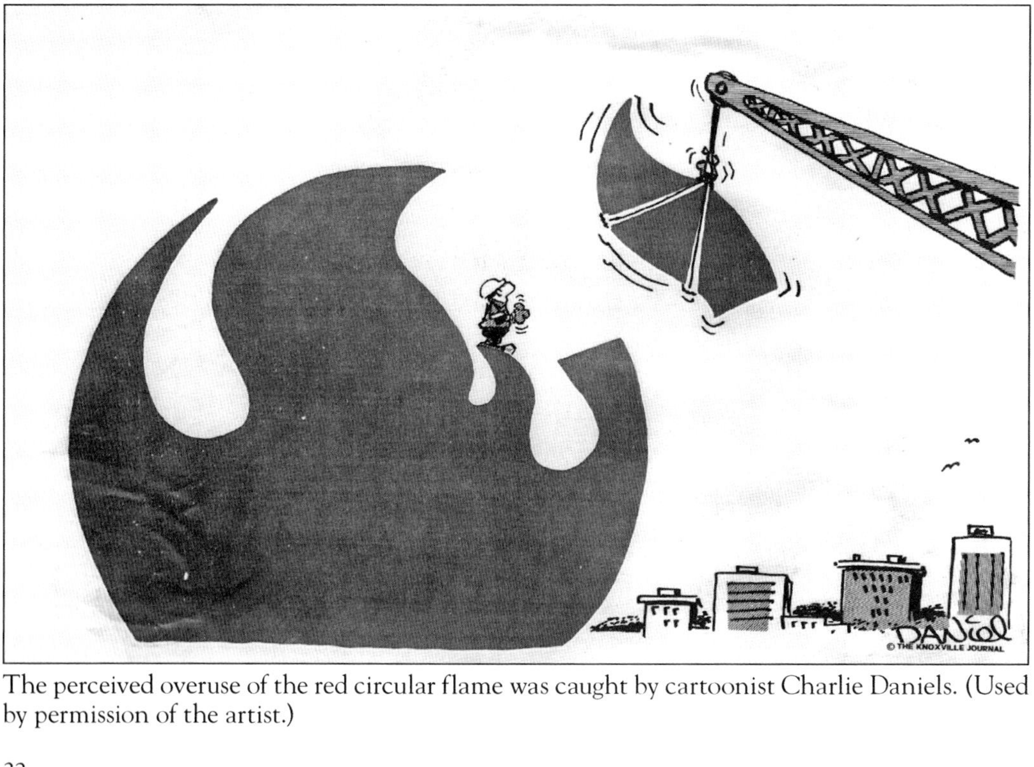

The perceived overuse of the red circular flame was caught by cartoonist Charlie Daniels. (Used by permission of the artist.)

Two

Pavilions and Countries

You will find the key to success under the alarm clock.

—Benjamin Franklin

Entering the 1982 World's Fair on Clinch Avenue from Henley Street, visitors would pass the New Hilton Hotel, attached to the Technology and Lifestyle Center. The Sunsphere was across the street from the Clinch Street Bridge. The bridge and the Sunsphere were covered in bright-yellow canopies.

The clear, blue waters of the man-made Waters of the World sparkled as canoes and paddleboats floated along filled with happy guests. The large, tent-like Tennessee Amphitheater was visible on the left, and the U.S. Pavilion could be seen at the edge of the lake, its solar panels twinkling in the sun.

The Candy Factory, across the bridge, contained the Folk Life Center, which hosted craftspeople who sold such things as quilts, books, carvings, wooden toys, handmade jewelry, foods, and more.

A right turn out of the Convention Center brought visitors to the Japanese Pavilion, which contained engineering marvels of the latest technology and featured a robot that could paint a picture using paints and a brush.

Next door to the Japanese Pavilion was the Elm Tree Theatre, named for an enormous, naturally growing elm tree. The outdoor site was a popular place for numerous performances as clowns, dancers, singers, and musicians entertained everyone with lively shows.

The country of Mexico's pavilion was another popular spot full of colors and aromas as authentic foods were available in a restaurant.

A highly decorated jeep, said to be owned by Ferdinand and Imelda Marcos, president and First Lady of the Philippines, was on display outside the pavilion for the country of the Philippines.

The continent of Europe was the next to be celebrated by pavilions from the countries of Italy and the European Economic Community, including Belgium, the Netherlands, Denmark, Ireland, Luxembourg, and Greece. The Federal Republic of Germany and the United Kingdom's pavilions were next, alongside the one for France. The pavilion for the Hungarian People's Republic was easily recognized by the 6-foot-high, revolving Rubik's cube. The Republic of Panama's pavilion rounded out the long line of light-blue buildings.

The pavilions for the Republic of Korea and the Royal Kingdom of Saudi Arabia were located behind the Tennessee Amphitheatre and drew large crowds.

As guests rounded the circle of the fair site, they passed merchandise shops on the way to the 13th pavilion on the "lower" side of the fairgrounds, which was the United States Pavilion, an oddly shaped building that looked like a skyscraper lying on its side surrounded by large metal-frame structures.

In order to access the remainder of the fair site, it was necessary to walk across Cumberland Avenue. Visitors were greeted by a garden of windmills beside the bright-blue pavilion from Australia. Next, the pavilion of Canada was easy to recognize from the red maple leaf motifs painted on the pavilion and because an officer from the Royal Canadian Mounted Police beckoned them inside.

After leaving the Canadian Pavilion, visitors would see the long line in front of the pavilions for the People's Republic of China, Egypt, and Peru, which were next door to one another and were some of the most popular pavilions of the entire fair. Leaving the pavilions, visitors could walk across Neyland Drive, board a showboat barge, and take a tour floating along the Tennessee River.

On Neyland Drive in front of the famous Neyland Stadium, visitors could ride amusement park rides and buy souvenirs; eat foods such as peanuts, popcorn, and candy; and drink fresh-squeezed lemonade.

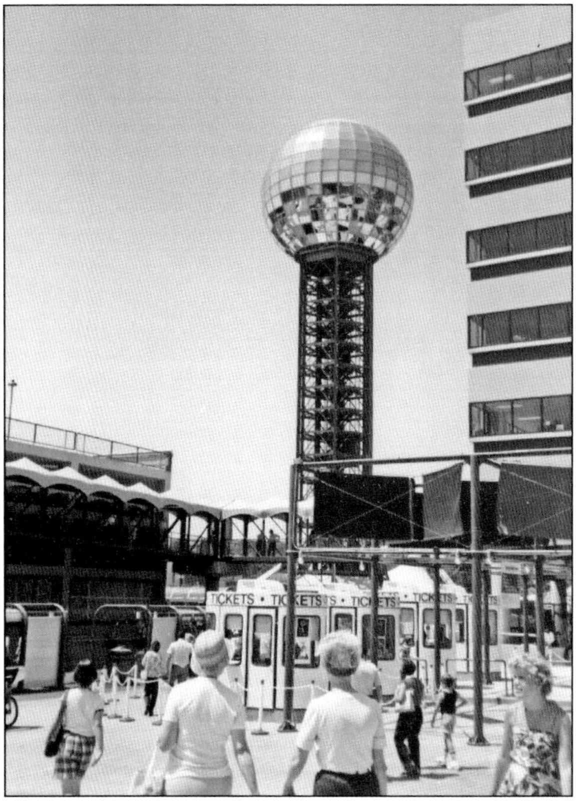

One of the first things visitors would see were the ticket booths near the new Hilton Hotel at the base of the Sunsphere. On one occasion, tickets were being sold so quickly that all booths ran out of them. After listening to complaints, the managers decided to allow people in free for the remainder of that day. (Courtesy of the Prather family.)

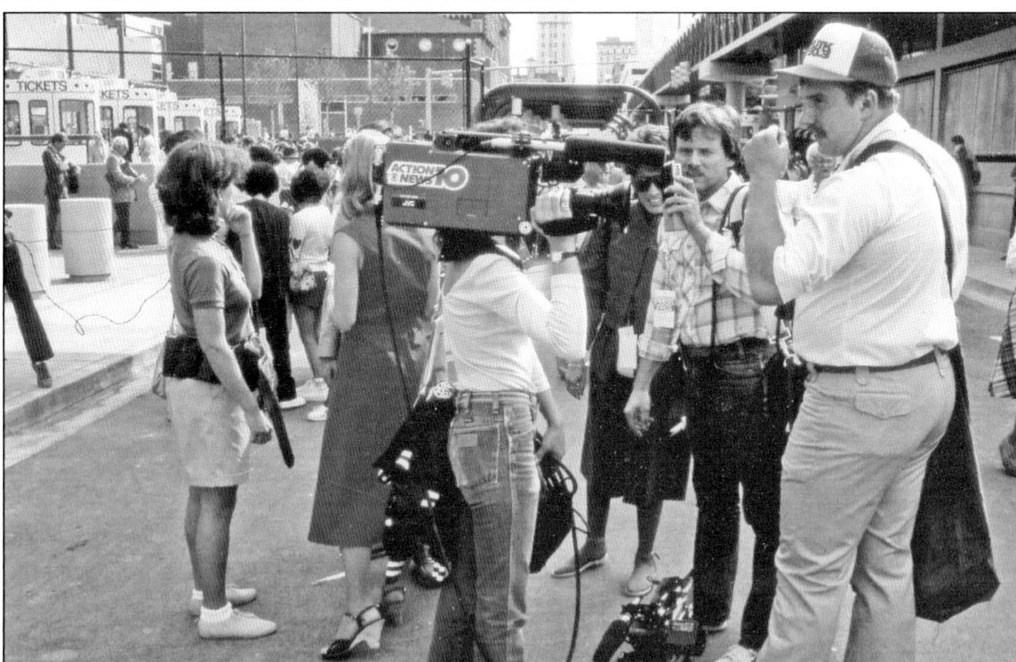

Camera crews roamed throughout the fairgrounds daily. Local television stations reported on events at the fair every hour for six months. (Courtesy of Charlie Brookes.)

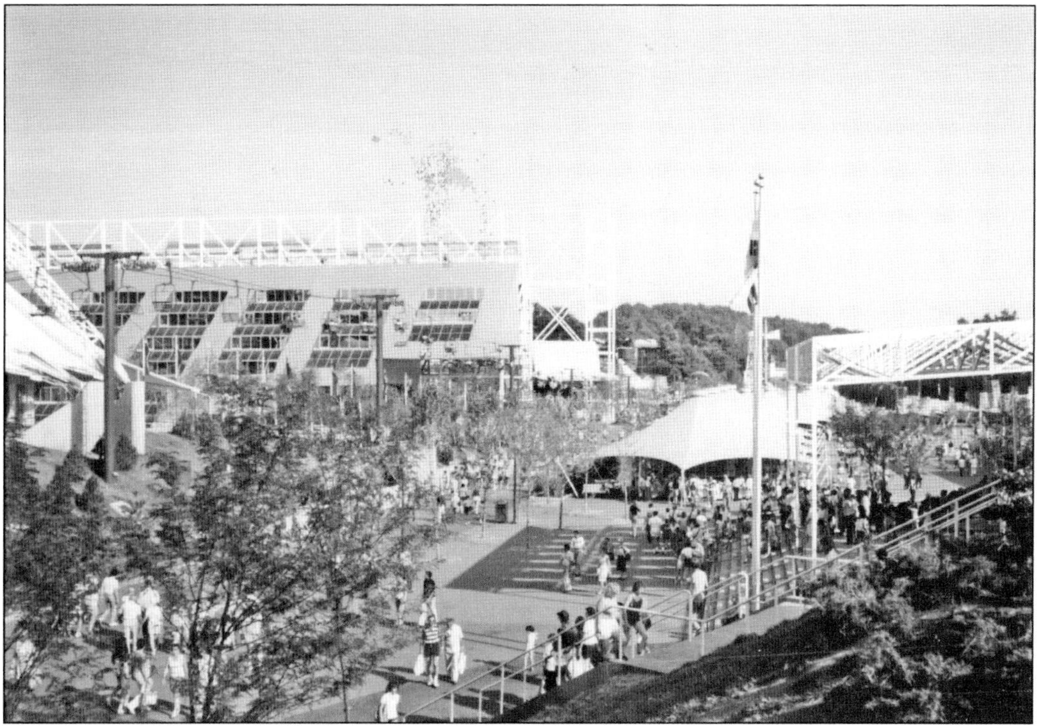

The United States Pavilion was an oddly shaped building that dominated the skyline of the lower section of the fairgrounds. (Courtesy of the Prather family.)

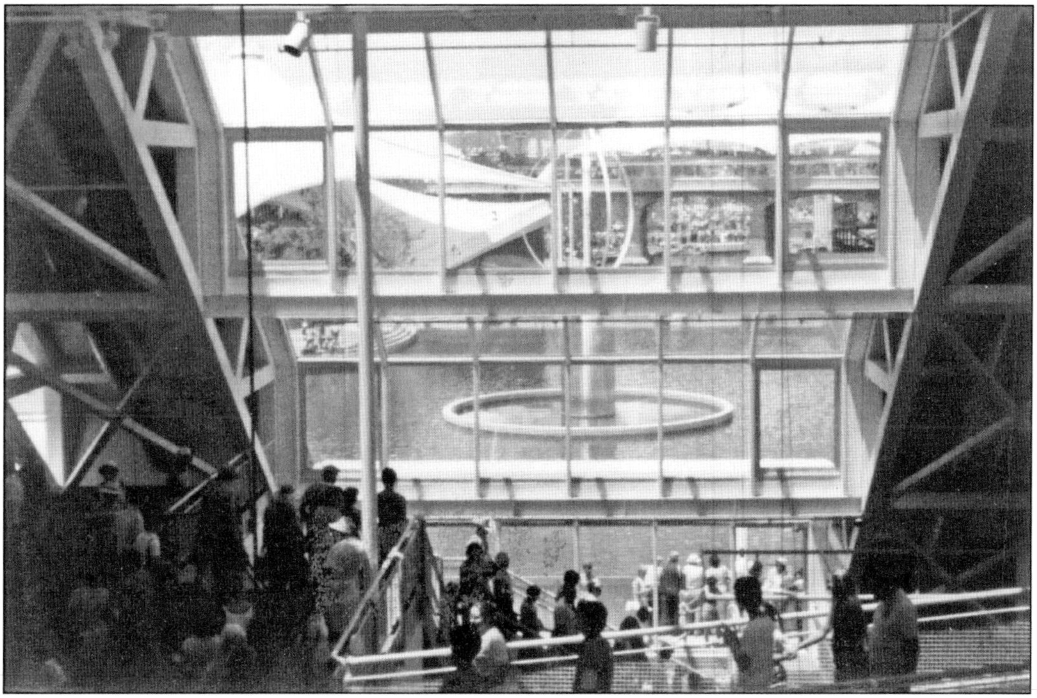

Inside the United States Pavilion, guests were carried up and down on escalators, which reminded many of the cartoon television show *The Jetsons*. (Courtesy of the Prather family.)

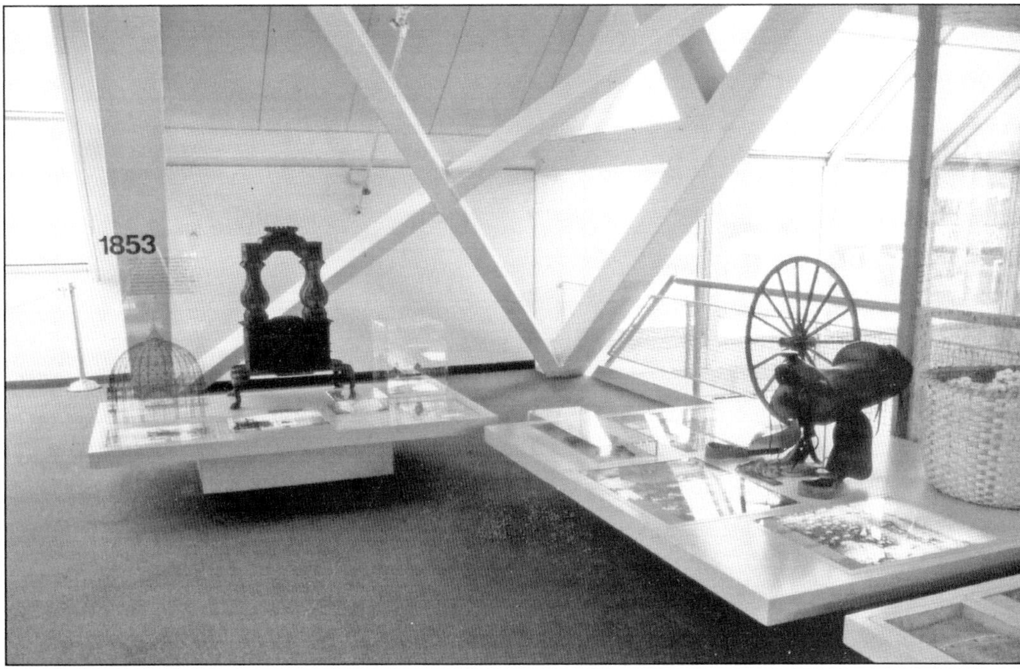

The history of energy was on display inside the United States Pavilion. (Courtesy of Miles Roberts.)

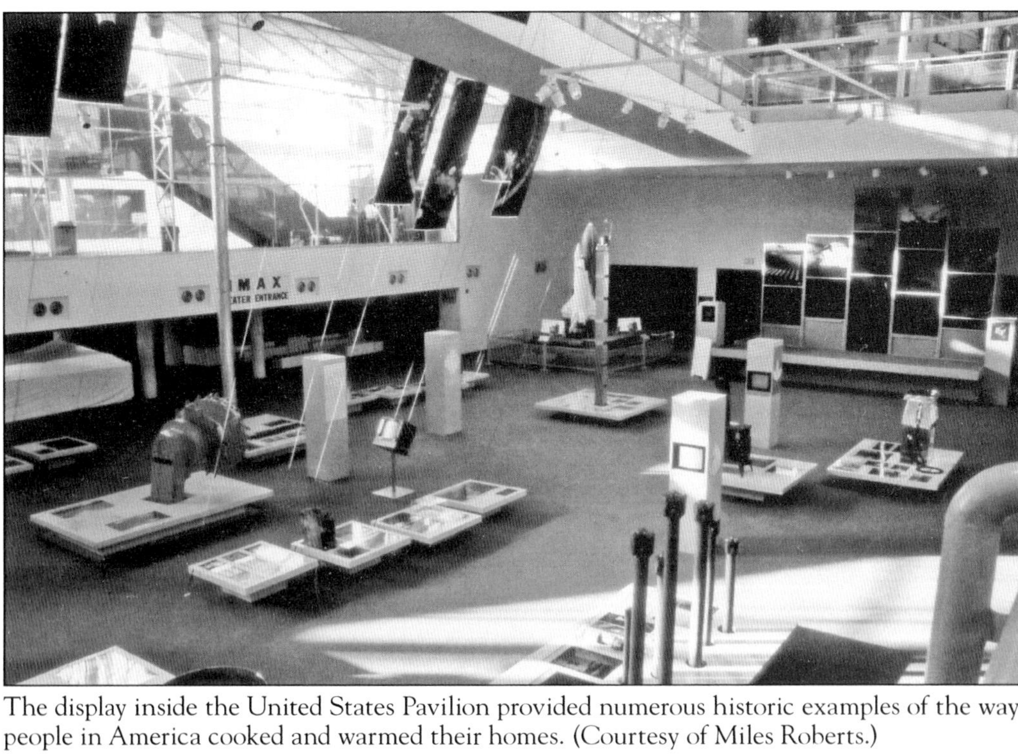

The display inside the United States Pavilion provided numerous historic examples of the ways people in America cooked and warmed their homes. (Courtesy of Miles Roberts.)

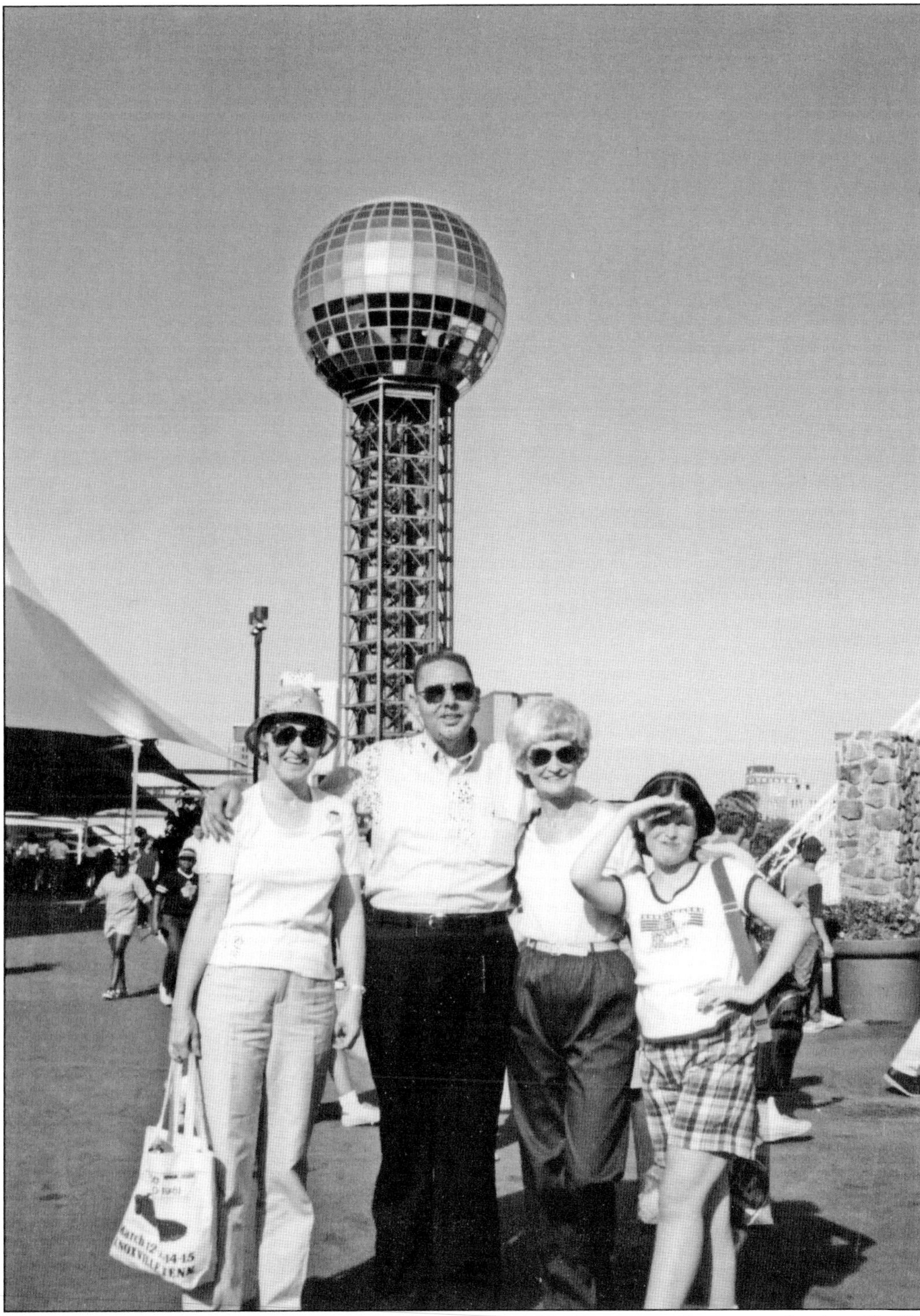

The Prather family of Norcross, Georgia, remembers having a grand time at the fair. Shelby Prather, wearing the straw hat, Jerry and Jackie Perry, friends of the family, and Mendy Prather, age 11, pose as Jim Prather snapped the picture. (Courtesy of Jim Prather.)

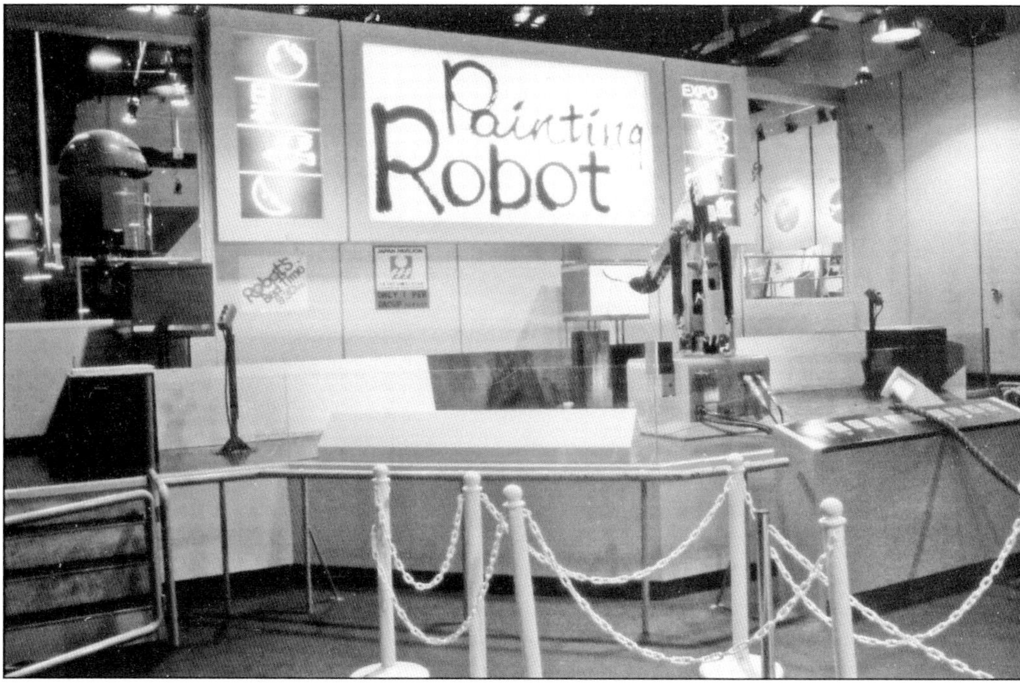

The exhibit inside the Japanese Pavilion was arranged around the topics of energy and future technology. One display included a painting robot. (Courtesy of Miles Roberts.)

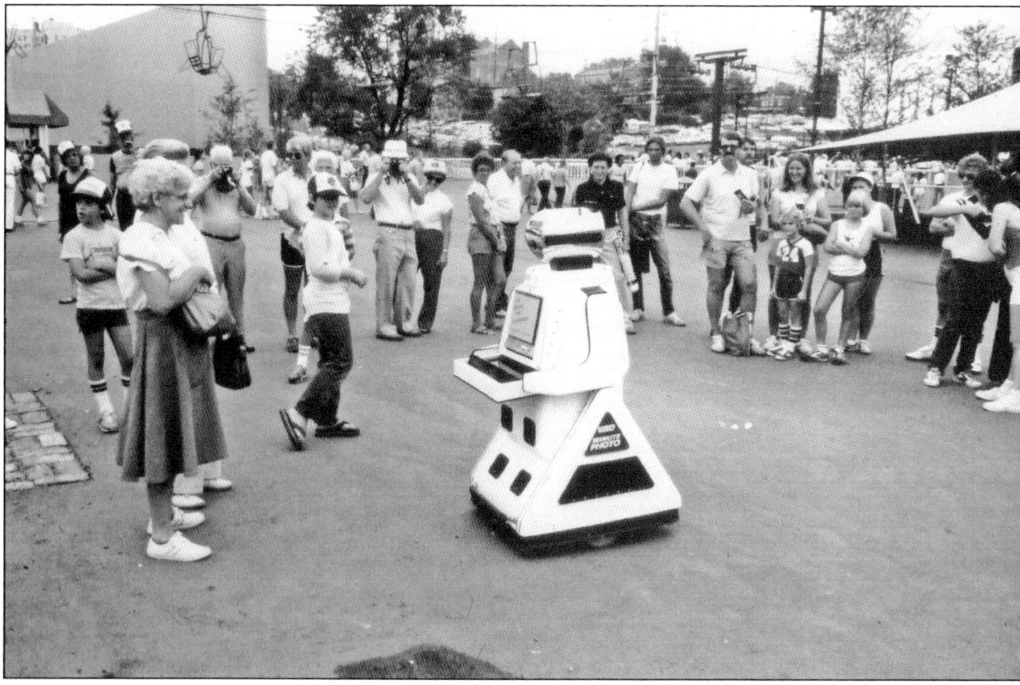

Visitors were delighted with the robot built for the Japanese Pavilion, which appeared to be human as it strolled throughout the fair. (Courtesy of Miles Roberts.)

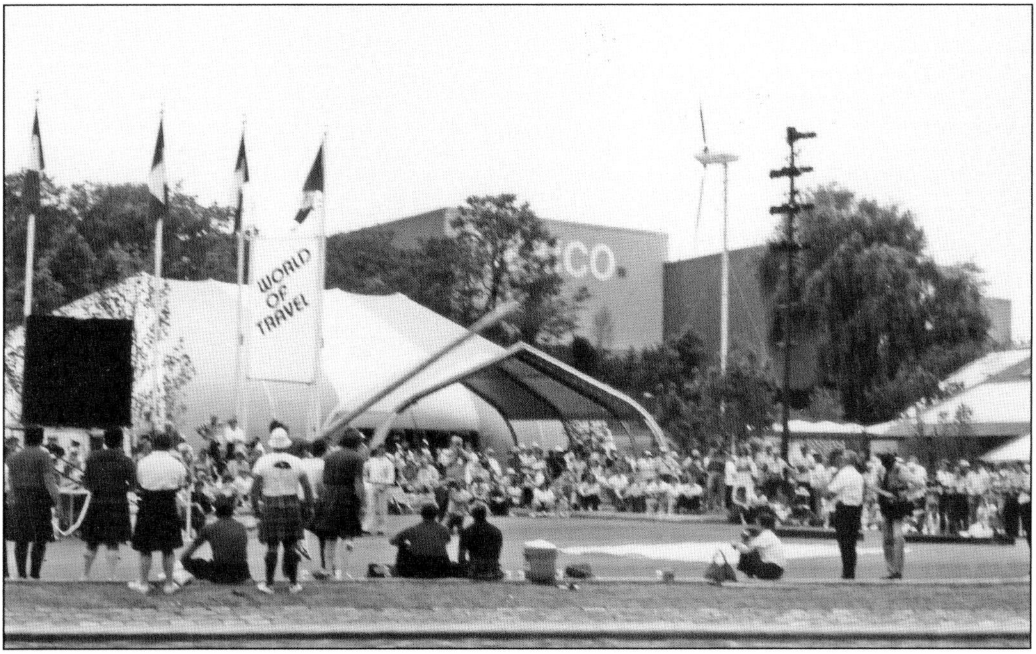

The exhibits in the Mexican Pavilion reflected its status and history as a major oil-producing country. (Courtesy of Miles Roberts.)

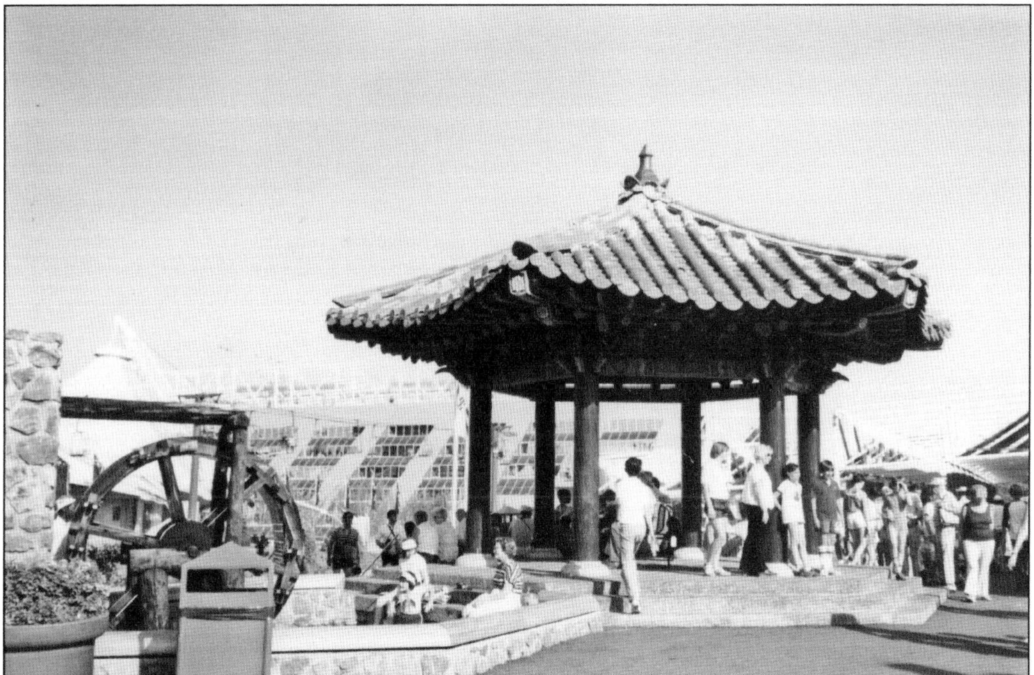
Korea's pavilion was easily recognized because of the pagoda. Visitors enjoyed the traditional architecture as well as the shade the tent-like structure provided from the hot sun. Pagodas are thought to have a spiritual connotation in Korea and are often placed near bridges and used near the openings of gates. (Courtesy of the Prather family.)

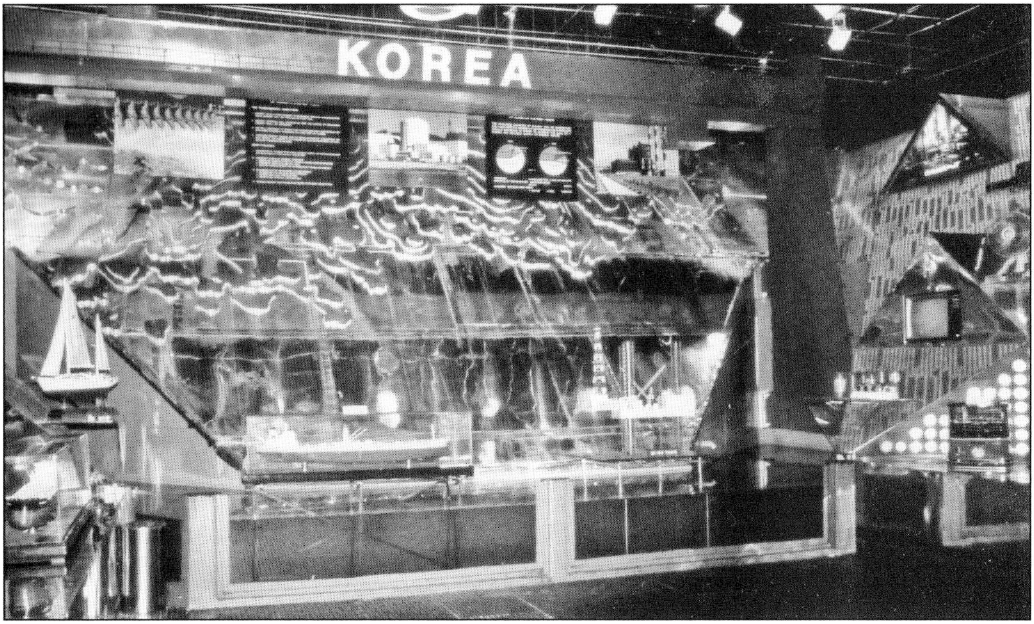

The historic perspective of the methods used in Korea for energy sources, including a large waterwheel to demonstrate the value of water power to the country, was shown in the pavilion, divided into three sections for the past, present, and future. (Courtesy of KIEE.)

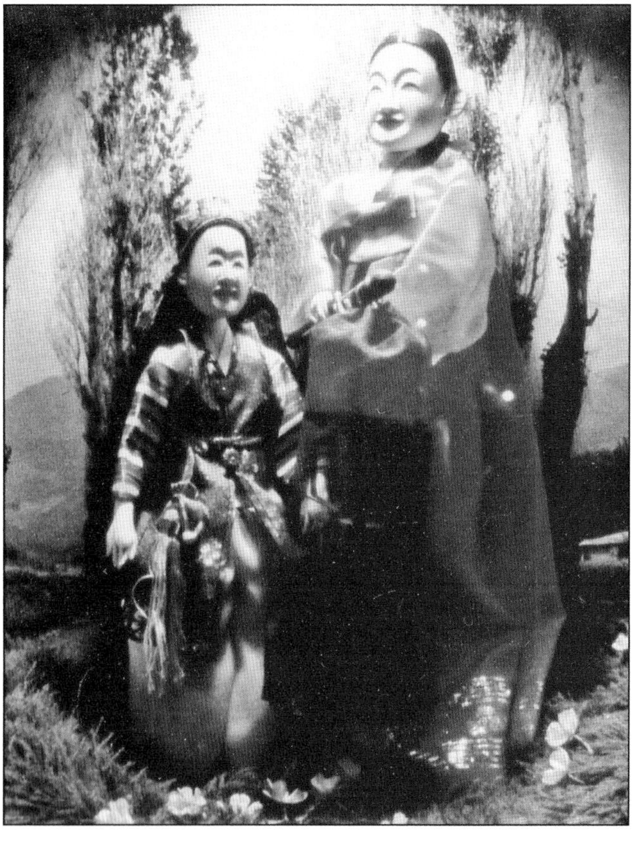

Mannequins were on display in front of the Korean Pavilion and were used to display examples of traditional Korean clothing. According to information presented on a pamphlet from the pavilion, the top blouse-like part of the outfit, which had long sleeves stretching down to the waist, is called a *jeogori* The skirt is called a *chima*. The coat, or outer garmet, is called a *durumagi* and is worn over regular clothes for warmth during cold weather. Commoners wore white, except during festivals and special occasions such as weddings. Clothes for the upper class were made of bright colors and indicated the wearer's social status. Various accessories such as foot gear, jewelry, and headdresses or hair pins completed the outfit. The mother and daughter pictured here must have been from the upper class because their ornate clothing was brightly colored. (Courtesy of KIEE.)

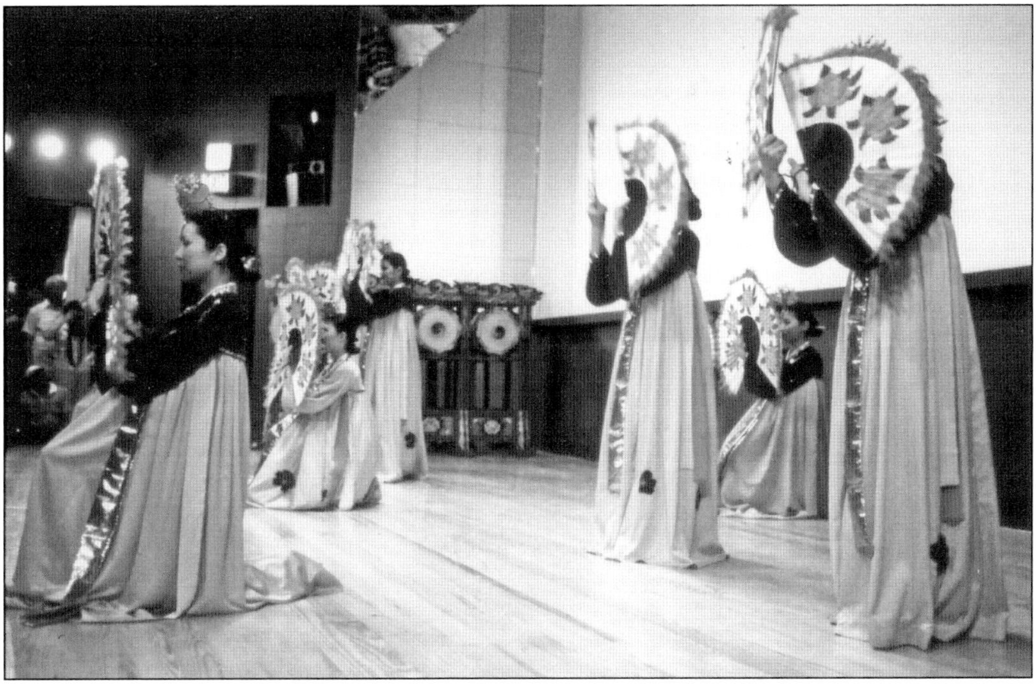

Korean dances originated thousands of years ago. They are noted for the use of props and colorful clothing. Drums, hats, swords, fans, and scarves are types of props often used. The central theme of the dances included such topics as harvest celebration, unrequited love, young love, war, or honor to ancestors. Traditional Korean dances, such as the fan dance, were presented inside the pavilion twice daily. (Courtesy of Charlie Brookes.)

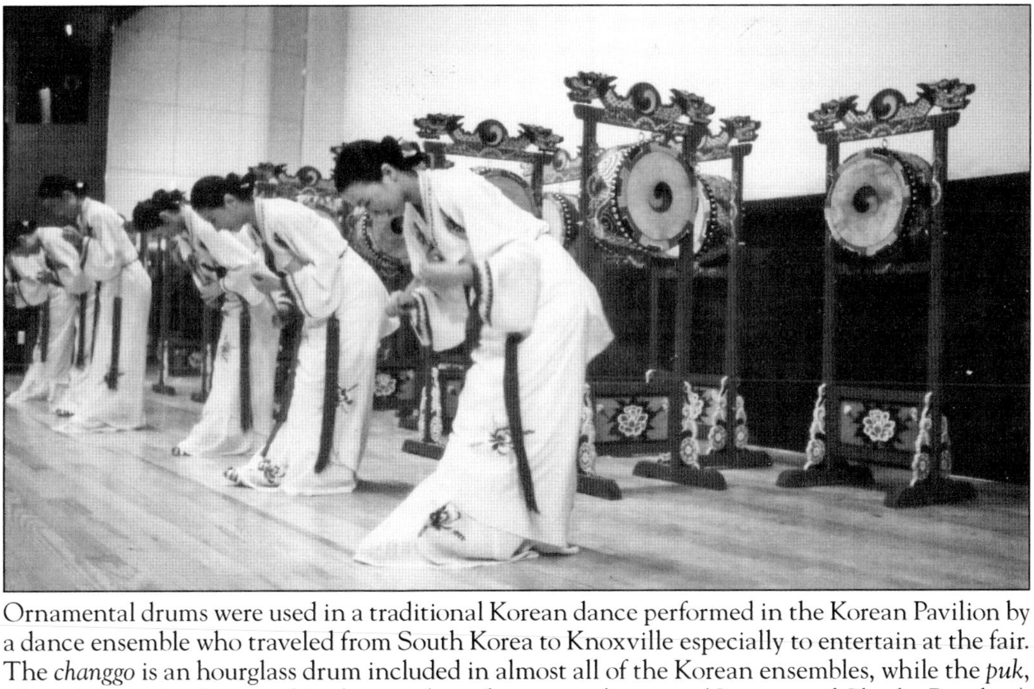

Ornamental drums were used in a traditional Korean dance performed in the Korean Pavilion by a dance ensemble who traveled from South Korea to Knoxville especially to entertain at the fair. The *changgo* is an hourglass drum included in almost all of the Korean ensembles, while the *puk*, a barrel drum, is often used in dances about farmers and nature. (Courtesy of Charlie Brookes.)

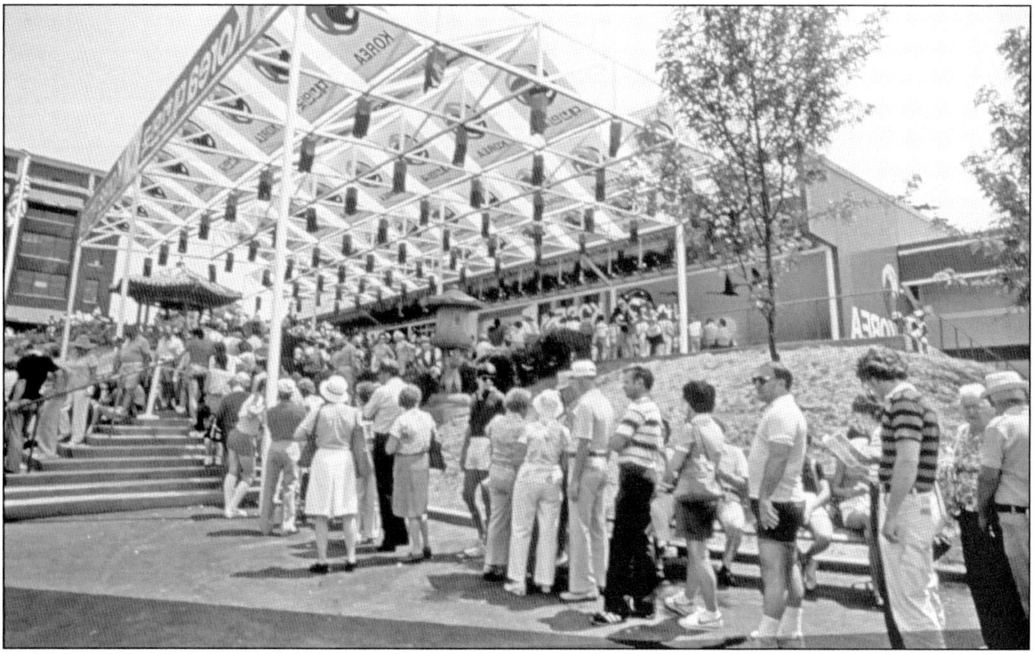

Visitors waited in long lines to visit the pavilion from the Republic of Korea. Inside the exhibit was an *ondoi*, a hot-floor heating system used since the prehistoric age. There was also a restaurant that served traditional Korean foods, and many items were for sale in a gift shop. (Courtesy of KIEE.)

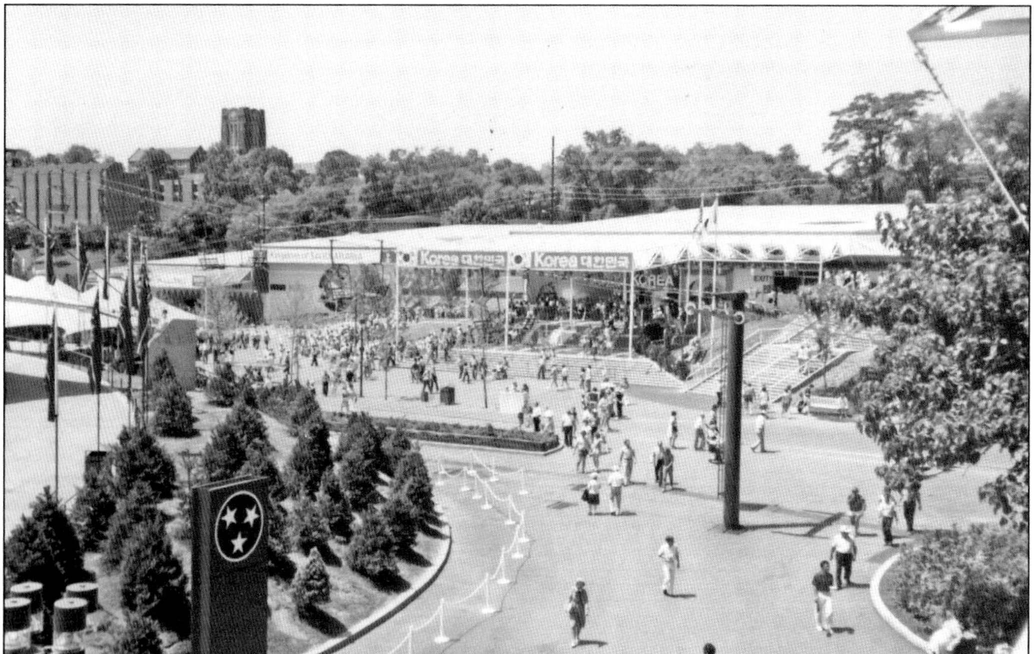

The Korean Pavilion was divided into three zones on the inside. One represented the present, one represented the past, and one represented the future. There were several multimedia presentations as well as live performances. (Courtesy of the Prather family.)

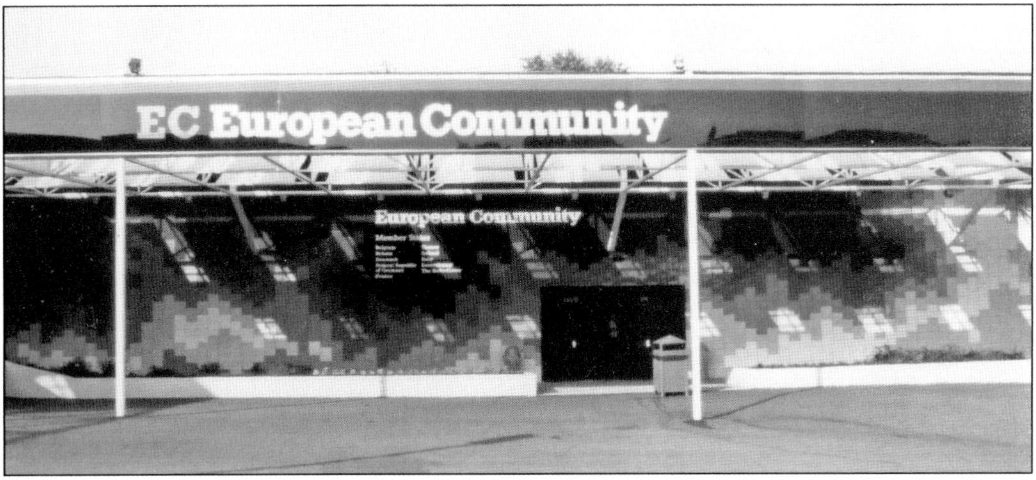

The European Economic Community (EEC), an organization established in 1958 by a treaty signed in 1957 by Belgium, France, Italy, Luxembourg, the Netherlands, and West Germany (now Germany), was known informally as the Common Market. The EEC was the most significant of three treaty organizations that were consolidated in 1967 to form the European Community. In 1982, the EEC listed 10 countires as host members for the fair's pavilion: Belgium, France, Germany, Italy, Luxembourg, the Netherlands, Iceland, United Kingdom, Denmark, and Greece. Other European countires such as Hungary and Ireland also participated in the fair. (Courtesy of Charlie Brookes.)

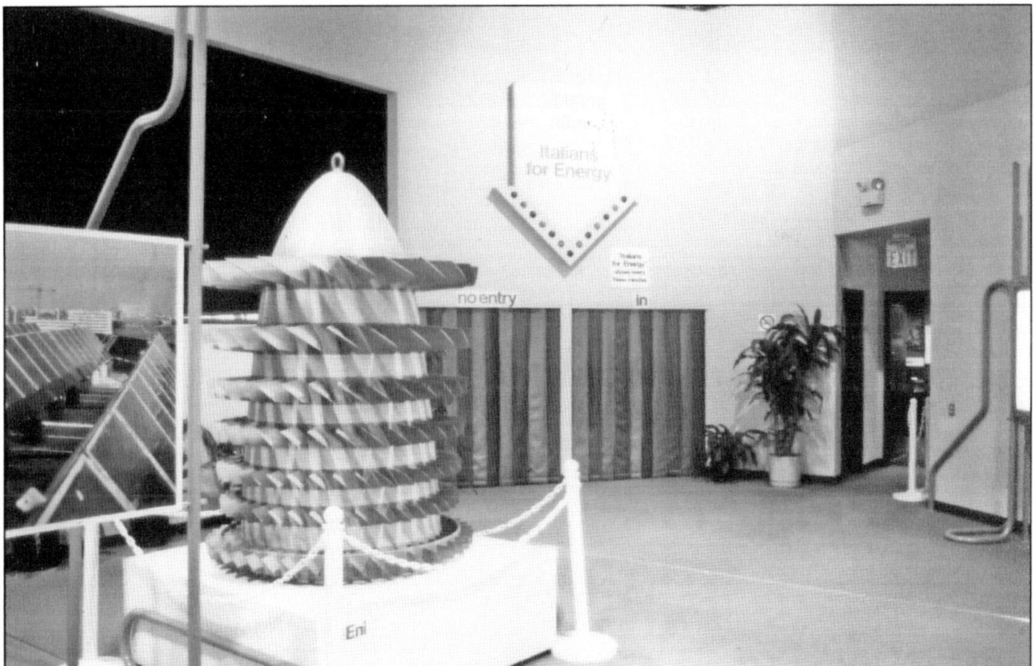

Italy's pavilion was cheerfully decorated in the red, green, and white colors of the country's flag. Focusing on the contribution made in the past centuries by famous Italian scientists, the pavilion included examples of machinery used in the production of energy. The pavilion was divided into four sections: production of energy, transmission of energy, renewable sources of energy, and energy saving. (Courtesy of Miles Brookes.)

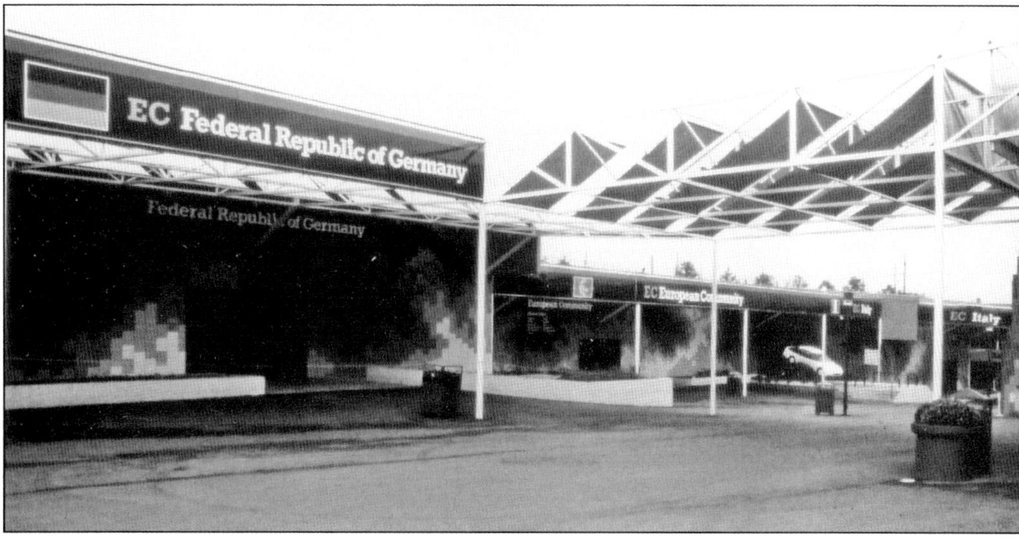

The 10 nations of the EC, or European Community—Belgium, France, Federal Republic of Germany, Italy, Luxembourg, the Netherlands, Iceland, United Kingdom, Denmark, and Greece—connected their pavilions into one long narrow building that was decorated with flags and bright colors. The fair's theme, "Energy Turns the World," was of particular importance to the EC whose goals are to improve and sustain economic well-being in Europe, to guarantee peace among the member states, and to help other nations with trade and aid. (Courtesy of Charlie Brookes.)

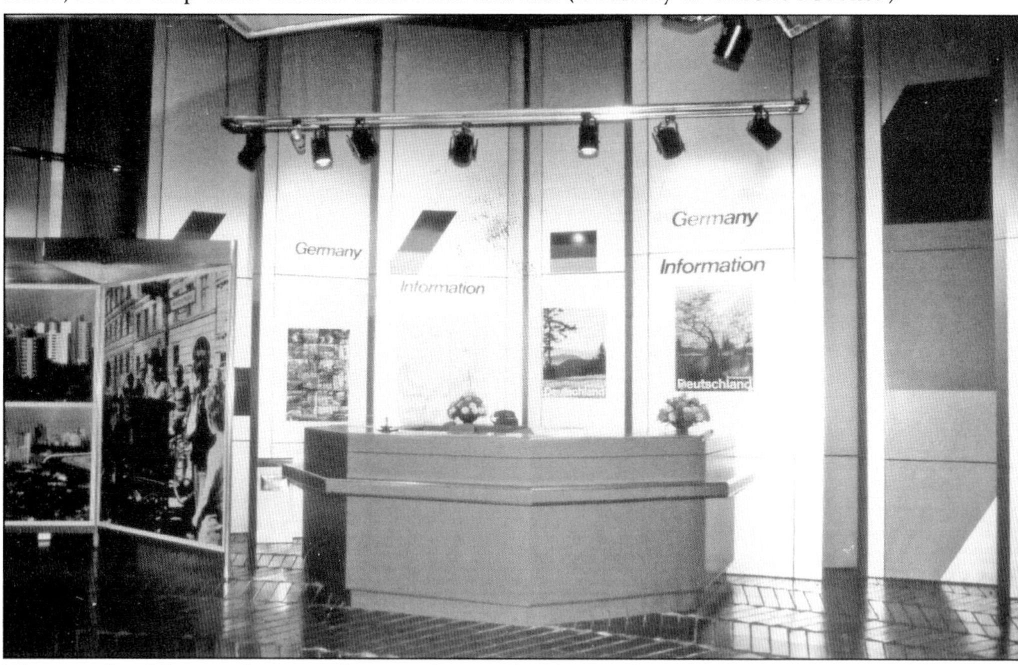

The outside of this pavilion was decorated using the three colors from the flag of Germany—black, orange, and yellow. The theme of the Federal Republic of Germany's pavilion was "Energy in Mind." The exhibit proceeded in steps that began with a history of Germany—its sociology, architecture, art, and culture. Emphasis was placed on the production, conservation, and future of energy with displays of solar panels, machinery, and wind and nuclear energy. Much of the information was presented on posters and photographs. (Courtesy of Miles Roberts.)

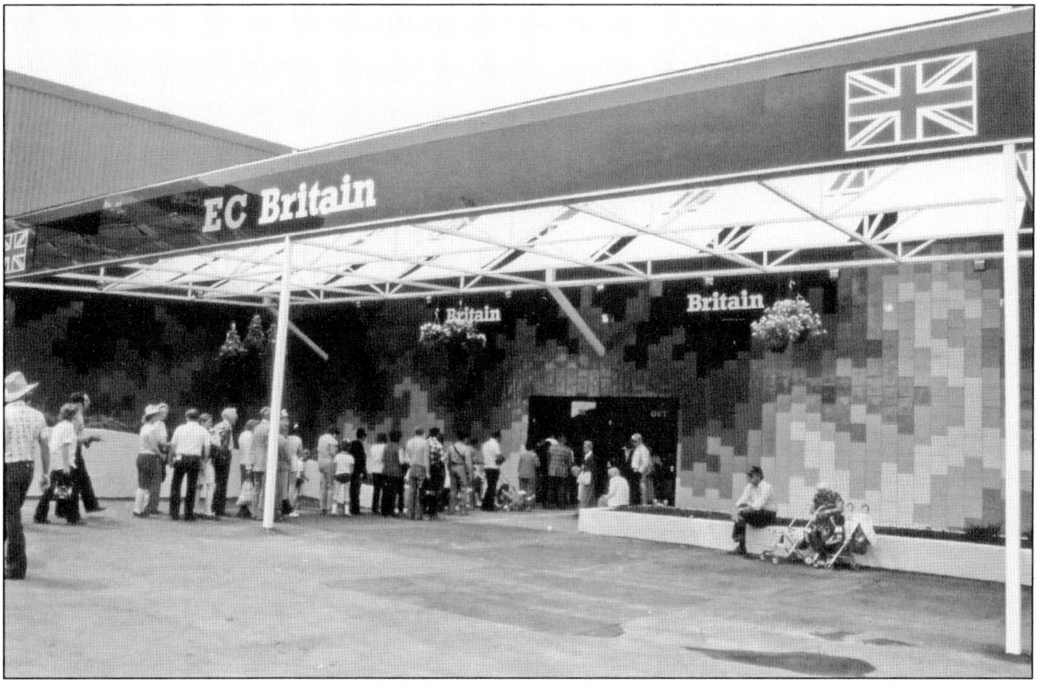

The United Kingdom's pavilion drew large crowds, who were disappointed by the displays of posters and photographs. The country's use of coal and oil and plans for new kinds of energy and technology were stressed. (Courtesy of Charlie Brookes.)

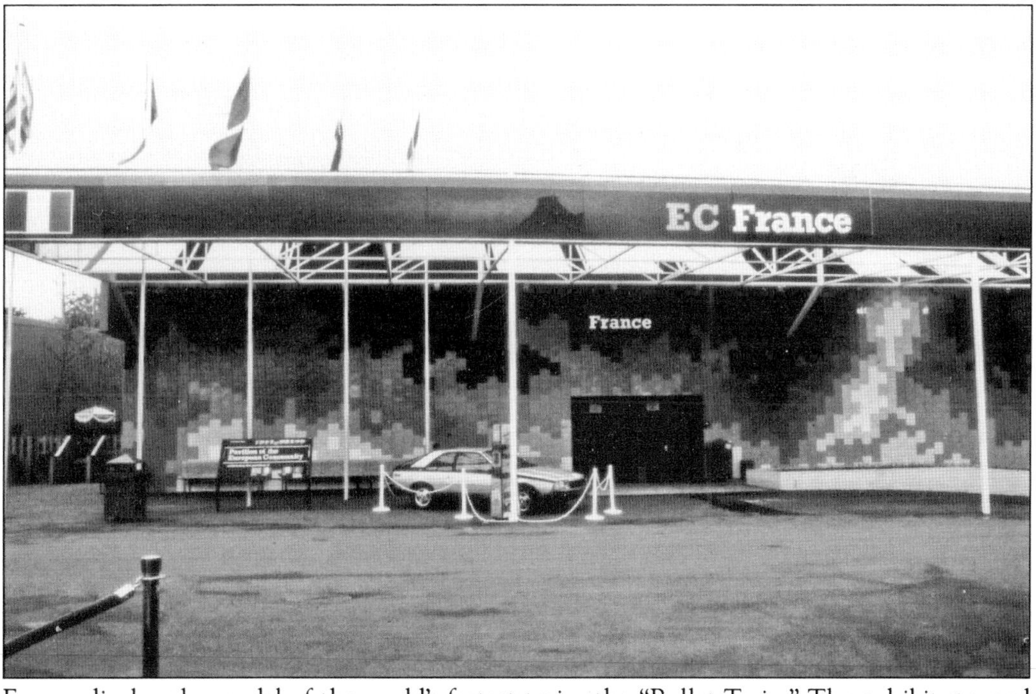

France displayed a model of the world's fastest train, the "Bullet Train." The exhibit stressed energy conservation. (Courtesy of Charlie Brookes.)

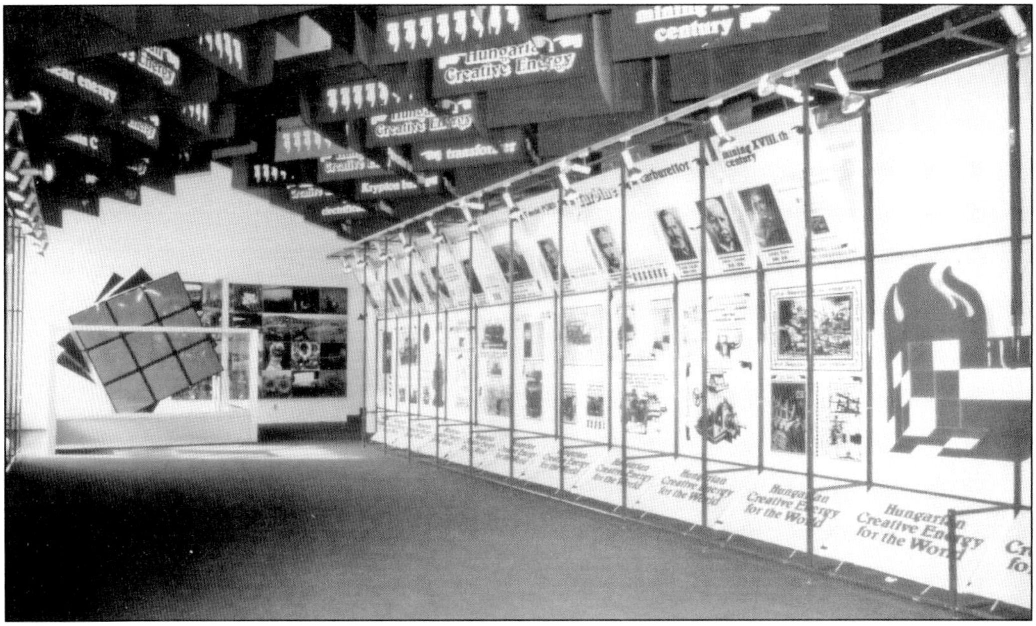

Hungary's pavilion was a "must see" for fairgoers because of the popularity of a toy invented by Erno Rubick in 1974. The mechanical puzzle, solved by turning sections of a four-sided cube until the colors matched, was all the rage at the fair. First called the "Magic Cube" by its inventor, it was purchased by a toy company and renamed Rubik's Cube. At one point, the new game was said to the be most popular toy in the world and by 2008 has sold an estimated 300 million copies. (Courtesy of Miles Roberts.)

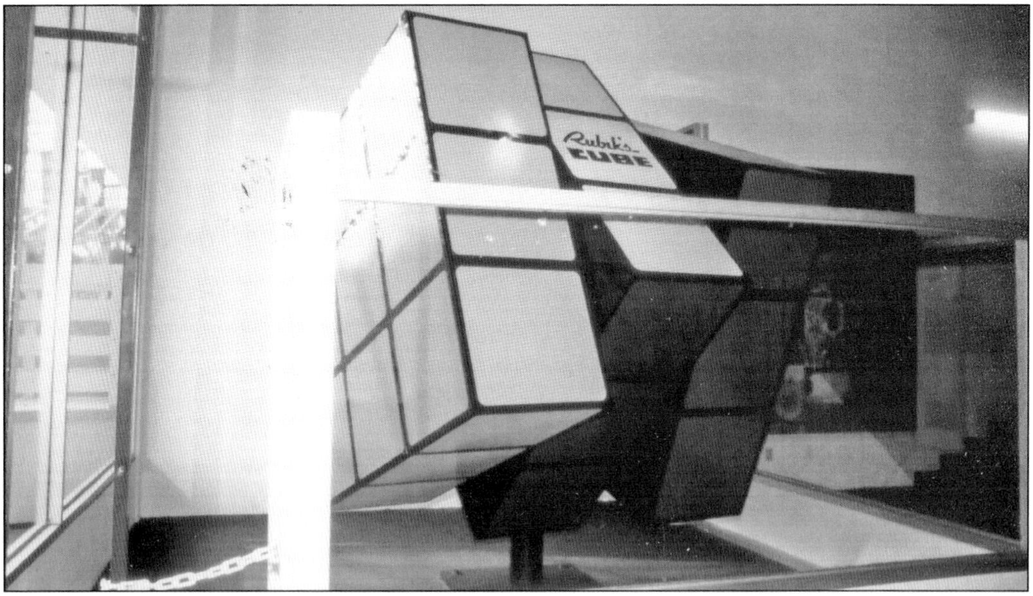

This large-scale model of a revolving Rubik's Cube was voted by visitors as one of the most popular displays at the fair. After the fair, the large diplay was sold and eventually moved to various spots around town. At one point, in the late 1990s, it was found sitting under a bridge near the fair site. After a public outcry from the community, it was rescued from despair, repaired, and placed back into service at a local museum. (Courtesy of Miles Roberts.)

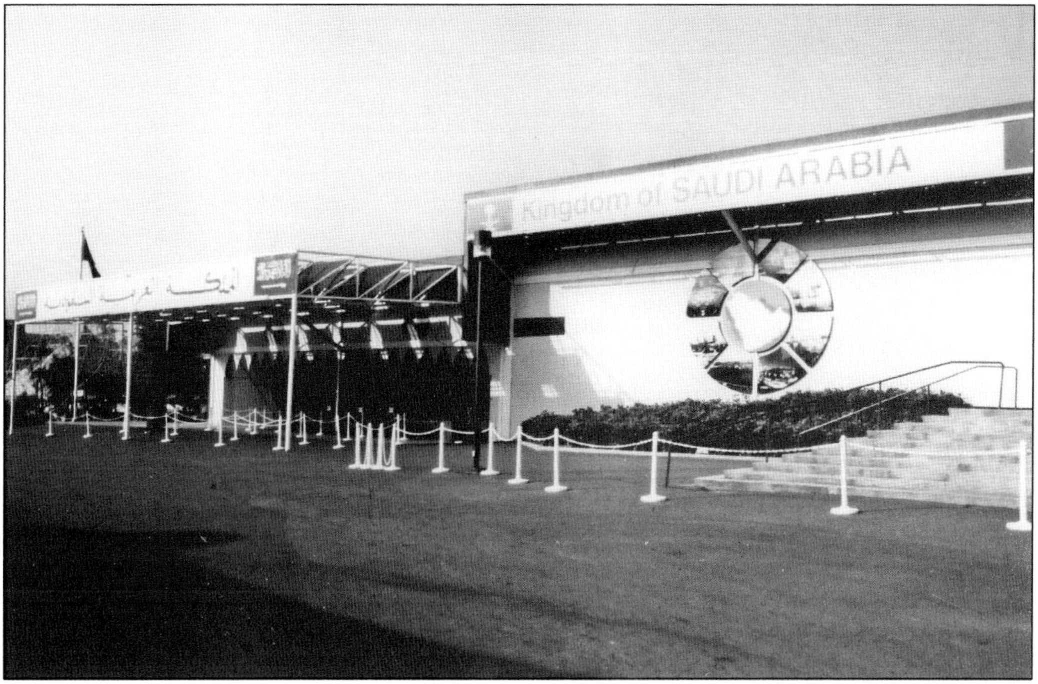

"Eternal Values in a Dynamic Nation" was the theme of the pavilion for the Kingdom of Saudi Arabia. Several exhibits included topics about Islam, Bedouin traditions, industrial development, human resources, and 50 years of U.S.-Saudi relations. The center of the pavilion was a model of the Grand Mosque of Mecca. (Courtesy of Miles Roberts.)

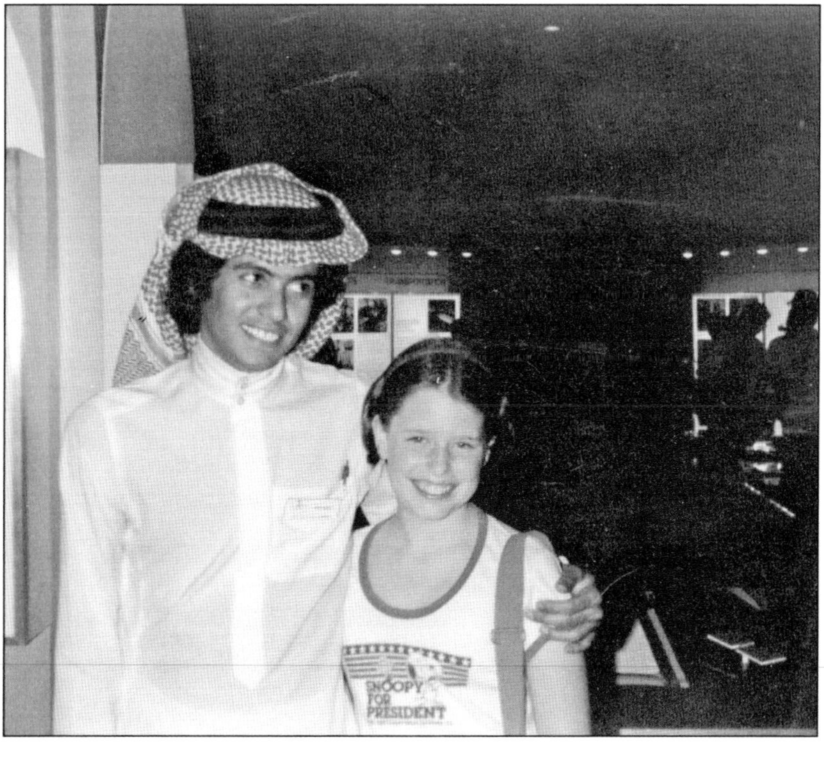

Mendy Prather of Norcross, Georgia, enjoyed meeting a young Saudi prince. (Courtesy of the Prather family.)

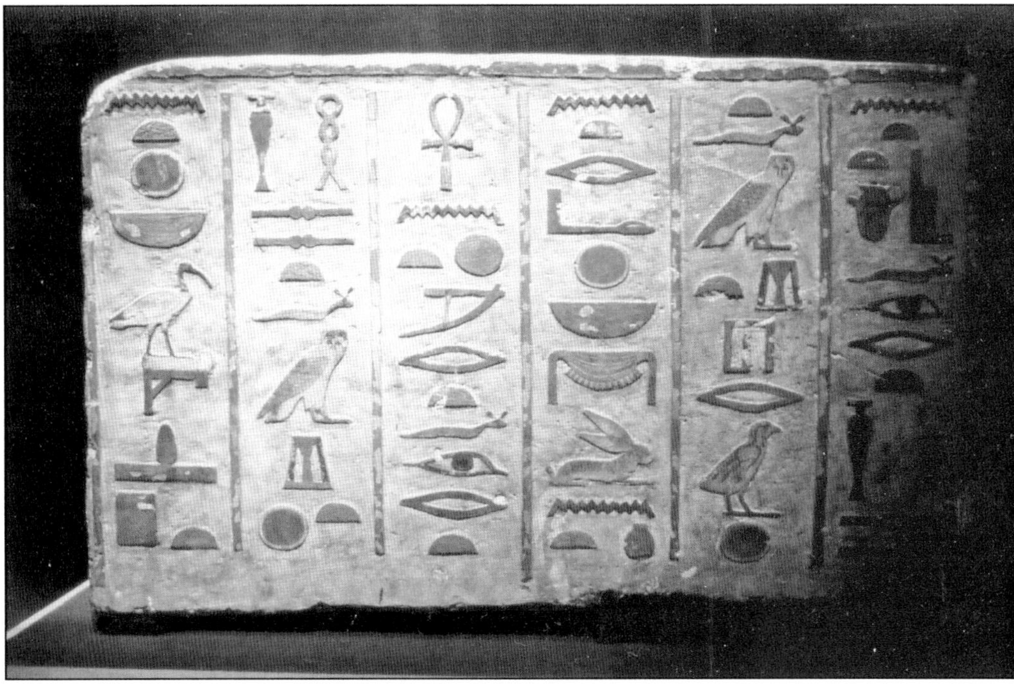

Egypt's exhibit of treasures from the tombs of ancient pharaohs was well received. Shown here is a stone table of hieroglyphic inscriptions, examples of some of the first written languages preserved on monuments. (Courtesy of Miles Roberts.)

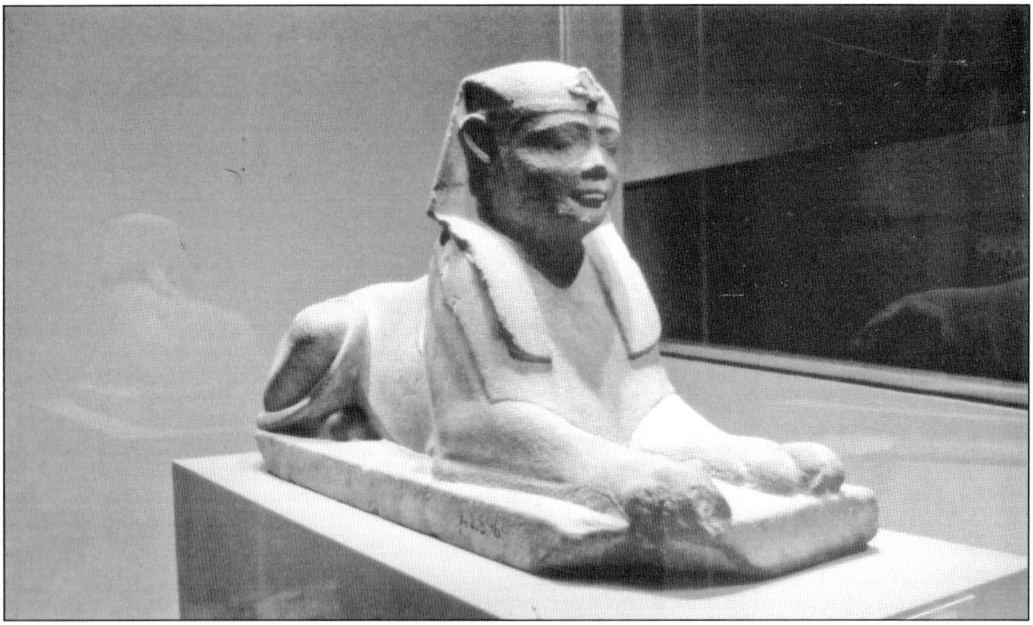

In Ancient Egyptian mythology, a sphinx is a zoomorphic figure, usually depicted as a recumbent lioness or lion with a human head. The figure had its origin in the Old Kingdom and is associated with the solar deity Sekhmet, who also was the fierce war deity and protector of the pharaohs. The role of the sphinxes was generally as temple guardians, and they may be found near royal tombs or religious temples. (Courtesy of Miles Roberts.)

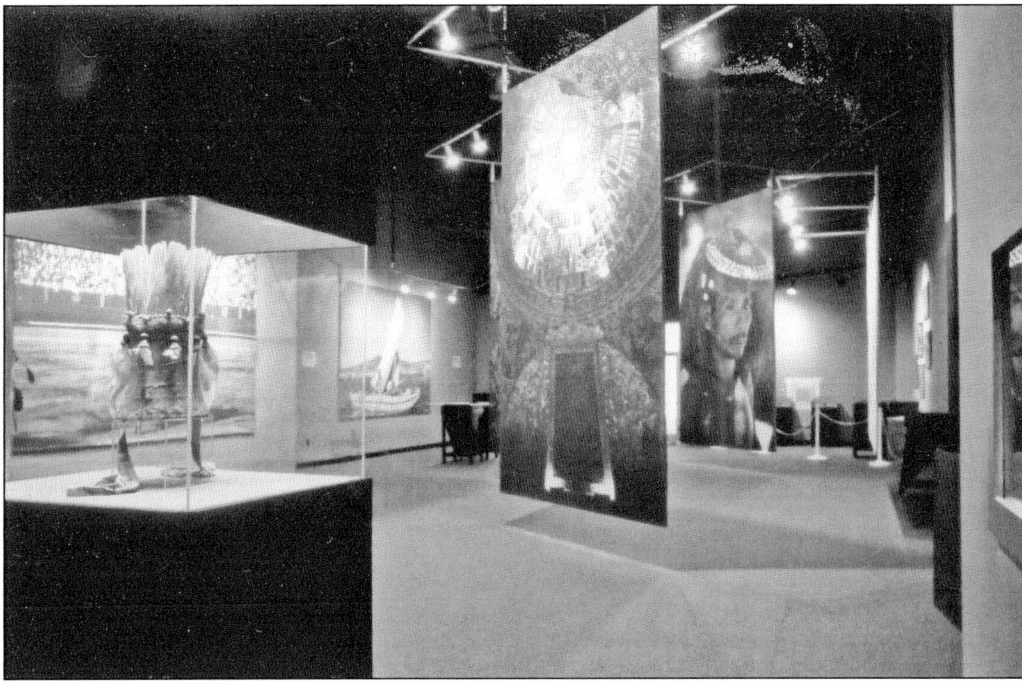

Located near the pavilions of the countries of China and Egypt, the pavilion for the country of Peru displayed over 250 golden treasures from the pre-Inca and Incan civilizations. (Courtesy of Miles Roberts.)

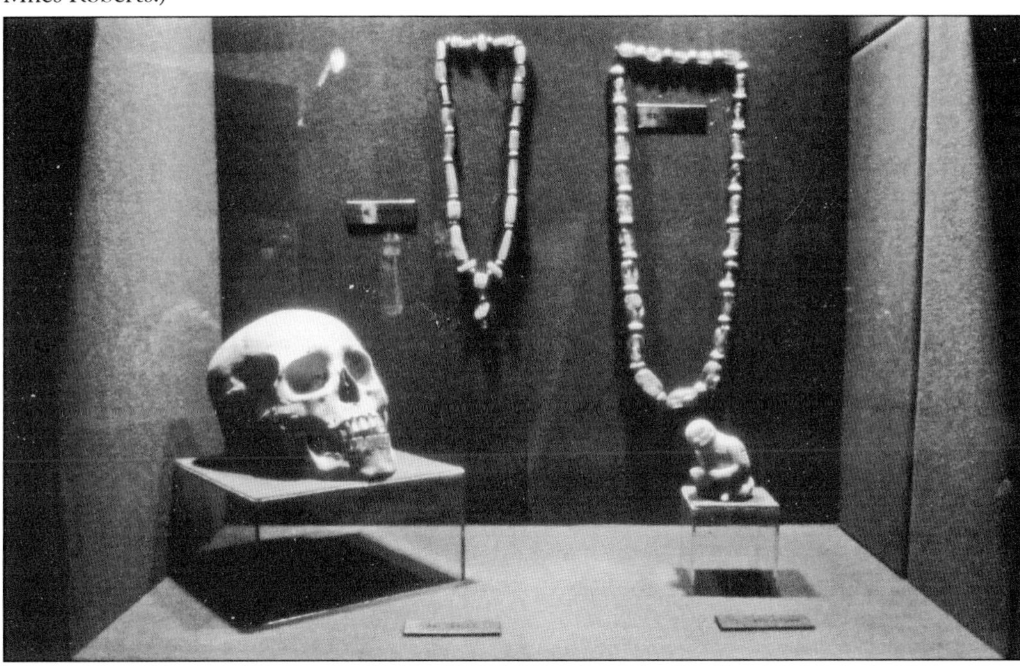

Peru's exhibit also included a skull and jewelry thought to be as much as 3,000 years old. Scientists from Peru, the Smithsonian Institution, the University of Tennessee, and other agencies unveiled a Peruvian mummy during a 15- to 36-day process. Experiments and analysis of the wrappings, hair, and microscopic insects on the body were studied. (Courtesy of Miles Roberts.)

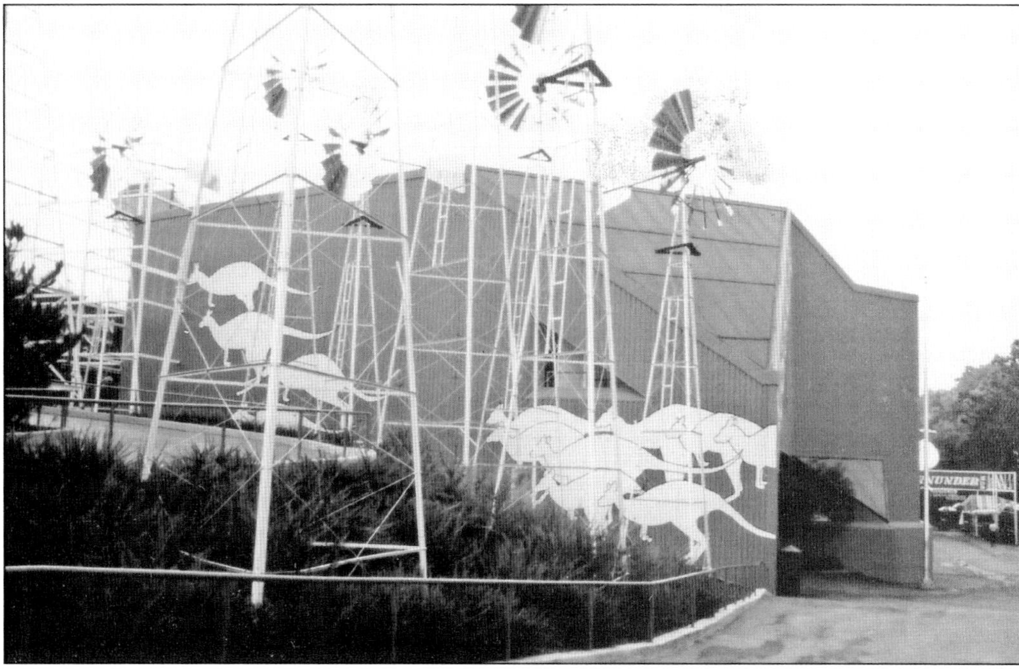

A garden of windmills provided beauty and interest to the Australian Pavilion, which won the top prize from the California-based *World Fair News* as the best international pavilion of the fair. (Courtesy of Miles Roberts.)

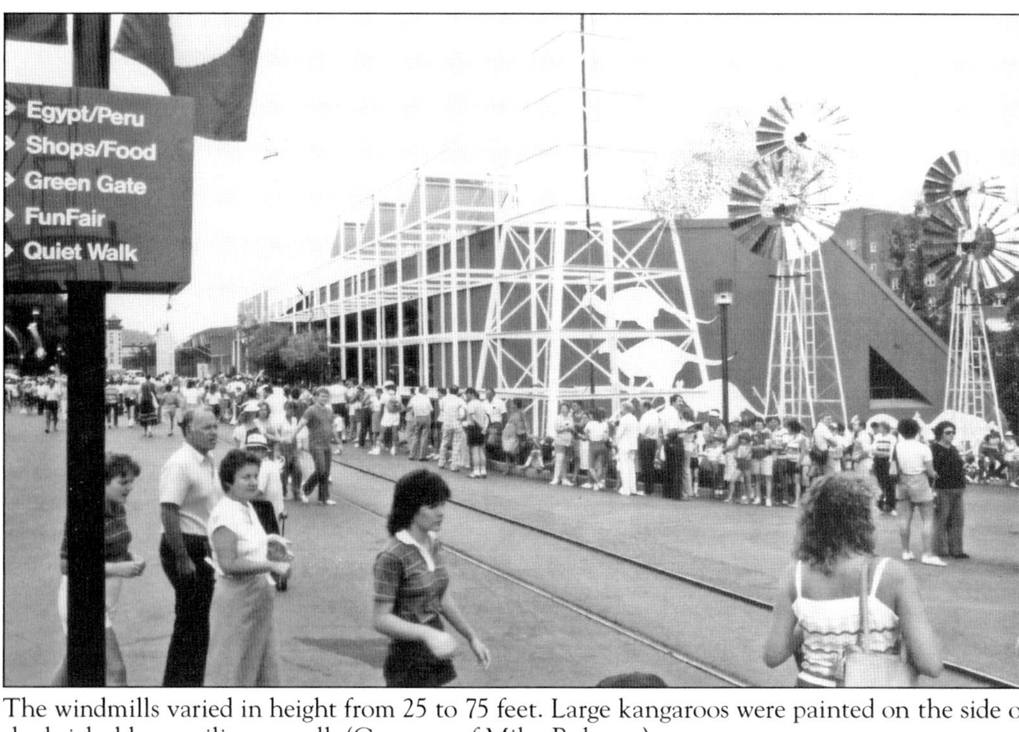

The windmills varied in height from 25 to 75 feet. Large kangaroos were painted on the side of the bright-blue pavilion as well. (Courtesy of Miles Roberts.)

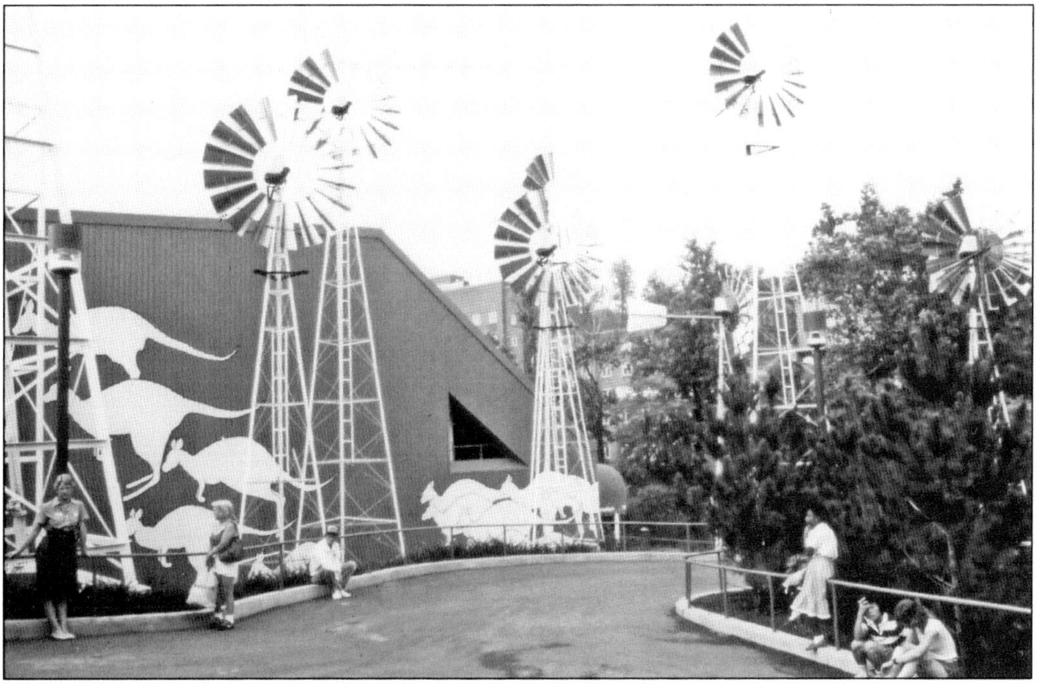

The topics covered inside the pavilion were energy resources, resource development, energy technology, and energy exports. (Courtesy of Miles Roberts.)

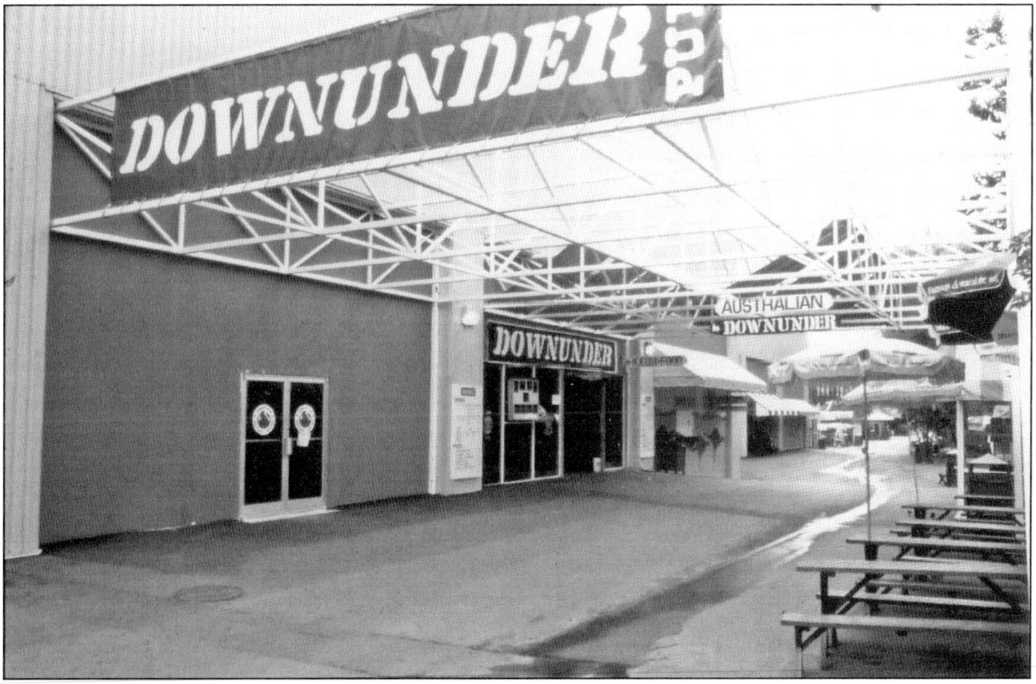

Australia's pavilion was Energy Down Under, which included the Down Under Pub serving cold beer and food. (Courtesy of Miles Roberts.)

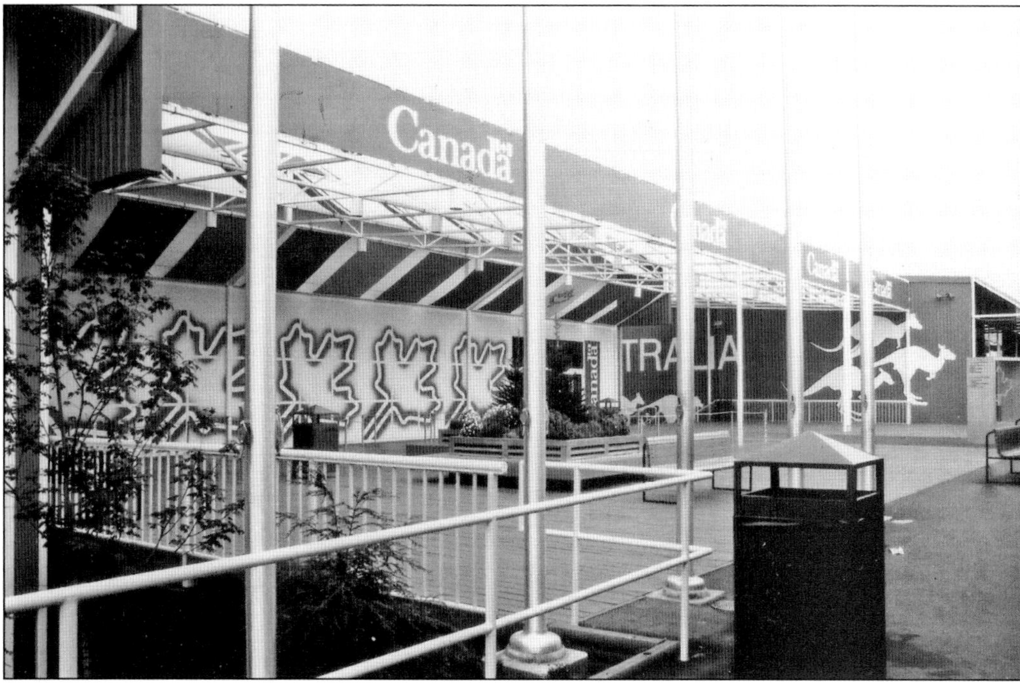

Flags and large maple leafs painted on the front of this building signaled the presence of the large country of Canada. (Courtesy of Miles Roberts.)

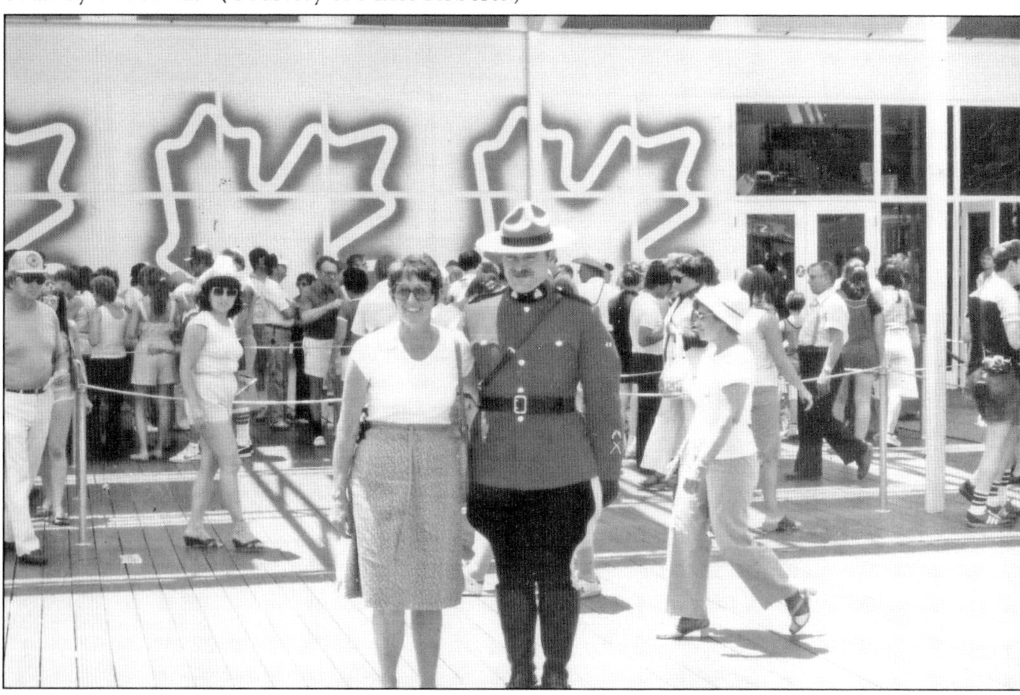

The Royal Canadian Mounted Police waved visitors into the pavilion, which introduced visitors to the "megaprojects" of Canadian energy development. A cinema gave a humorous interlude and transition to the second exhibit, about the need for efficient and economical transportation of energy across the 3.8 million square miles of the country. (Courtesy of Miles Roberts.)

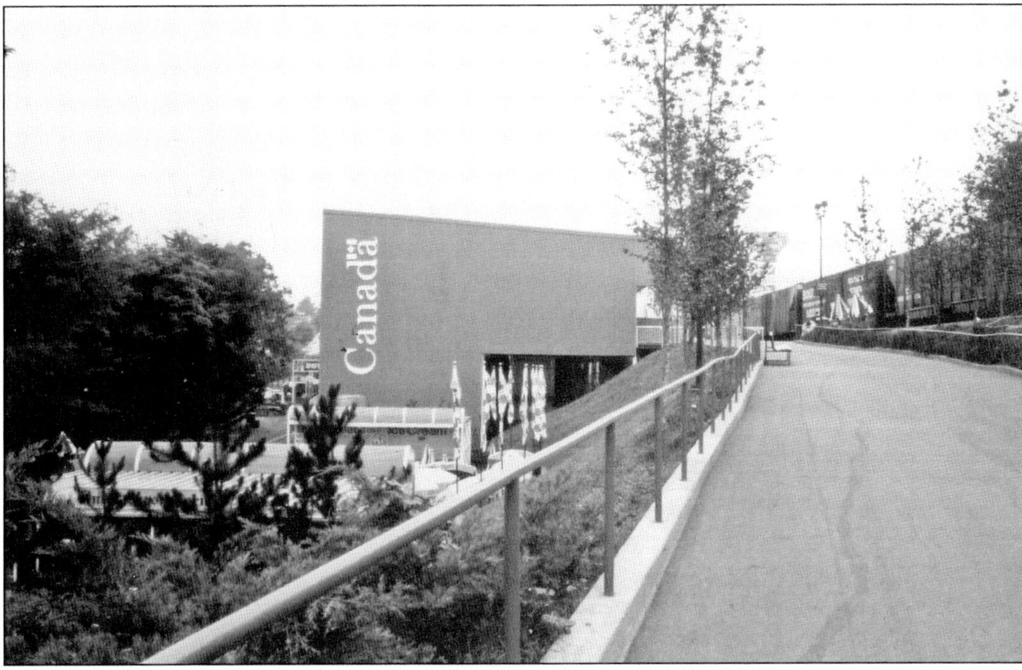

The dark blue pavilions were easily spotted on the trails that wound around from the Fun Fair back to the main level of the fairgrounds across Cumberland Avenue. (Courtesy of Miles Roberts.)

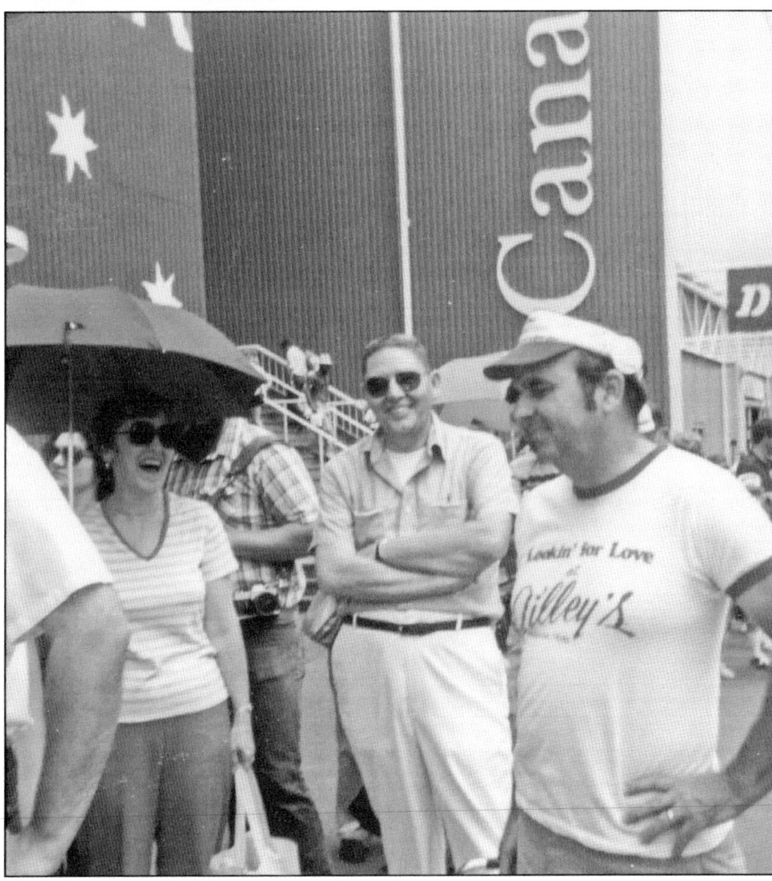

The Prather family visited the fair during the month of July. Jim Prather, seen in the Gilley's T-shirt, provided many photographs for this book. (Courtesy of the Prather family.)

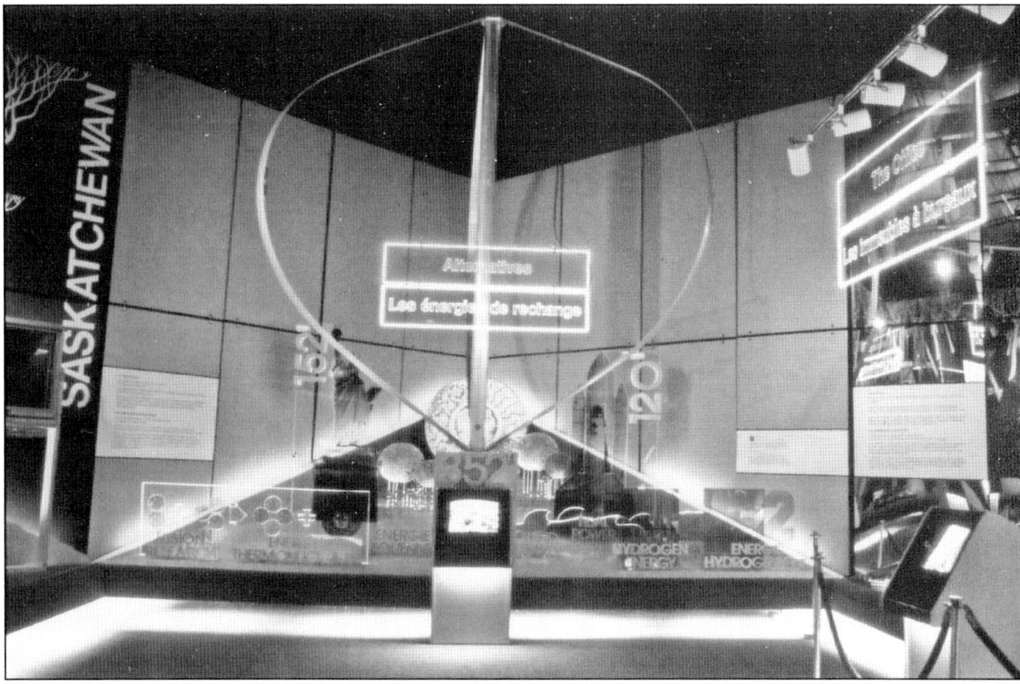

Inside the Canadian Pavilion, a light show as well as a short movie taught visitors about Canada's many sources of energy. (Courtesy of Miles Roberts.)

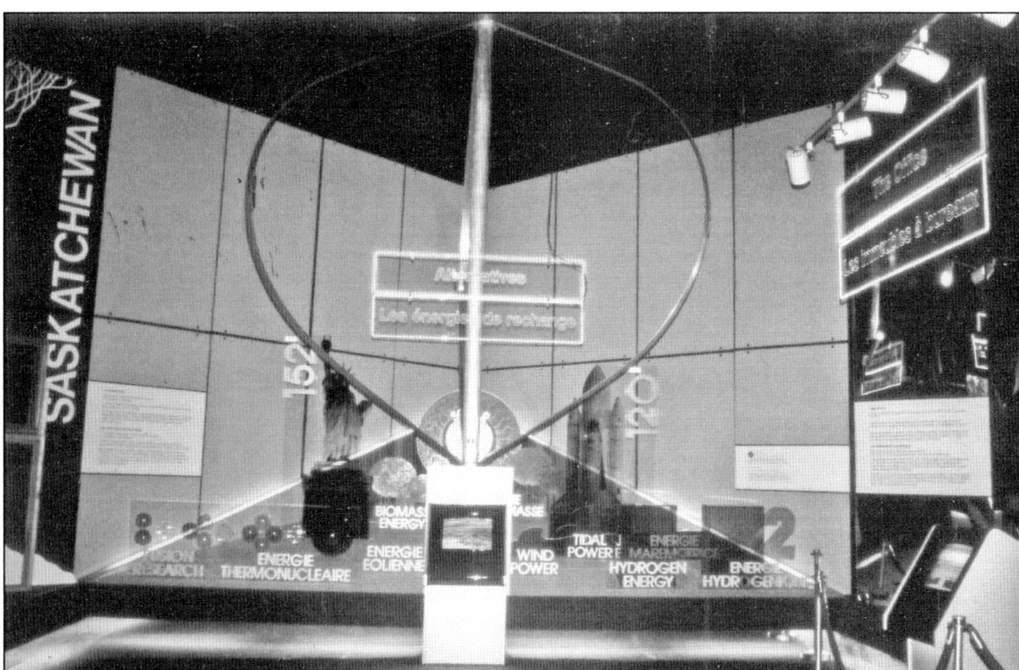

The world's largest wind turbine and Canada's search for alternative sources of energy were part of the exhibits provided by the provinces of Alberta, British Columbia, Ontario, and Saskatchewan. (Courtesy of Miles Roberts.)

This was a typical day as many visitors hurried to find the exhibits from Canada, Australia, and China. (Courtesy of KIEE.)

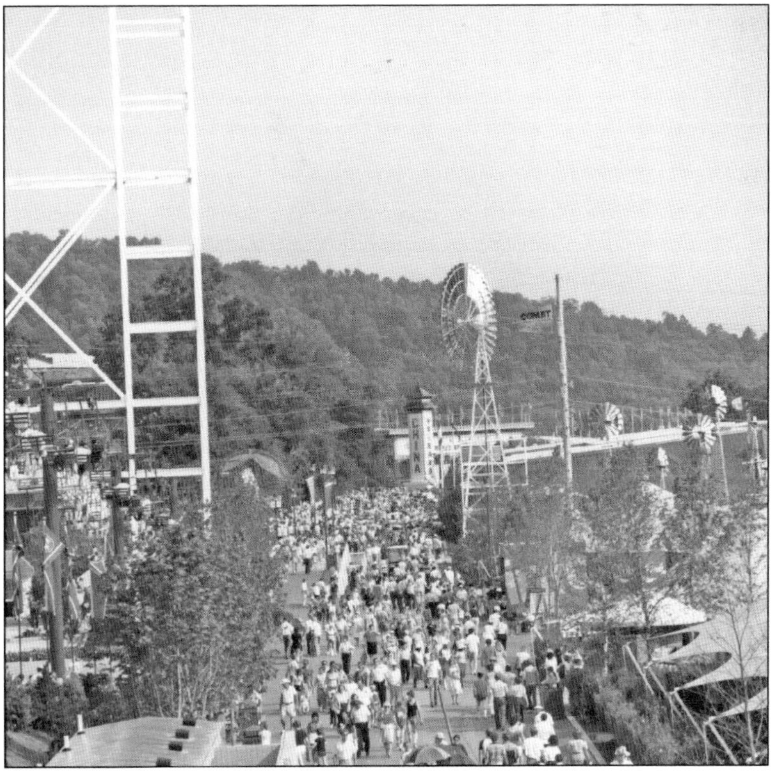

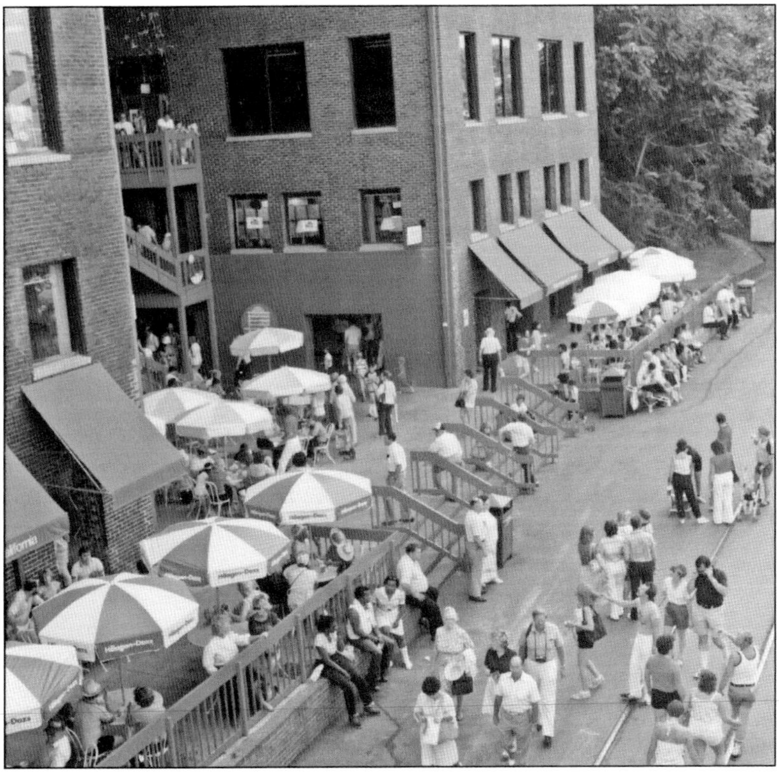

Picnic table umbrellas looked like large pieces of candy, creating a festive feeling on the fairgrounds. (Courtesy of KIEE.)

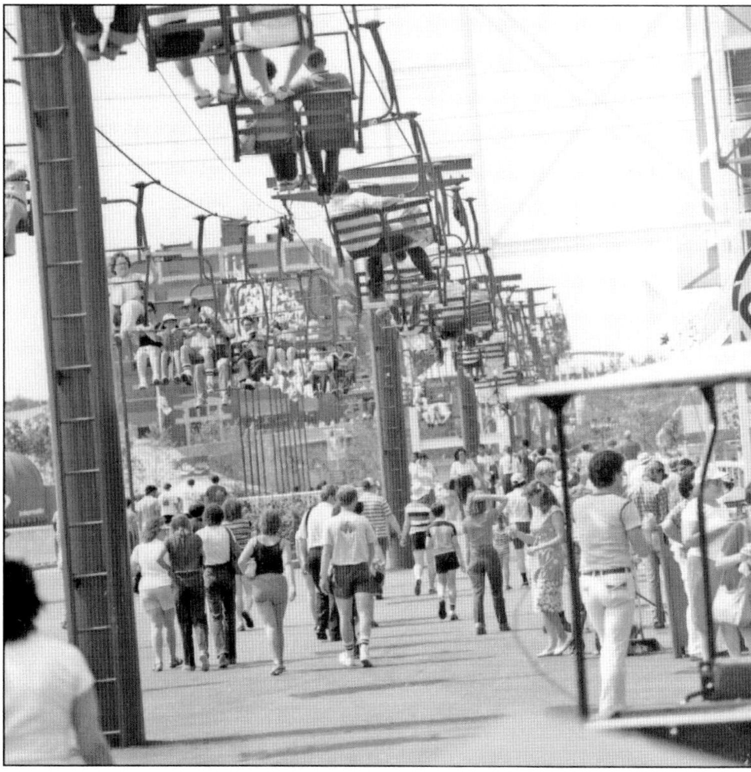

Fairgoers enjoyed riding the chair lift from the center of the fairgrounds to the Canadian Pavilion. The ride was provided by Sky Transpo, a Von Roll corporation based in Switzerland. (Courtesy of KIEE.)

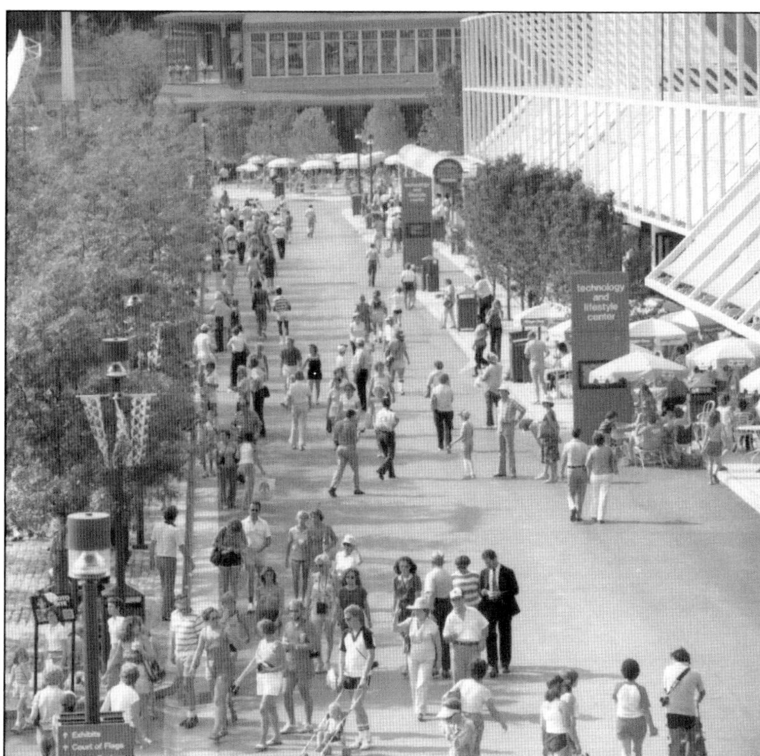

As temperatures began to fall and the days ticked by, visitors continued to rush across the fair site hoping to take in as much as they could in one day. (Courtesy of KIEE.)

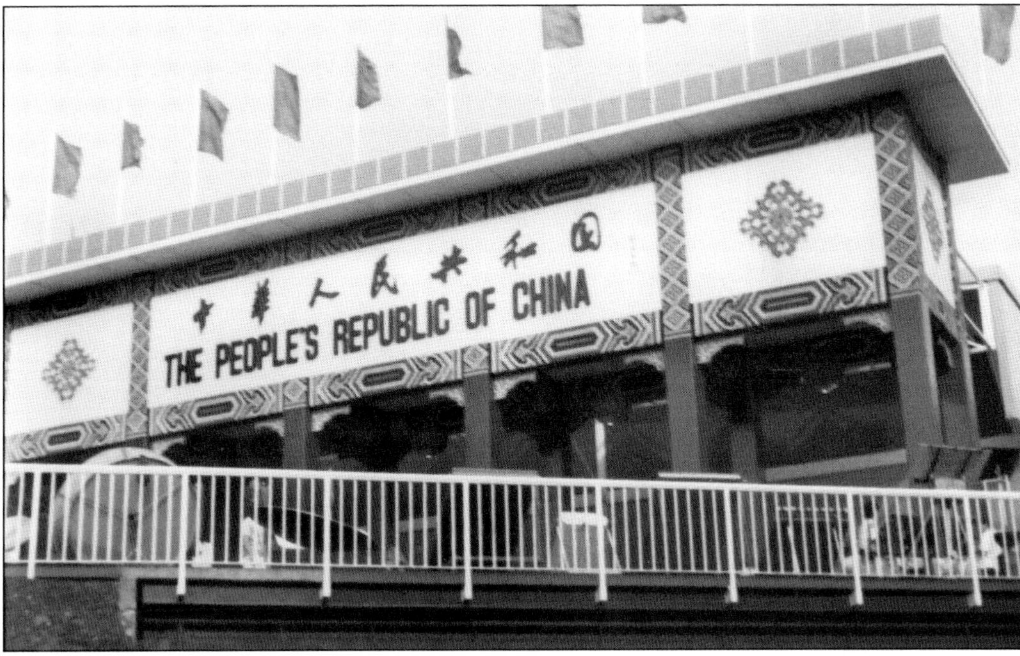

Visitors who came to the fair early in the morning could be seen running across the fairgrounds in order to be first in the lines for the Chinese Pavilion. (Courtesy of Miles Roberts.)

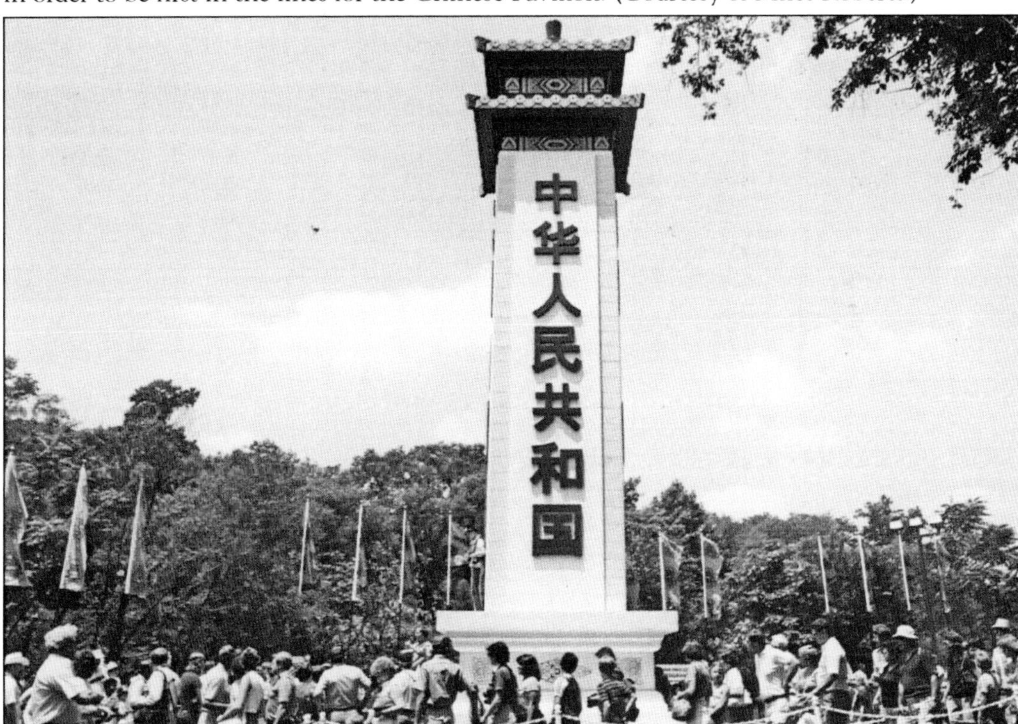

The symbol tower of the Chinese Pavilion and the red flags of the People's Republic of China led the way to the exhibit, which became the most popular spot in the fairgrounds. (Courtesy of KIEE.)

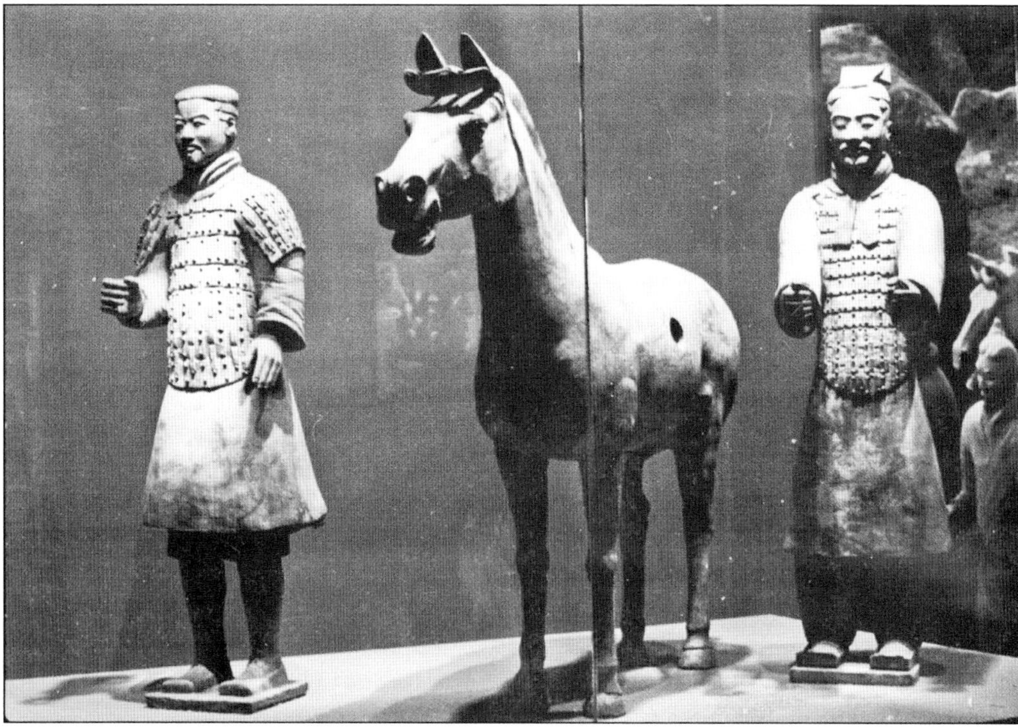

Statues of terra-cotta warriors and a horse, said to be over 2,000 years old, were found while archeologists were digging near the tomb of the first emperor of Qin. (Courtesy of KIEE.)

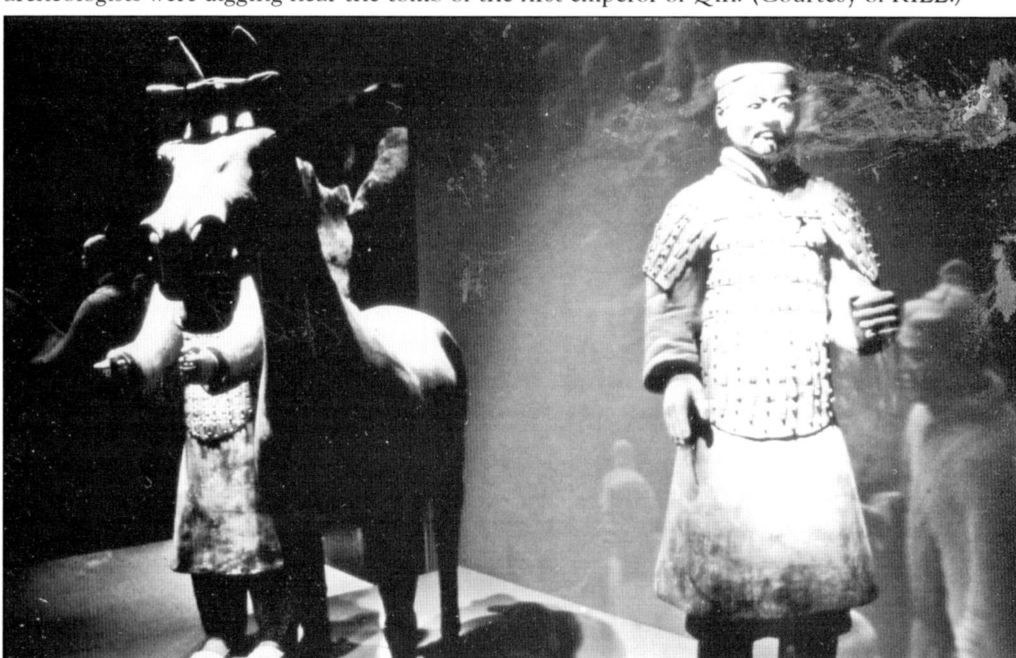

Although the horse and soldiers had been covered in dirt for many years, archeologists were able to save them and place hundreds of them on display. Others were left in place near the tomb where they were found in China. (Courtesy of Miles Roberts.)

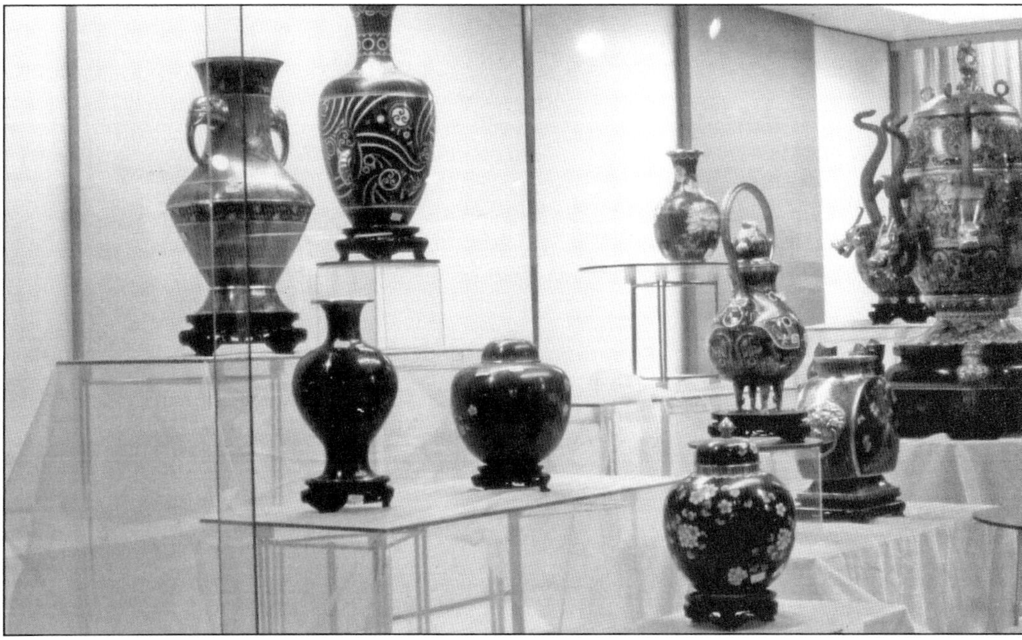

China's long-lost techniques of the celebrated ancient porcelain kilns such as Longquan, Jun, Ru, Guan, Cizhou, and Yaozhou were displayed through various examples of jars and vases. Often using themes from nature, the pottery on display was described by the hostess in the pavilion as being "like old trees putting forth new blossoms." Guests were also told that the colors of the pottery were determined from the type of soil and could range from deep blue to light brown. (Courtesy of KIEE.)

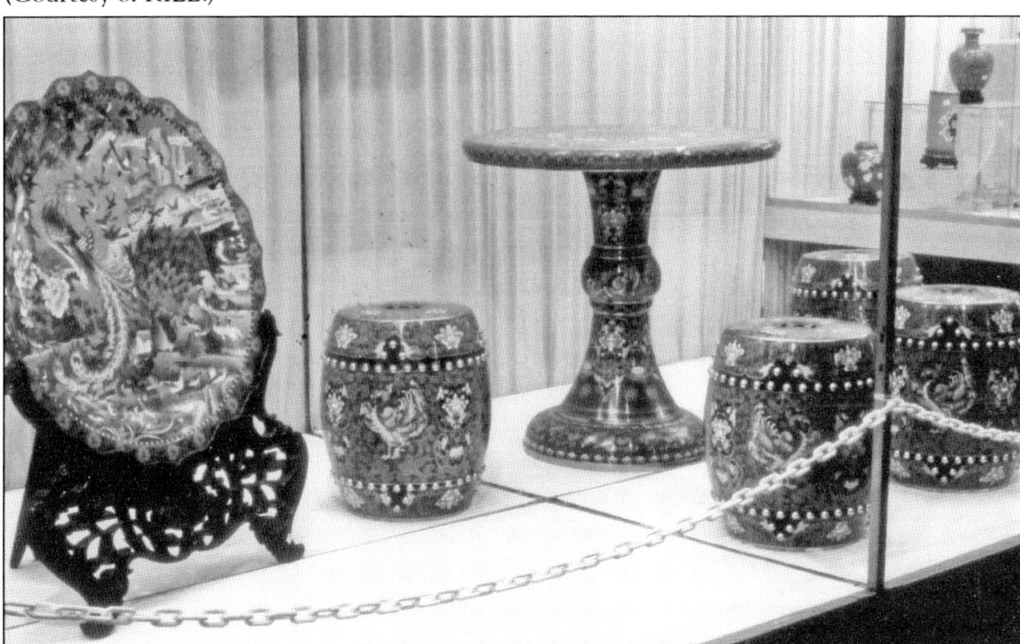

Porcelain items were often used to transport foods or herbs and also as furniture. Painting the items of pottery was an important part of the artwork. (Courtesy of KIEE.)

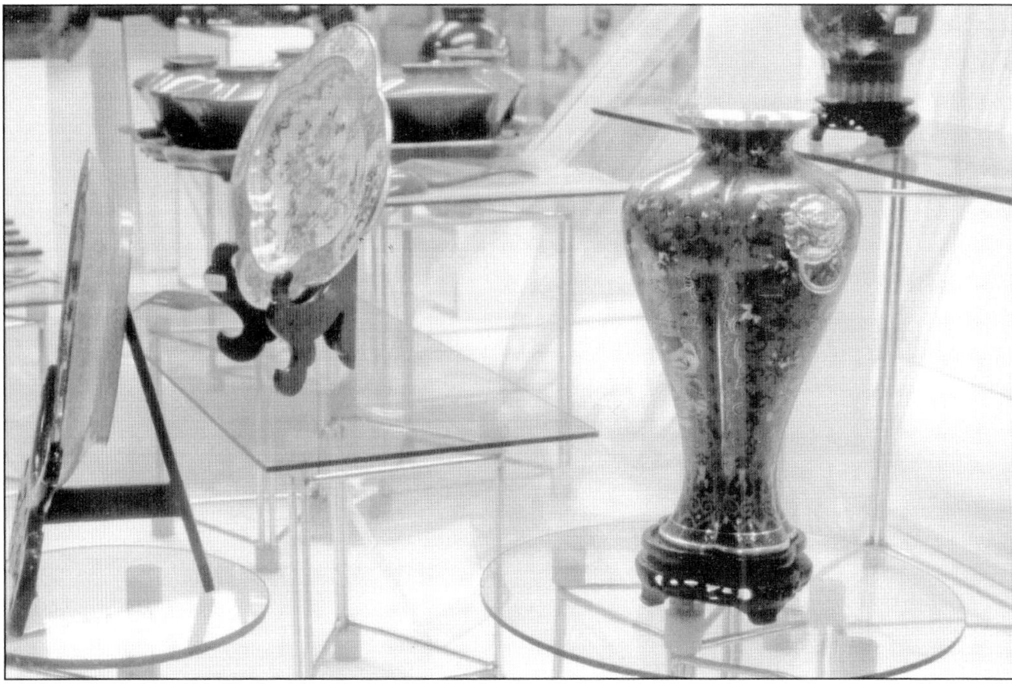

Visitors who stood in long lines just to get inside the Chinese Pavilion were heard to say, "What does all this pottery have to do with energy?" The representatives from China answered, "The energy and genius of the Chinese people is clearly shown by the displays of art and pottery." (Courtesy of Miles Roberts.)

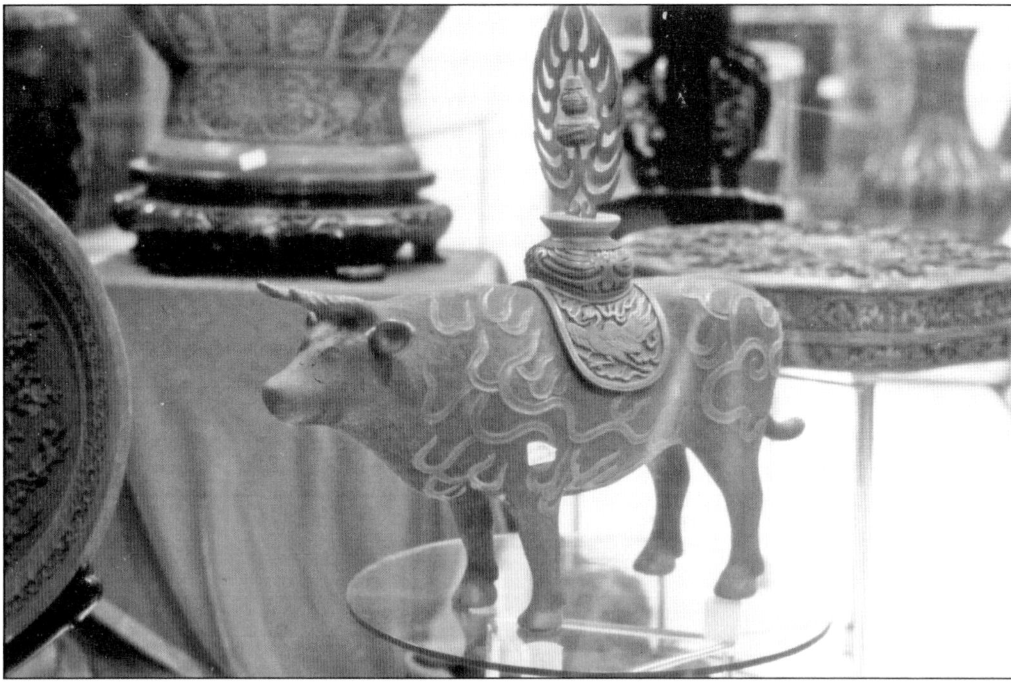

Chinese artists often use animals and nature as themes for their pottery. The ox is celebrated because of its strength and usefulness. (Courtesy of Miles Roberts.)

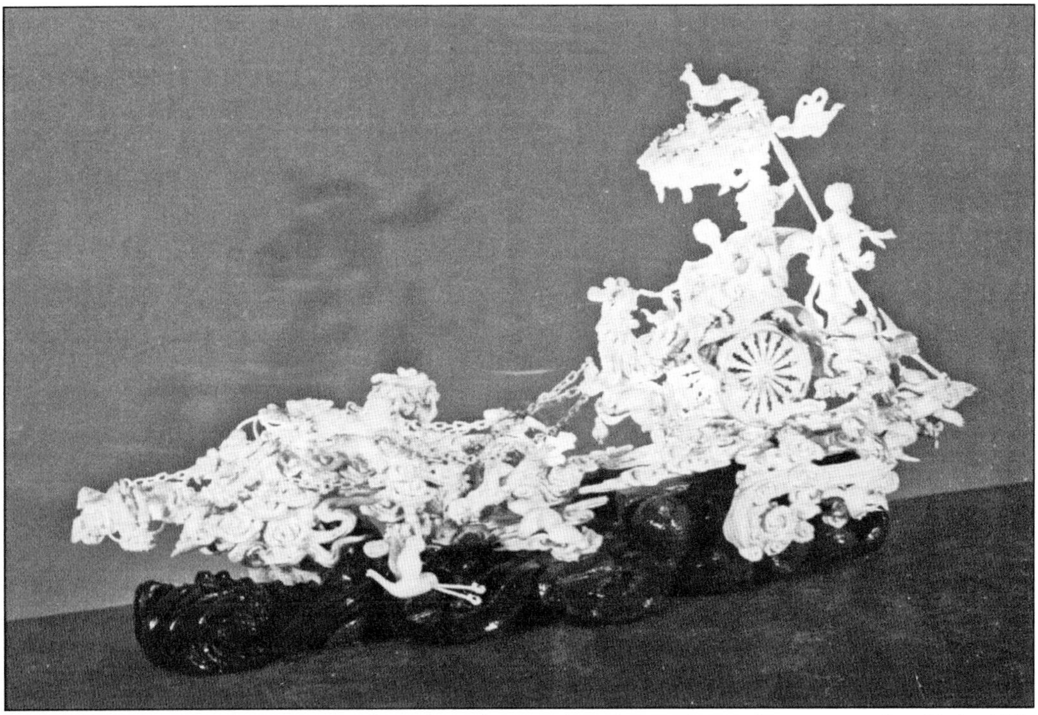

Hand-carved ivory statues were found in the tombs of the Shang dynasty in the 18th–12th centuries BC. (Courtesy of KIEE.)

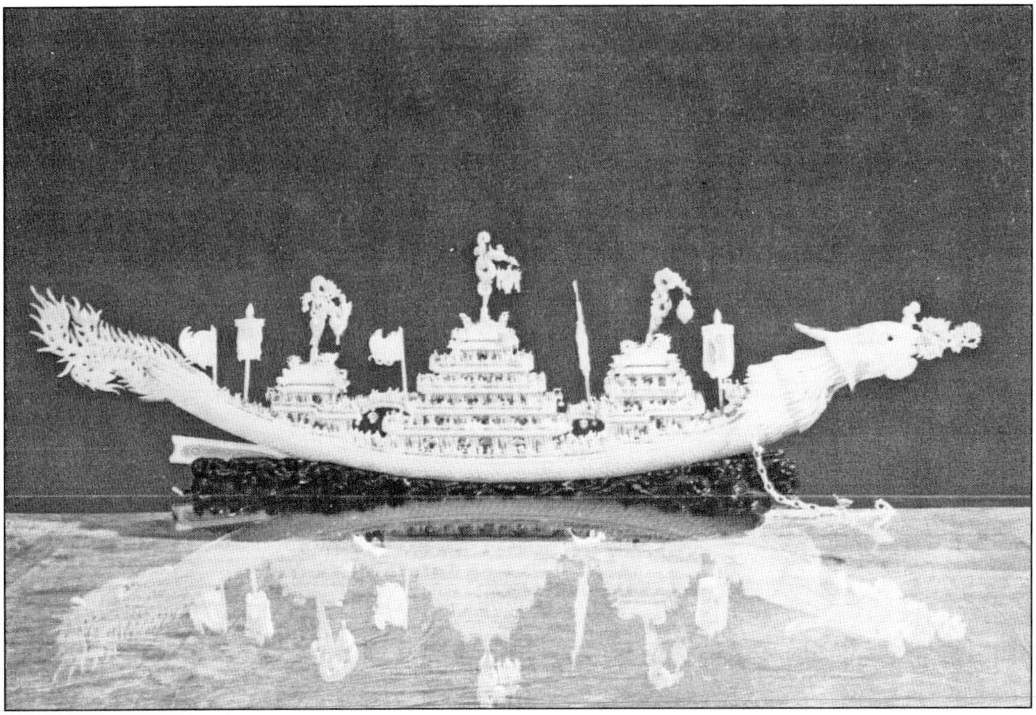

A hand-carved ivory Phoenix boat, said to take 546 working days to complete, was another example of the skill of the Chinese artisans. (Courtesy of KIEE.)

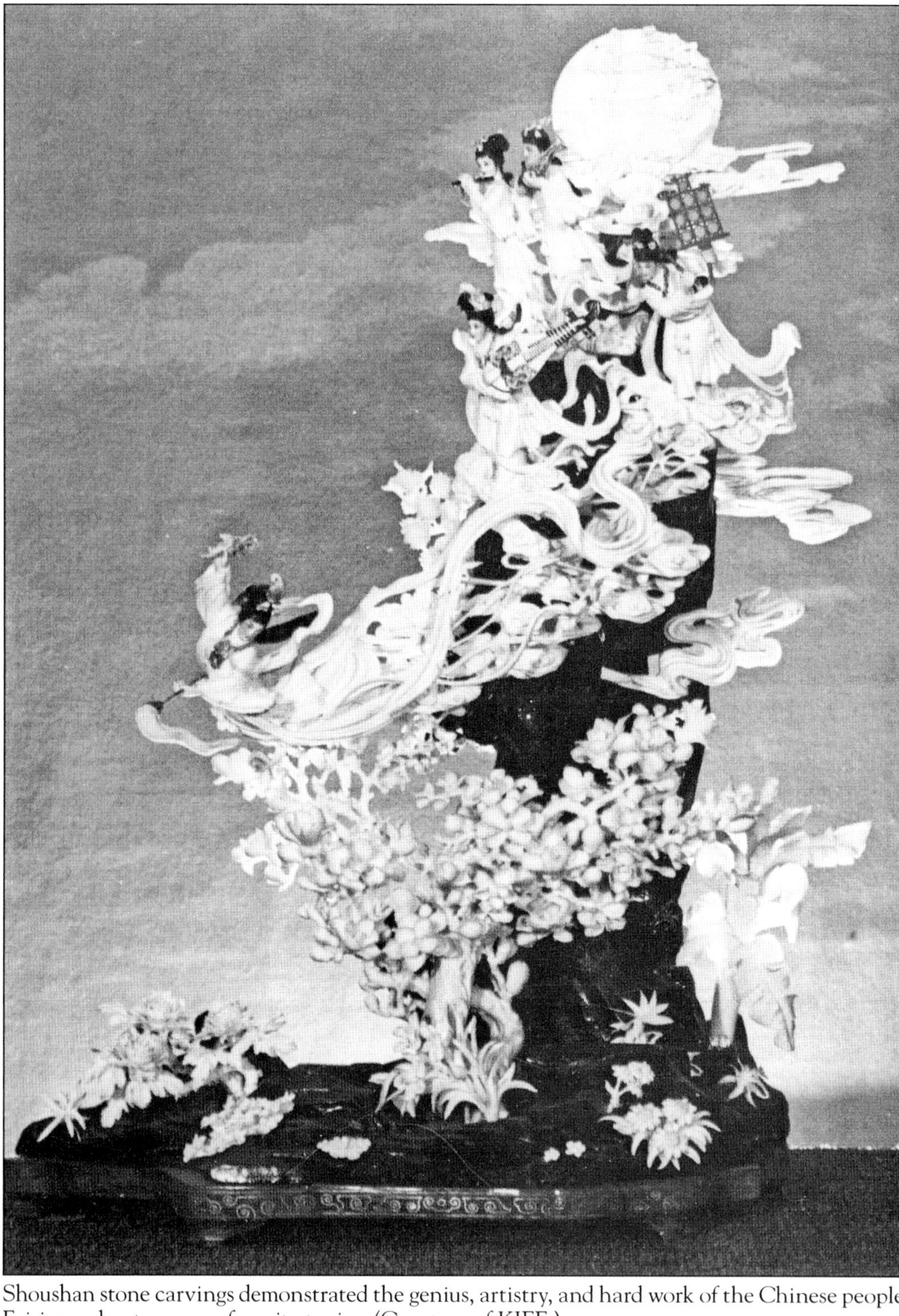

Shoushan stone carvings demonstrated the genius, artistry, and hard work of the Chinese people. Fairies and nature were favorite topics. (Courtesy of KIEE.)

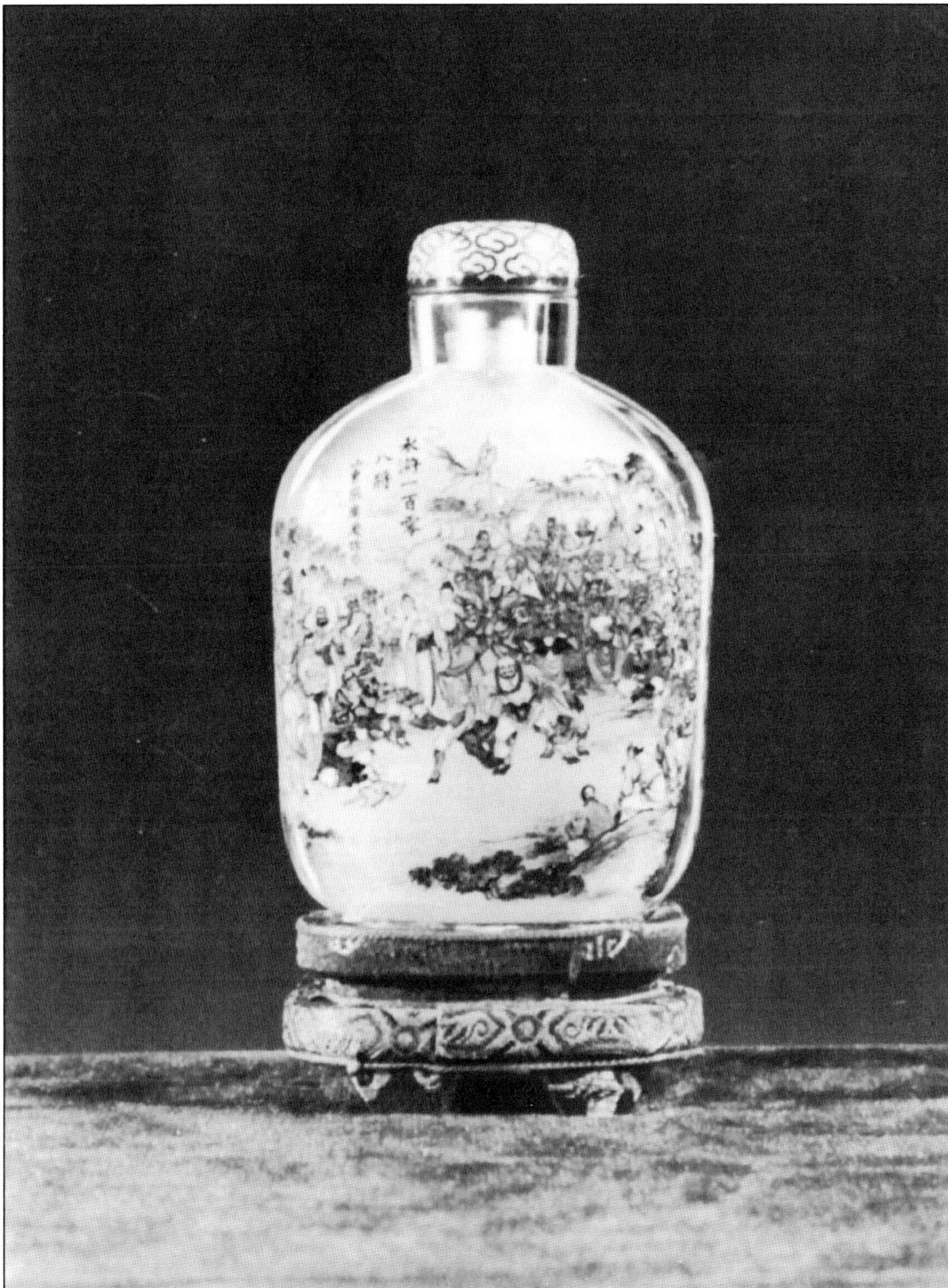

Snuff bottles were used by the Chinese during the Oing Dynasty and contained powdered tobacco. Smoking was illegal, but the use of snuff was allowed because the Chinese considered snuff to be a remedy for common illnesses such as colds, headaches, and stomach disorders. (Courtesy of KIEE.)

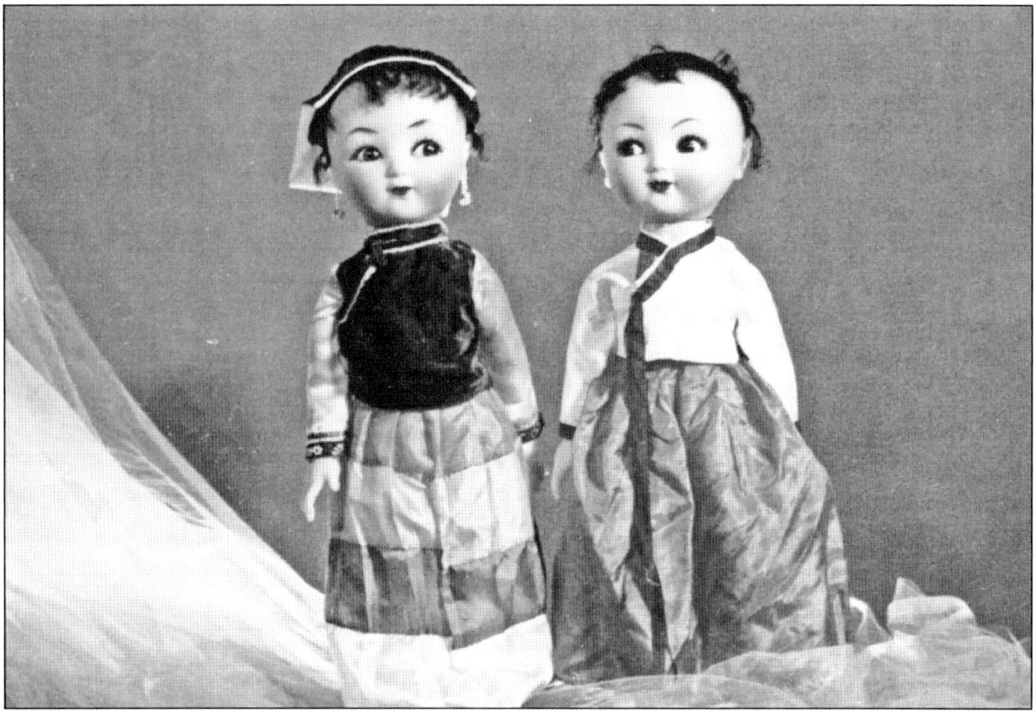

Chinese folk dolls were on display and were also for sale as the country known for communism became capitalistic for the duration of the fair. (Courtesy of KIEE.)

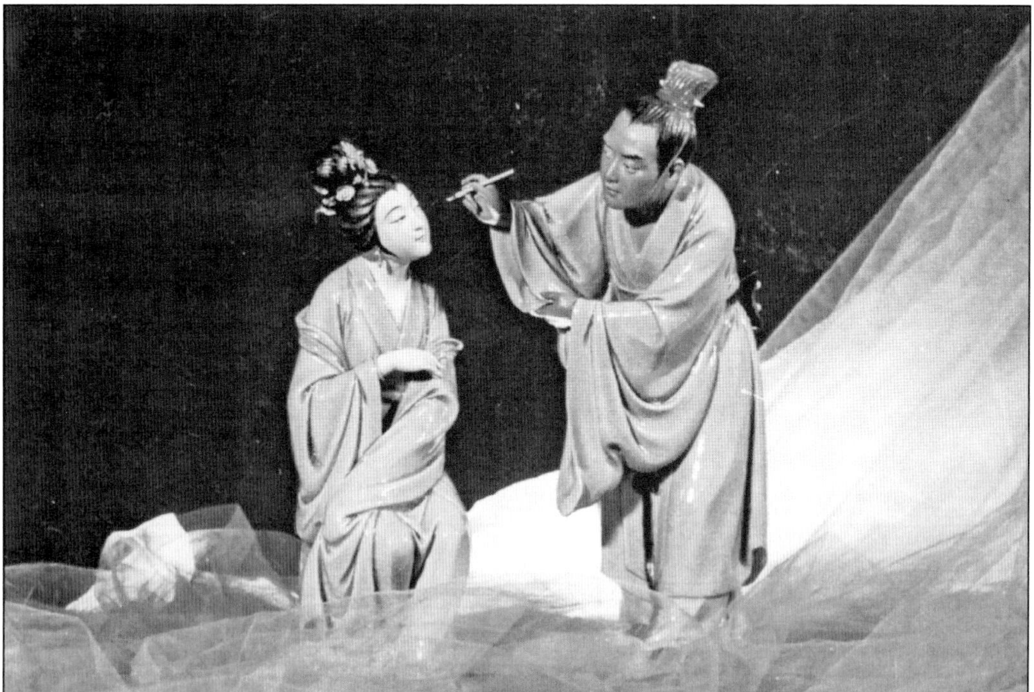

Zhag Chang, a prefect, or high-ranking member of the culture in the time of Emperor Xuan of Han Dynasty, painted eyebrows for his wife to show their conjugal love. (Courtesy of KIEE.)

Four

EXHIBITS AND ACTIVITIES

If you shoot for the stars and hit the moon, it's OK. But you've got to shoot for something. A lot of people don't even shoot.

—Robert Townsend

Plenty to see, plenty to do, plenty of places to go, and plenty to eat is what could be expected during a visit to the 1982 World's Fair. Bringing the numerous things together to bring the fair into reality took planning, time, money, and a lot of hard work from a wide variety of people.

There were over 200 companies and organizations that participated in the fair. Exhibits inside the "lower" fairgrounds included the Strohaus, the L&N Hotel, the L&N Station, the Solar Home, the Home of the Future, the World of Travel, the Knoxville Health Pavilion, Baptist Ministries, Tenneco/Occidental, Conergy, A.C.T. '82, the Budweiser Clydesdale horses, American's Electricity Energy, Gas Energy, Federal Express, Tennessee Valley Authority, and more.

The fair was called the "largest restaurant" in the world, having over 180 food venues. Two fledgling companies, Buddy's BBQ and Petroleum Belly's, successfully launched new foods during the fair and remain in business to this date. Buddy's is famous for barbeque ribs, chicken, and pork sandwiches, while Petro's is a mixture of chili and fresh vegetables served in a Frito's bag.

No one could miss the International Court of Flags, from which flew the 22 flags of the participating countries alongside the flags from the United States and the states of Tennessee, Alabama, Georgia, Kentucky, North Carolina, Oklahoma, South Carolina, West Virginia, Alaska, and Hawaii.

Visitors could ride across the fairgrounds in a gondola from the Clinch Street Bridge to the L&N Hotel or on a chairlift that carried them from the Clinch Street Bridge to the Canadian Exhibit.

Across the path from the Canadian Pavilion was an area that contained the Second Creek Gazebo. Visitors could stop and rest under green trees and watch as others walked by on the pavement.

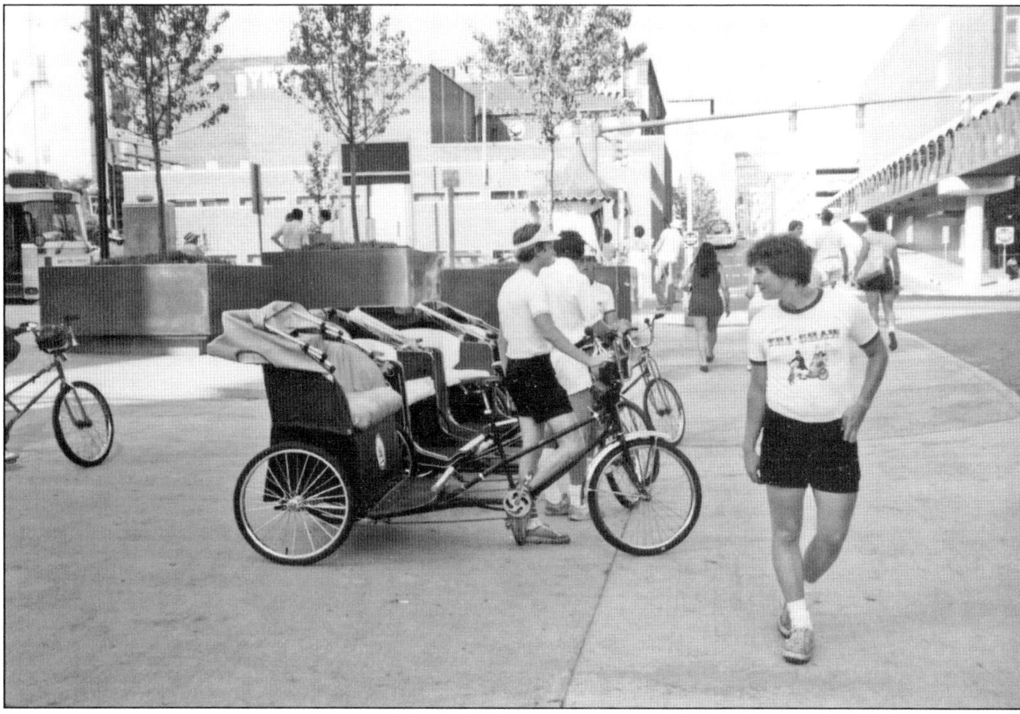

Visitors who were tired of walking could rent a ride on a modern-day rickshaw; however, it was called a pedicab since the young men who hauled guests rode a bike instead of running on foot. (Courtesy of the Prather family.)

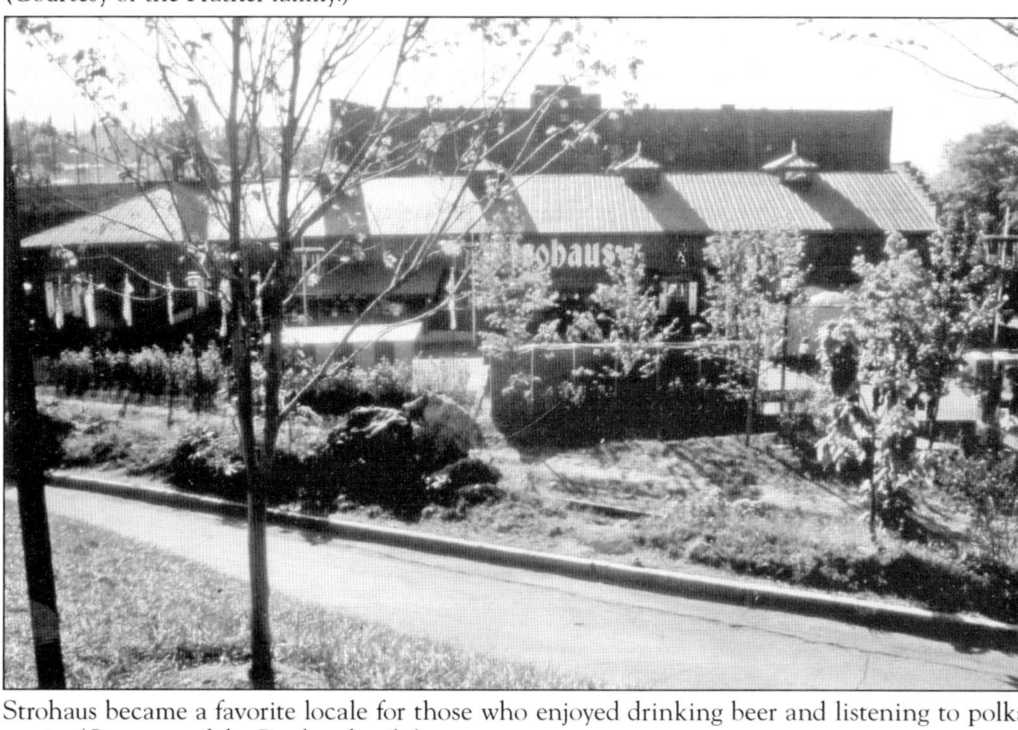

Strohaus became a favorite locale for those who enjoyed drinking beer and listening to polka music. (Courtesy of the Prather family.)

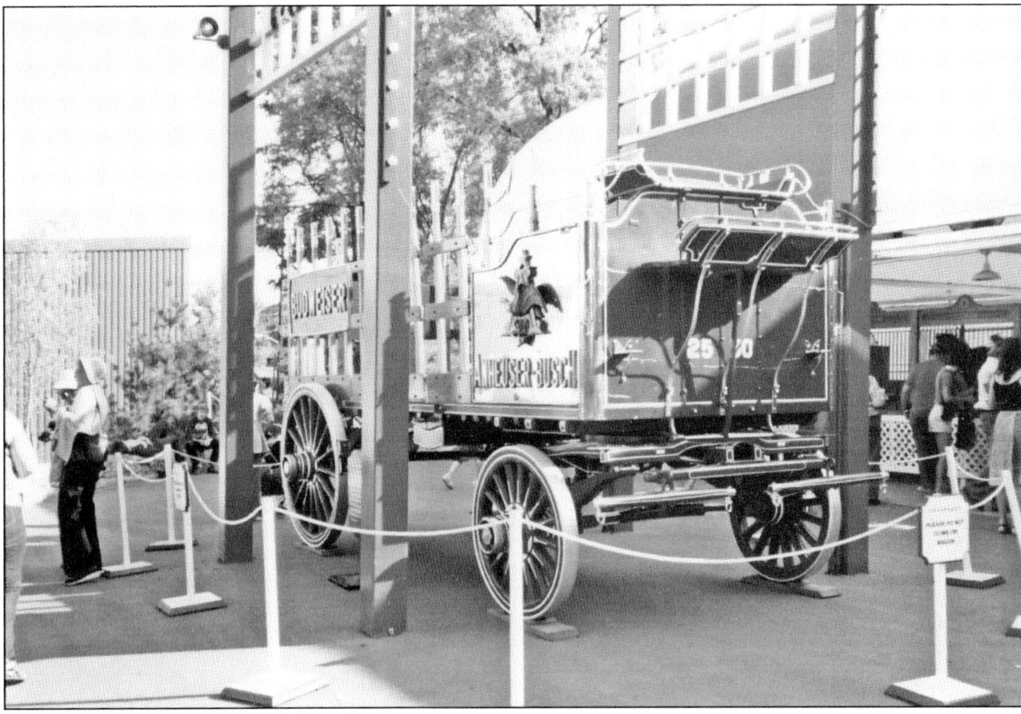

One of the surprises of the fair was the popularity of the beer wagon and Clydesdale horses, sponsored by Anheuser-Busch. (Courtesy of the Prather family.)

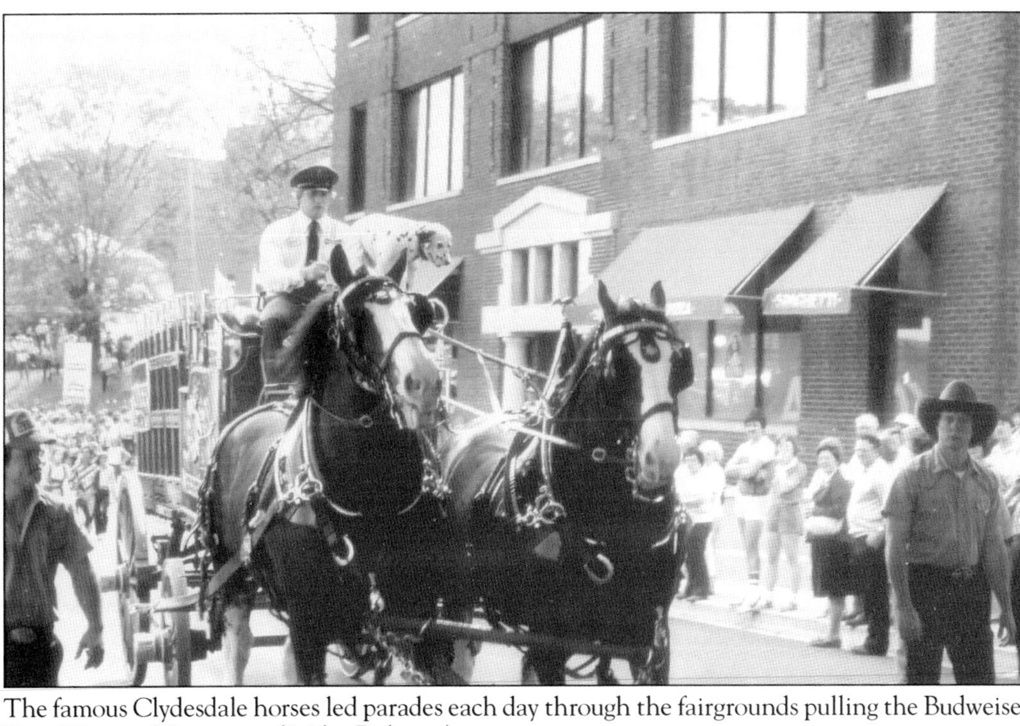

The famous Clydesdale horses led parades each day through the fairgrounds pulling the Budweiser Beer Wagon. (Courtesy of Miles Roberts.)

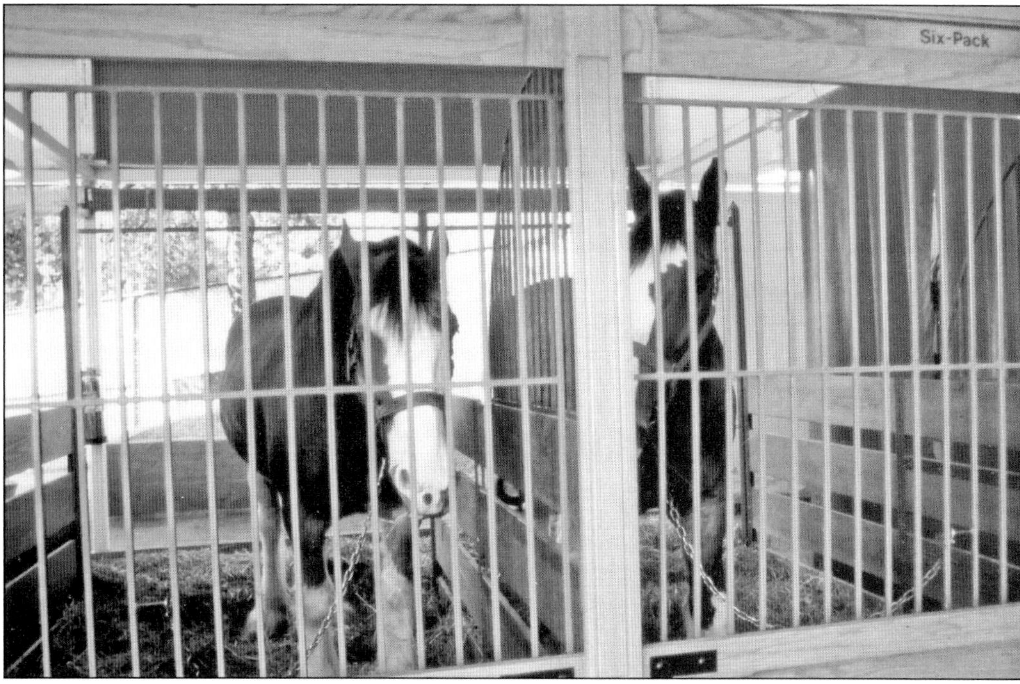

The Clydesdale horses were on display and were available for petting. (Courtesy of Miles Roberts.)

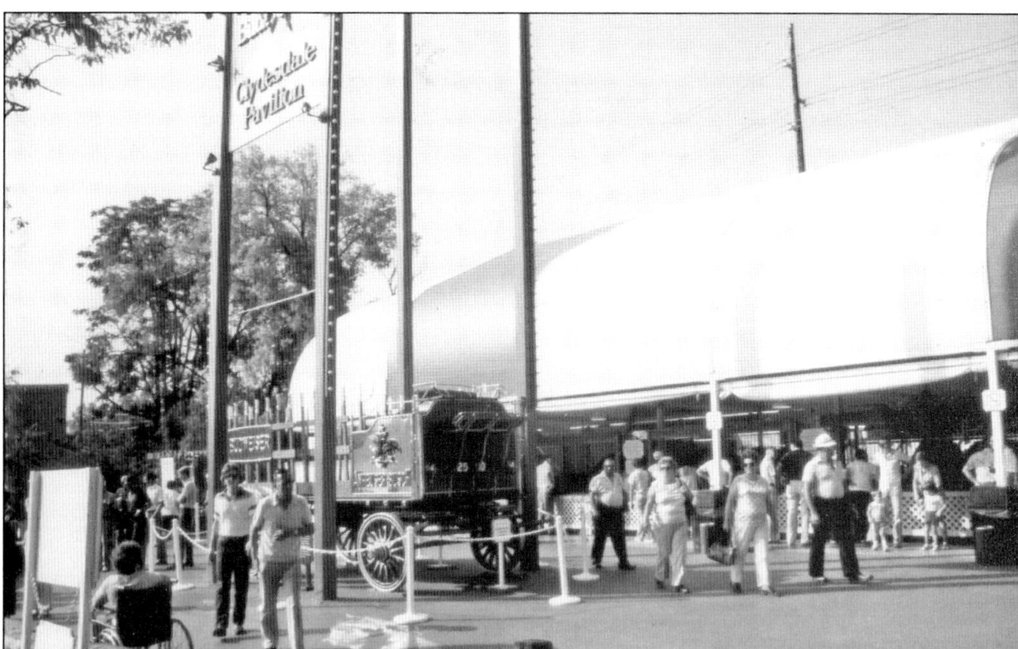

The Clydesdale horses and beer wagon were one of the most famous advertisements running on television during the 1980s. This made their stable a "must see" for guests. (Courtesy of Miles Roberts.)

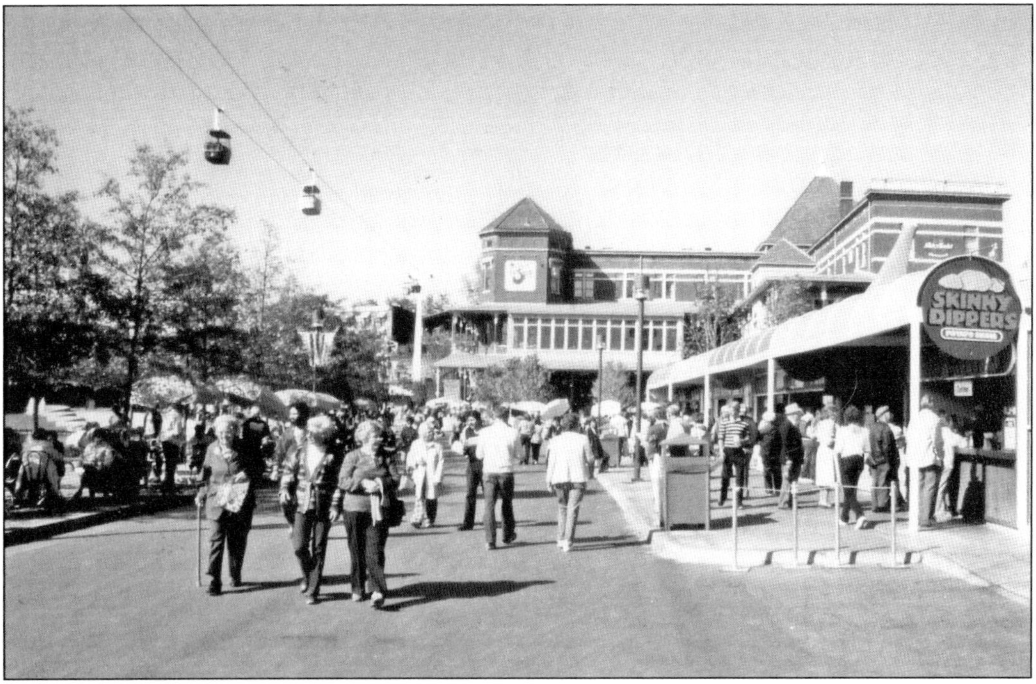

A variety of food vendors offered snack foods as guests strolled along the street in front of the Lifestyle and Technology Center near the L&N Railroad Station. (Courtesy of Miles Roberts.)

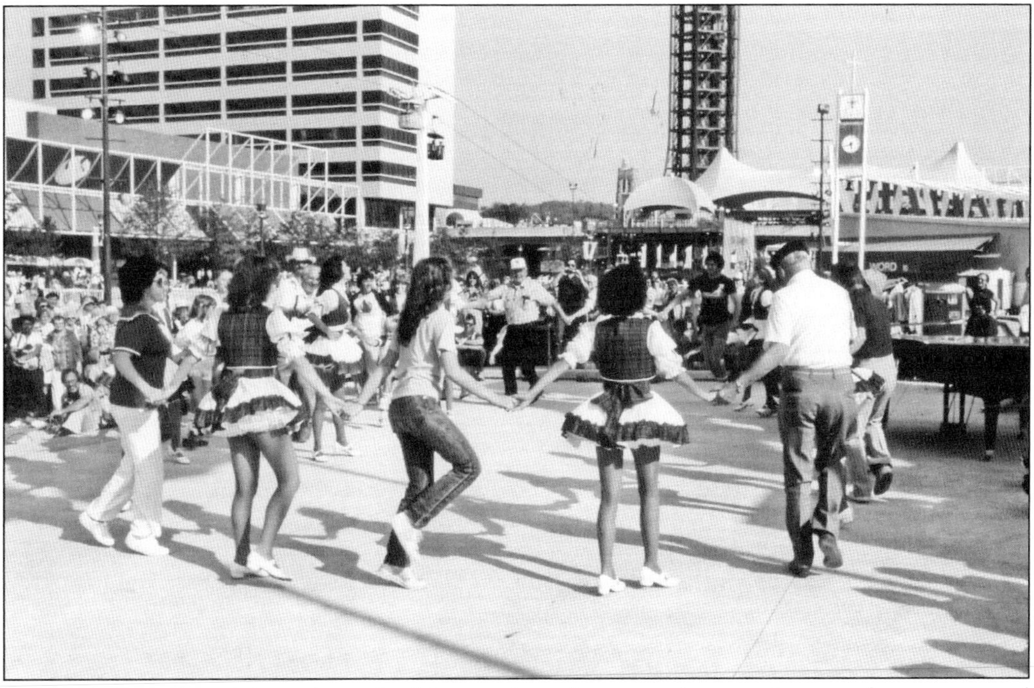

Lively music was heard throughout the fairgrounds as cloggers and square dancers often encouraged guests to join in on the fun. (Courtesy of Charlie Brookes.)

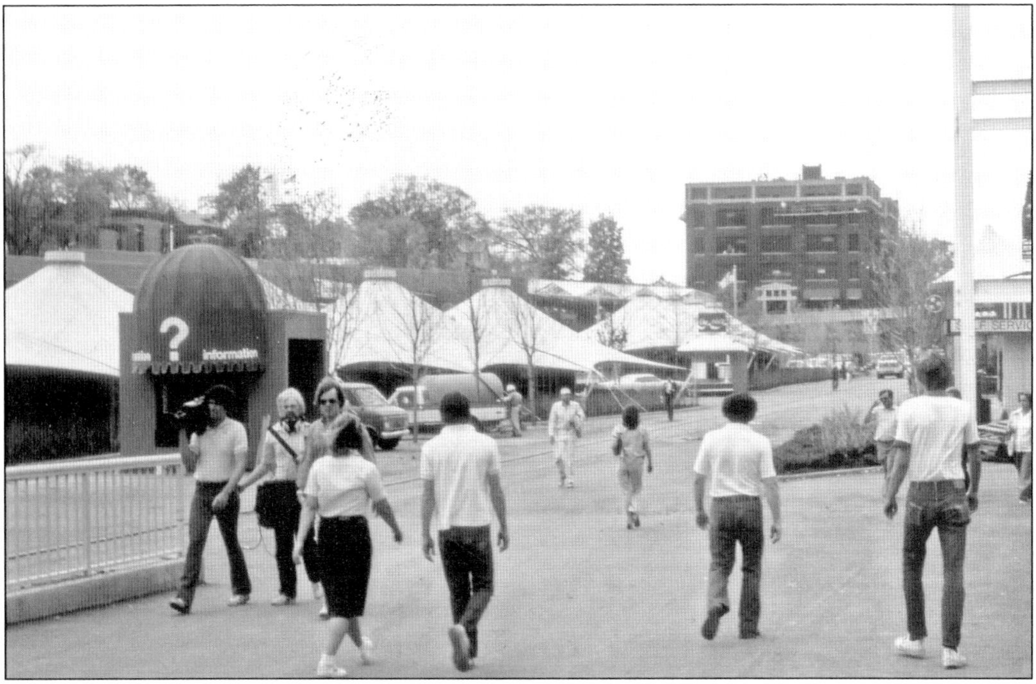

The attendance dropped some days in September to as low as 23,000 and 24,000. (Courtesy of Miles Roberts.)

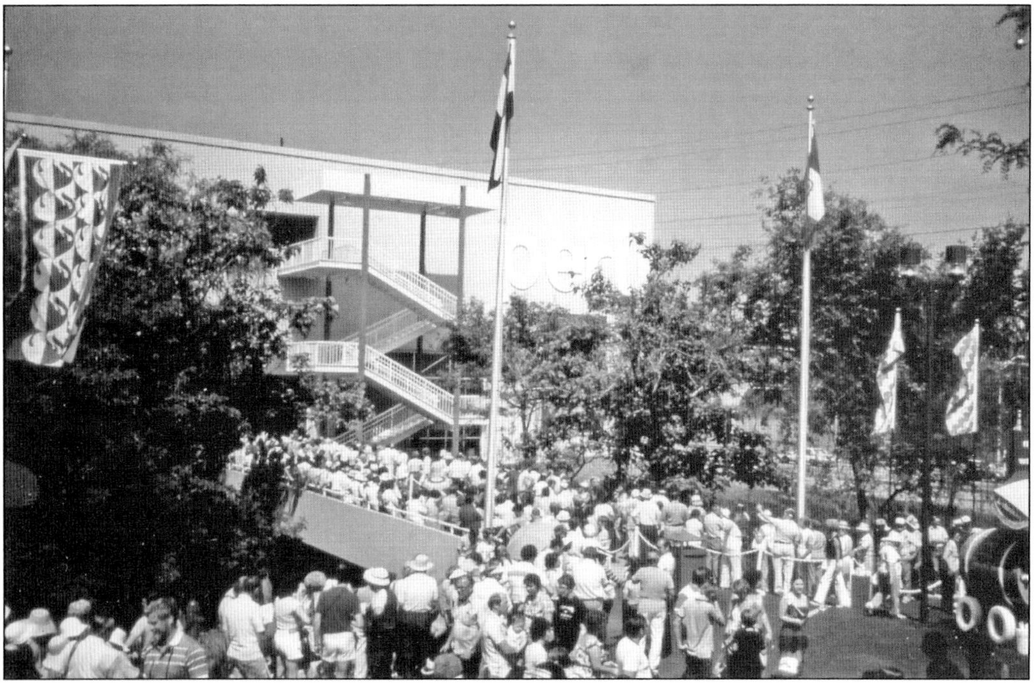

The highest numbers in attendance occurred during the summer months while school was out of session: numbers ranged from 70,000 to 80,000 daily. (Courtesy of Charles Brookes.)

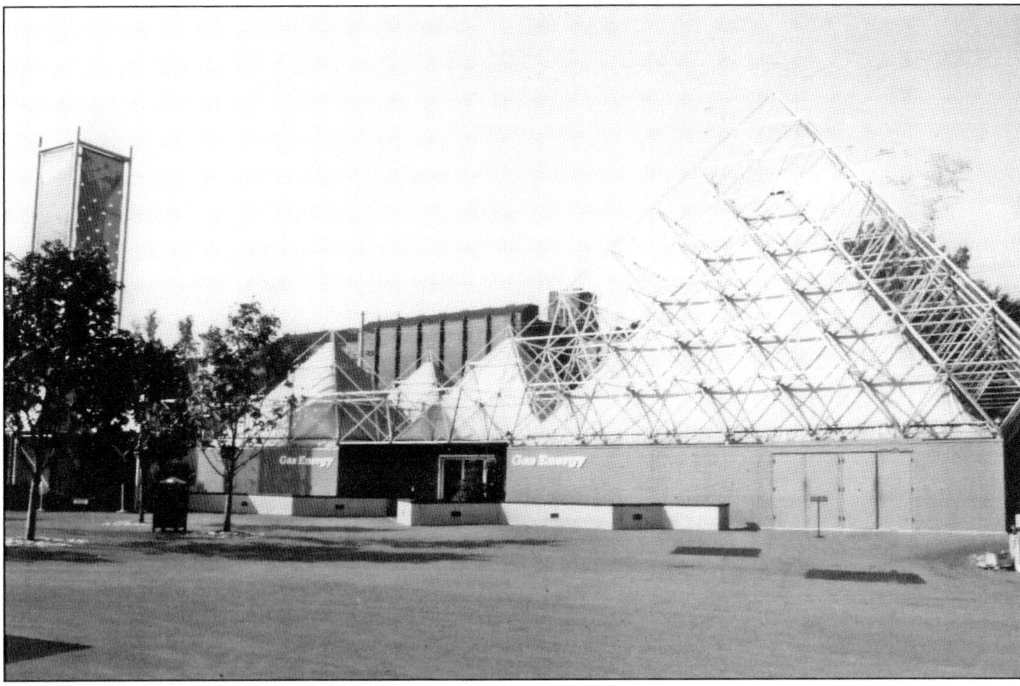

The Gas Energy Pavilion was a 55-foot-tall, 5,000-square-foot, pyramid-shaped exhibit about technology that required audience participation. The exhibit also contained video games that simulated natural gas exploration. (Courtesy of Miles Roberts.)

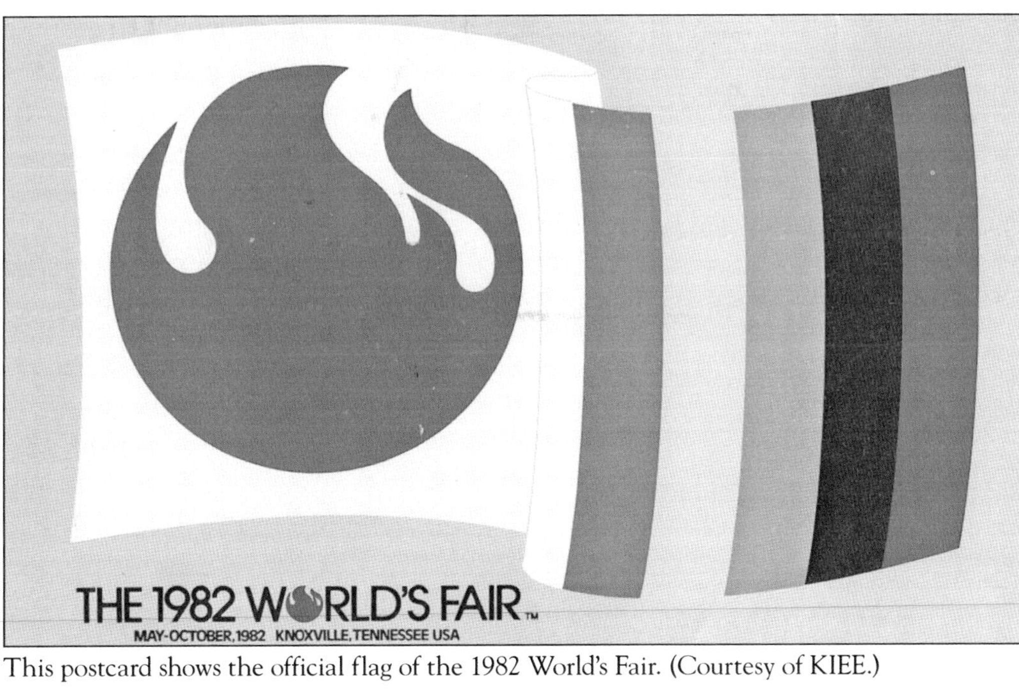

This postcard shows the official flag of the 1982 World's Fair. (Courtesy of KIEE.)

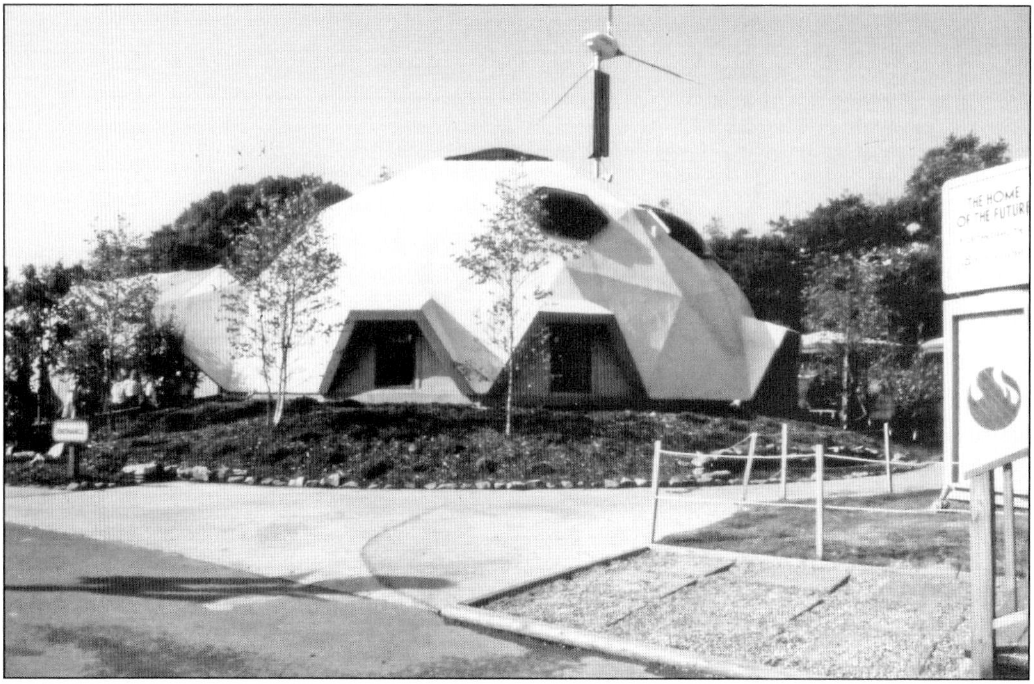

Cathedralite, Inc., and South Central Bell presented the "Home of the Future." The 2,300-square-foot home was full of modern technology. The reflective roof and skylights increased the passive solar and photovoltaic capabilities of the home. (Courtesy of Miles Roberts.)

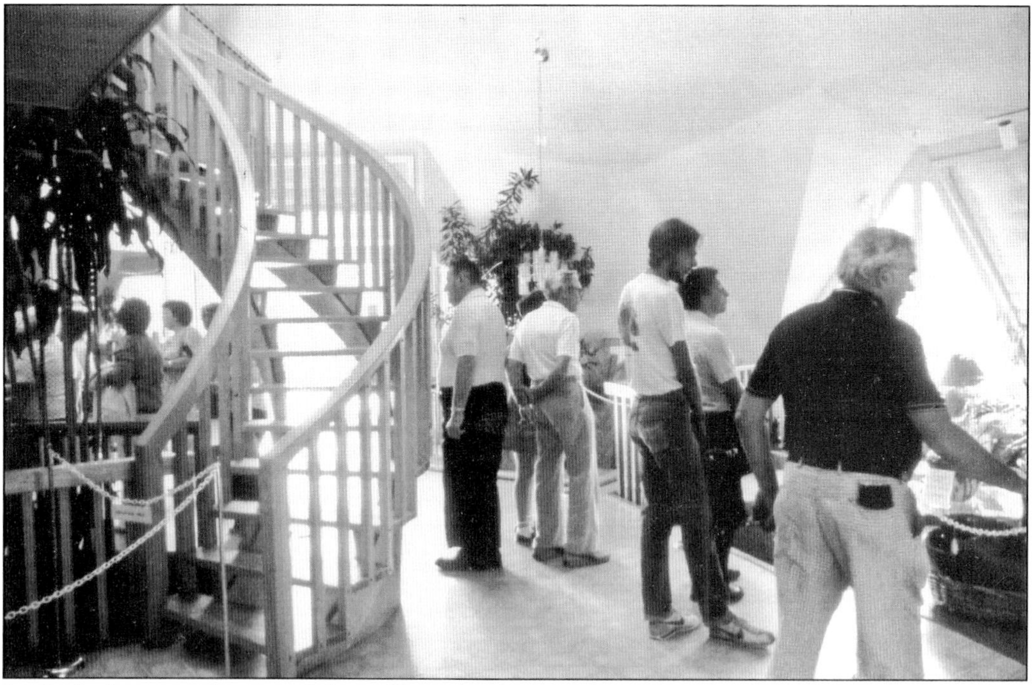

Inside the home, a teleterminal showed how the phone and computer could be used for recordkeeping, banking, and maintaining appointments—and all with the touch of a few buttons. (Courtesy of Miles Roberts.)

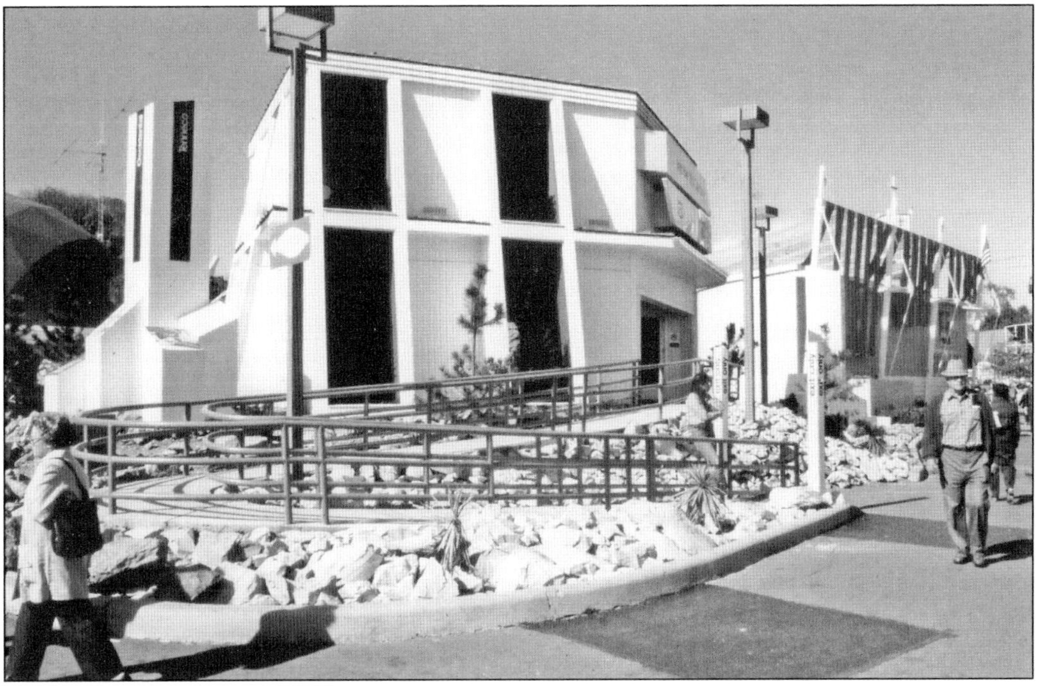

Tenneco/Occidental, headquartered in Houston, Texas, sponsored an educational exhibit in a futuristic building that focused on oil shale and the processes used to release oil from it. (Courtesy of Charlie Brookes.)

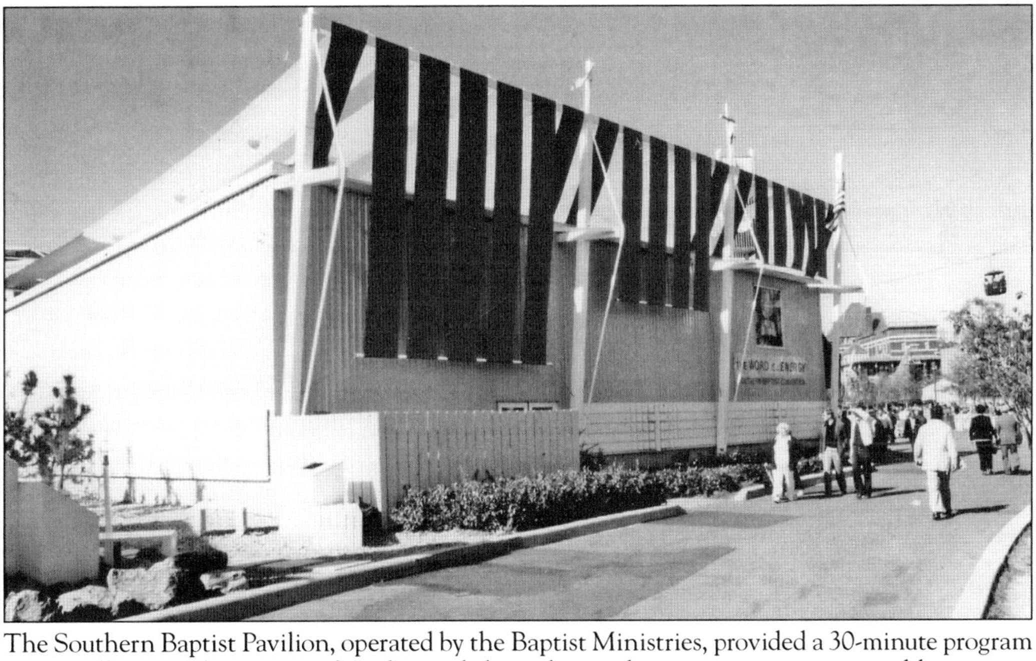

The Southern Baptist Pavilion, operated by the Baptist Ministries, provided a 30-minute program used to illustrate the energy of God's word through a multi-image presentation and live music. There were performances of choirs from across the United States on most days as well as a display case holding Bibles from the first Bible publisher, A. J. Holman and Company. (Courtesy of Miles Roberts.)

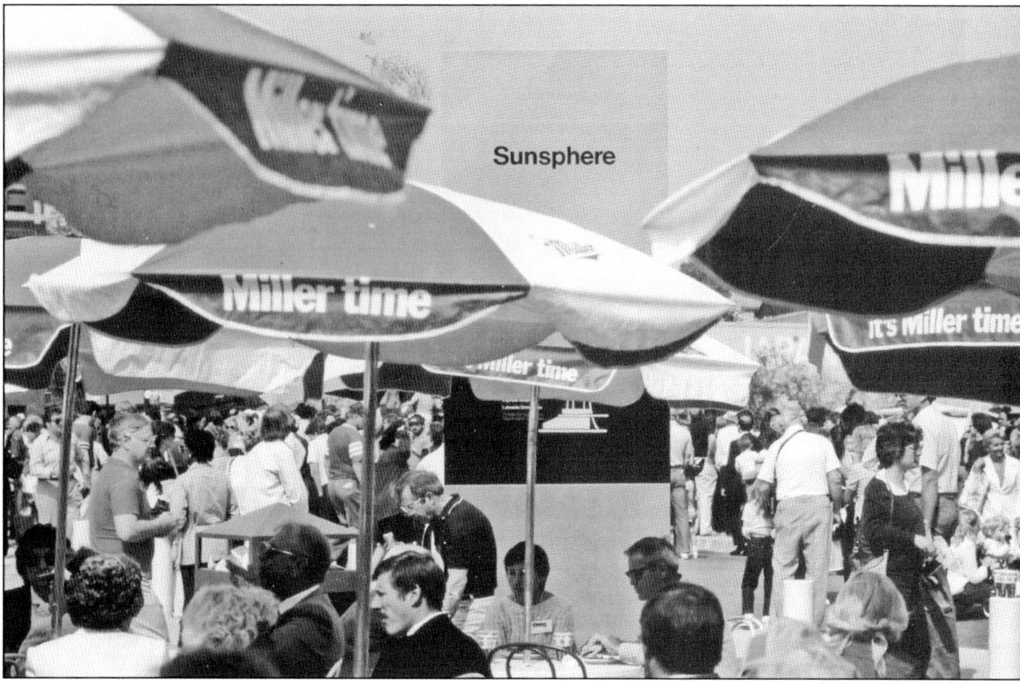

Colorful umbrellas provided shade from the hot sun as visitors stopped by the Hardee's fast-food restaurant, located in a temporary building on one side at the base of the Sunsphere. (Courtesy of Charlie Brookes.)

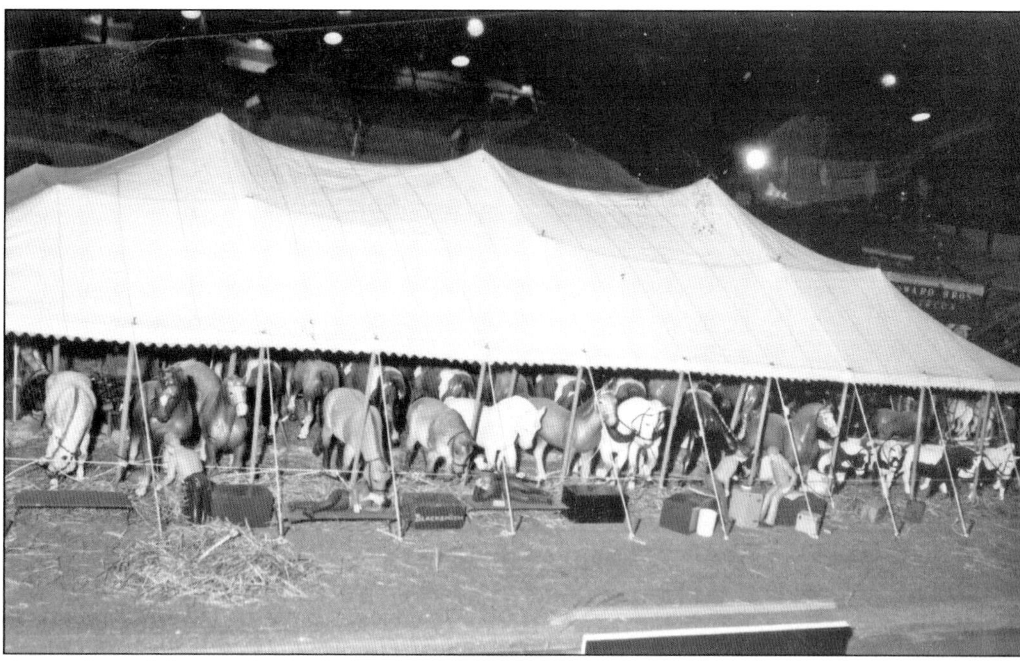

A popular exhibit inside the Lifestyle and Technology Center was the miniature circus, "The Biggest Little Show on Earth," built by Howard C. Tibbals. Tibbals asked Ringling management if he could use their name for his circus when he started building it, but they refused. So he called it the Howard Brothers Circus instead. (Courtesy of the Prather family.)

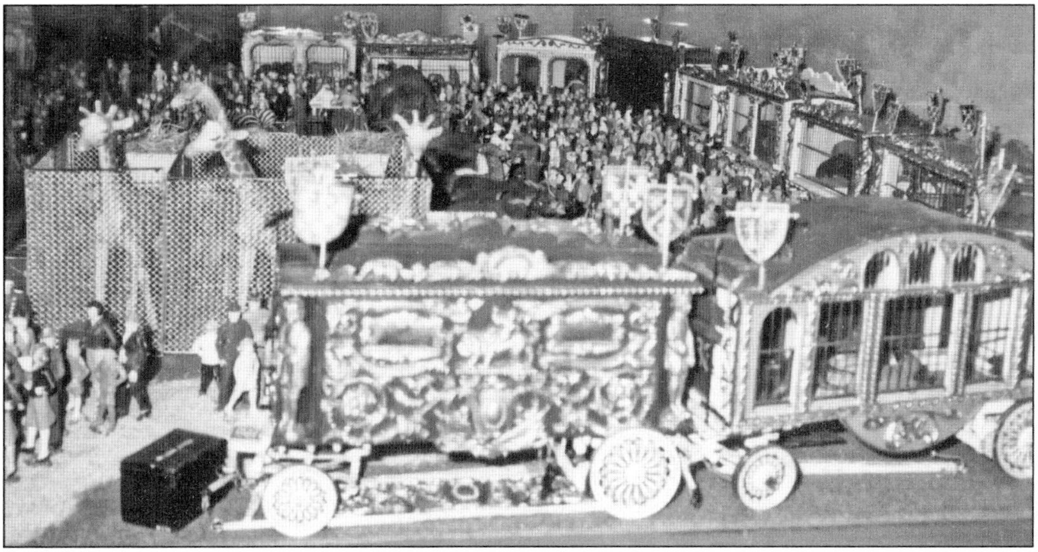

Howard C. Tibbals began toying with circuses in 1943, at the age of 7. At 12, he was given a lathe and jigsaw, which advanced his model building. He started working on the model in earnest in 1956, using a collection of posters owned by Harold Dunn as research for his models. Much of the circus was completed by 1974, but it did not premiere until the 1982 World's Fair in Knoxville, Tennessee. (Courtesy of Prather family.)

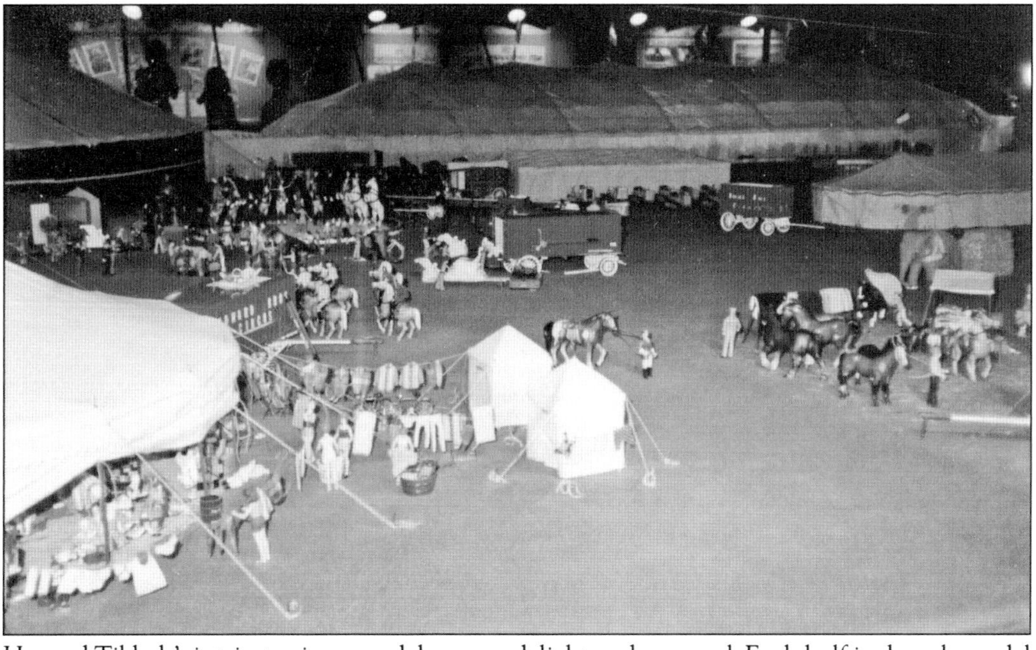

Howard Tibbals's intricate circus models were a delight and a marvel. Each half-inch scale model scene was meticulously reproduced by Tibbals using actual circus posters and pictures from the collection of Harold Dunn. In 1958, Dunn and Tibbals came together to produce the displays, which were divided into two sections. One section was set on a surface and measured 30 feet by 64 feet so fairgoers could see how an entire circus would look on a city lot. The second part consisted of 15 plexiglass cases which contained tiny vignettes of animals, people, and all the details of daily circus life. (Courtesy of the Prather family.)

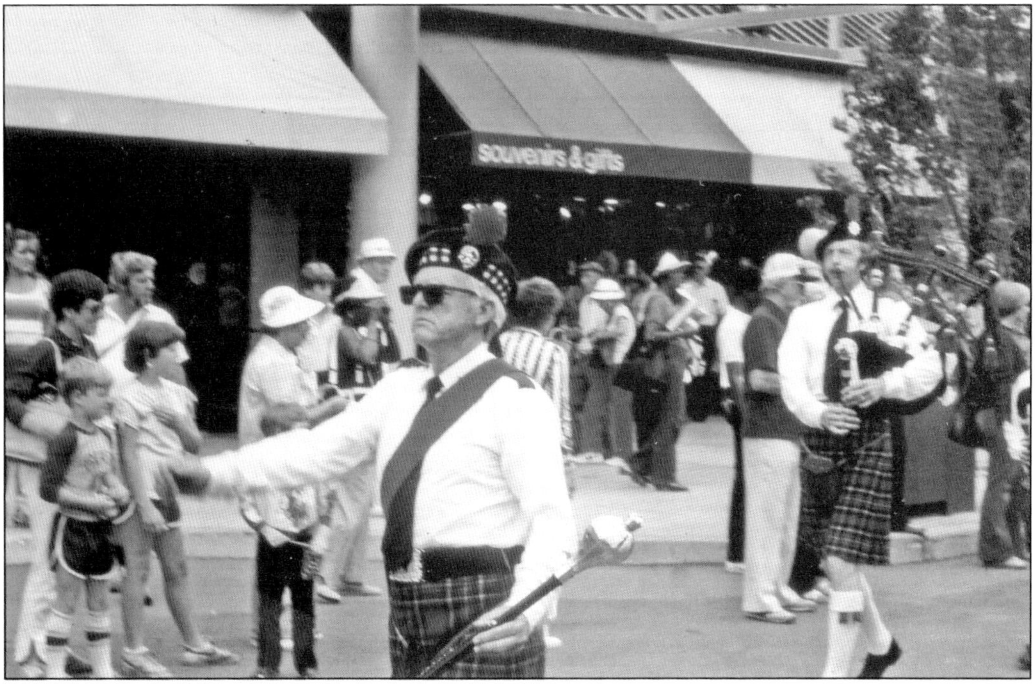

A group of bagpipers from Ireland entertained the crowds by marching in one of the daily parades. (Courtesy of Miles Roberts.)

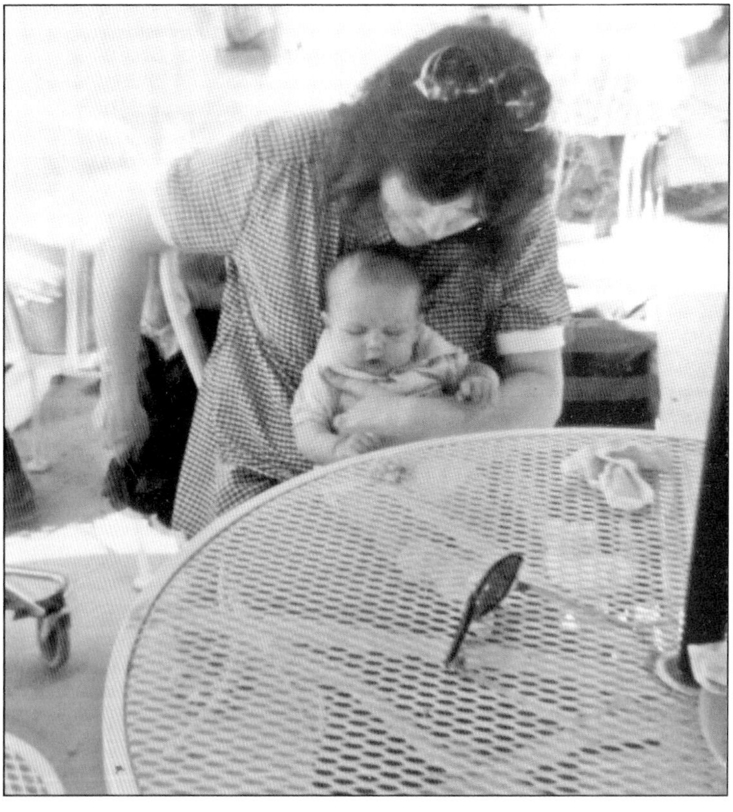

Linda MacDonald and Toni Erin Penery (the baby), daughter of this writer, enjoyed lunch at Hardee's near the base of the Sunsphere. (Photograph by Martha Rose Woodward.)

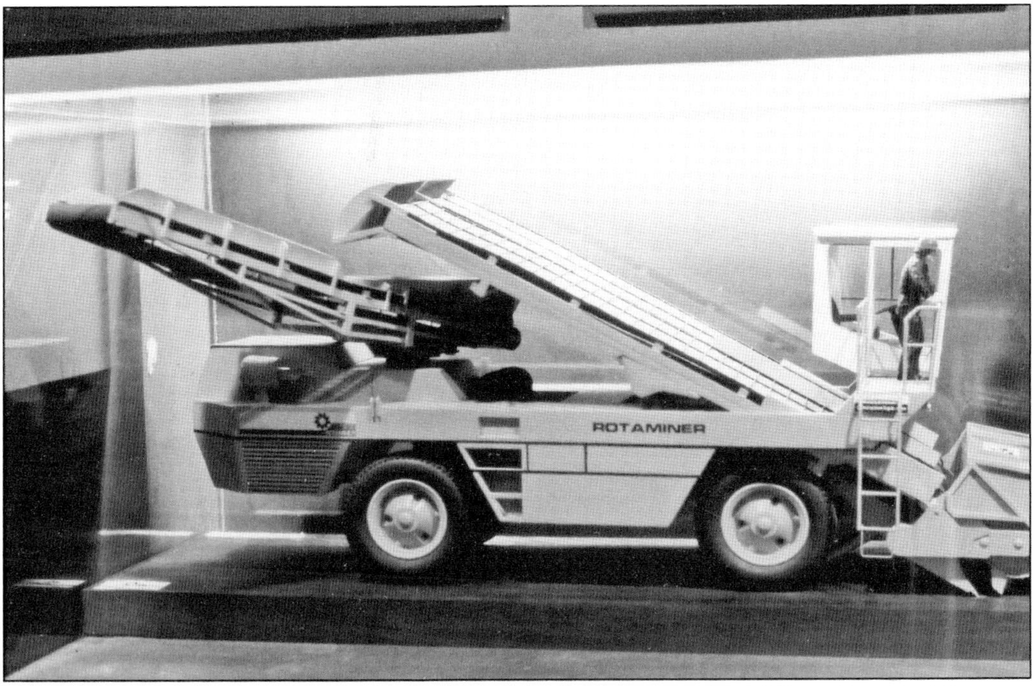

The production of coal was on display in the exhibit from the country of Great Britain. (Courtesy of Miles Roberts.)

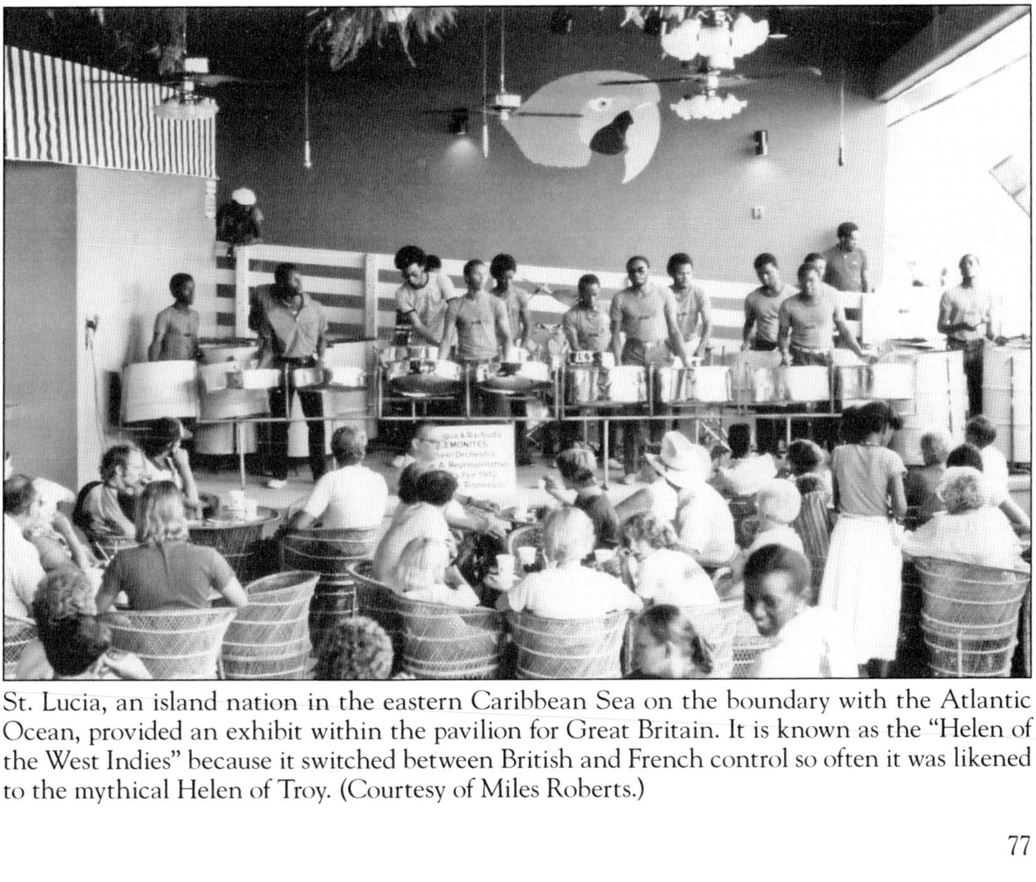

St. Lucia, an island nation in the eastern Caribbean Sea on the boundary with the Atlantic Ocean, provided an exhibit within the pavilion for Great Britain. It is known as the "Helen of the West Indies" because it switched between British and French control so often it was likened to the mythical Helen of Troy. (Courtesy of Miles Roberts.)

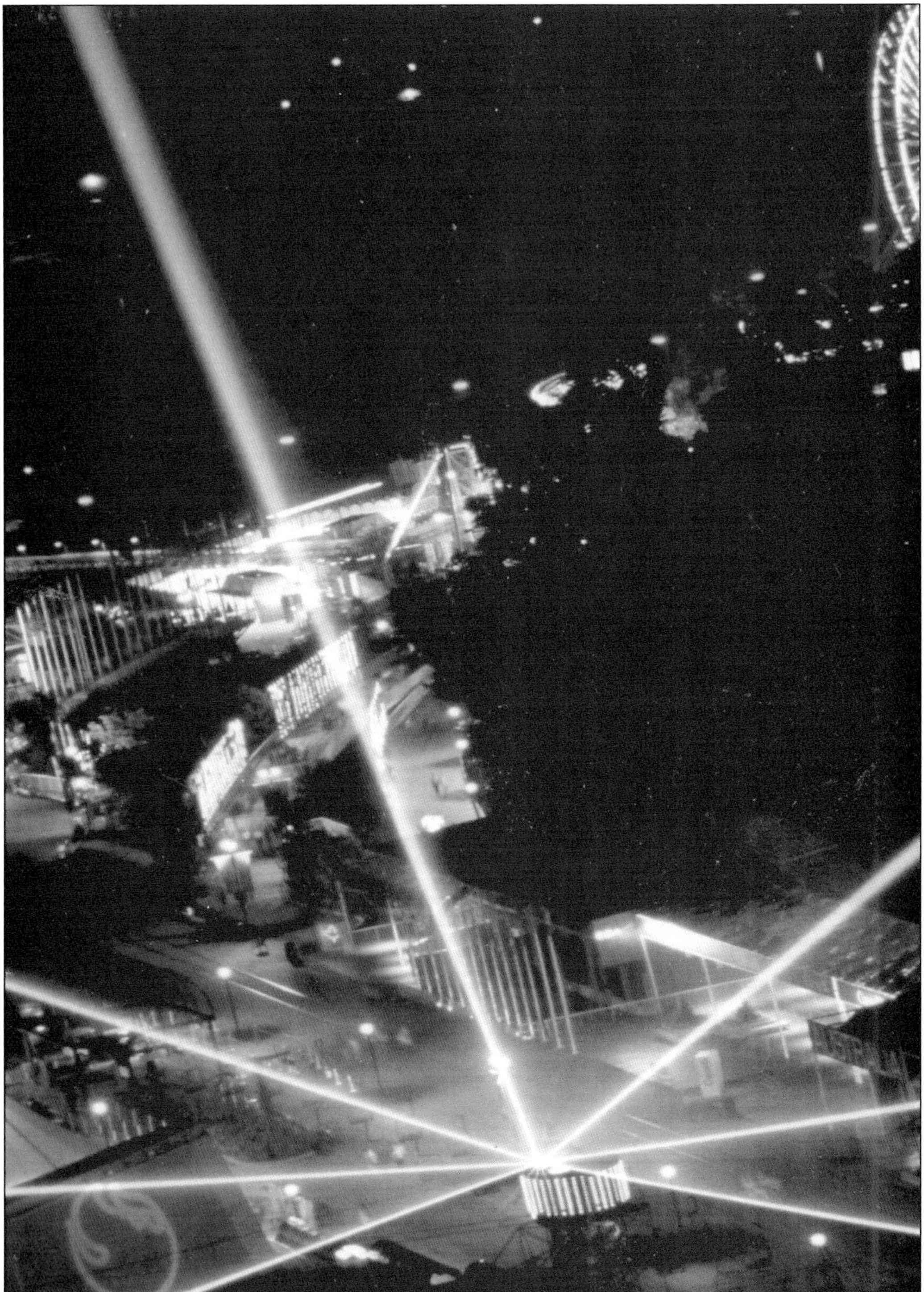

The fair took on a much different look at night as a laser light show gave a futuristic feeling to the night skies. (Courtesy of Miles Brookes.)

Five

FAMILY FUN FAIR

It's kind of fun to do the impossible.

—Walt Disney

In itself, the word "fair" means a gathering of stalls and amusements for public amusement or entertainment. Thus the word "amusement rides" became the description for the numerous ways in which people were transported throughout the fairgrounds. In 1851, in the earliest known fair in Europe, people were given rides on donkeys and in goat carts. As the modern fair has developed, the term "rides" has come to mean any of the electronically driven types of mechanical structures on which people are twirled, whirled, spun, or driven around, such as the carousel, Ferris wheel, log flume, swings, bumper cars, and hundreds of others.

The amusement rides are a big part of the reason why children and teenagers want to attend any fair, with the 1982 World's Fair being no exception. As plans were being made for the 1982 fair, the section of the fairgrounds assigned as the place for the amusement rides was "Family Fun Fair." The largest Ferris wheel in the world was in service for every day of the fair as well as a roller coaster, airplanes and other "kiddie" rides, a log flume, and even a ride on an actual showboat barge that carried visitors up and down the Tennessee River.

Fun Fair was located near Neyland Stadium and the Tennessee River. The site currently hosts a greenway, walking trail, and parking lot.

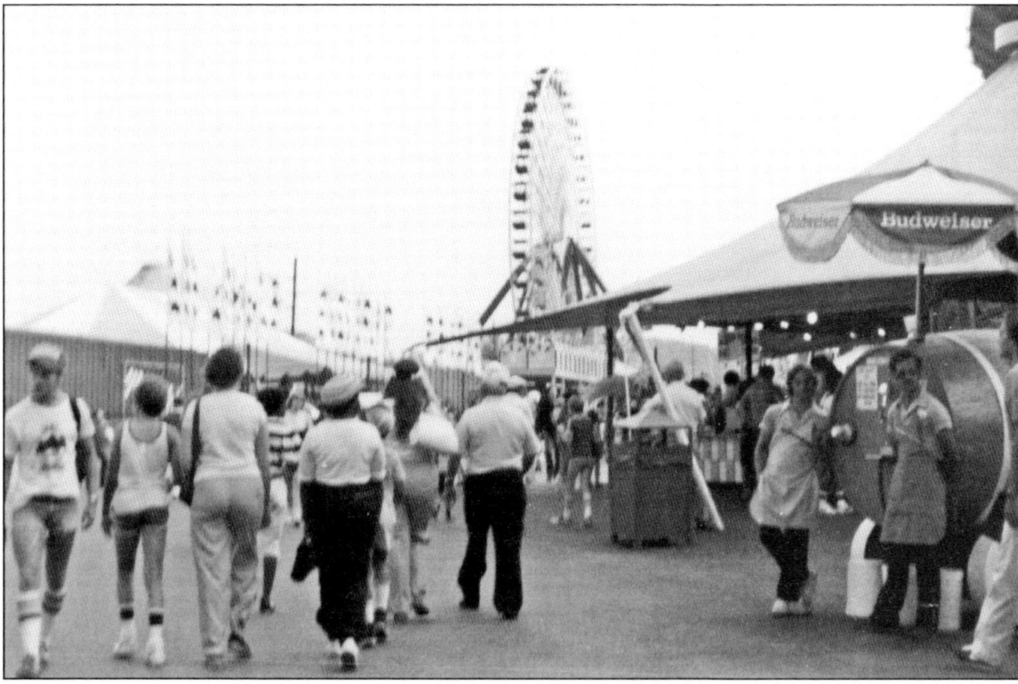

Visitors were drawn into the Fun Fair section with colorful tents and aromatic foods such as popcorn or fried onions. Youngsters and the young at heart happily hurried to enjoy the rides. (Courtesy of the Prather family.)

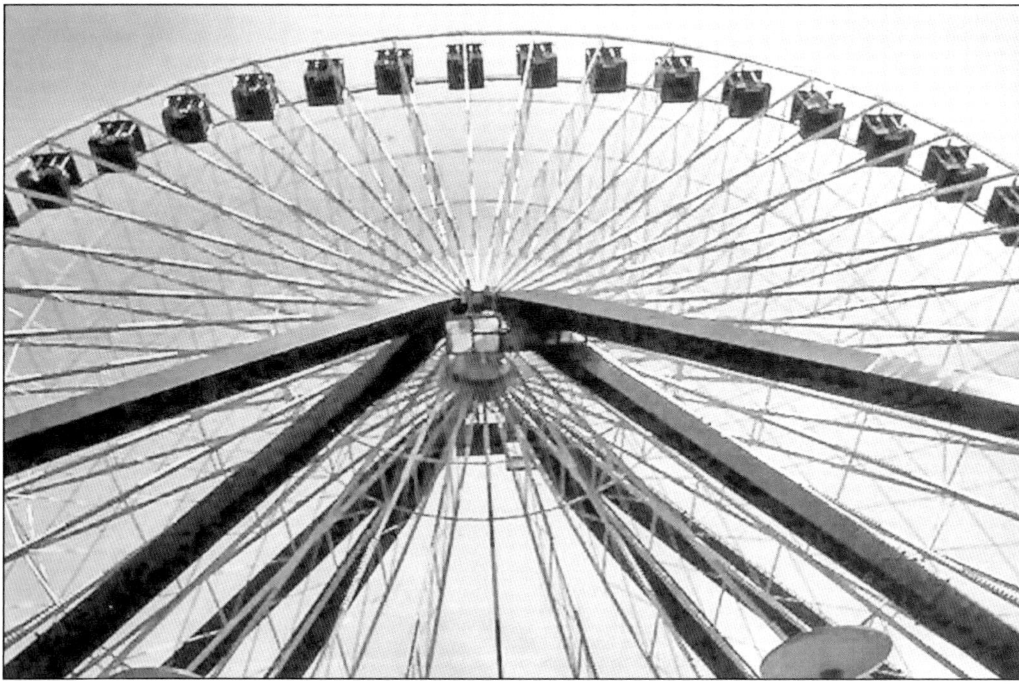

A Ferris wheel, said to be the largest one in the world, could be seen throughout the fairgrounds and provided a spectacular view of the entire fair from high atop the bucket seats. (Courtesy of Miles Roberts.)

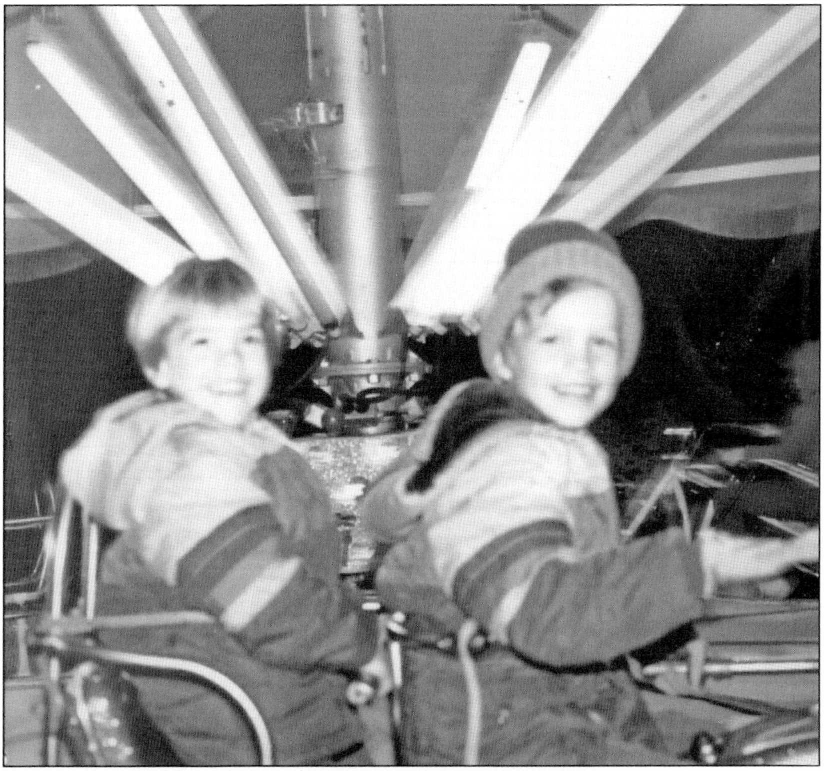

Local residents Suzanne and Geoff Emery took their two young sons, Geoffrey, age 4, and Turner, age 7, to ride the kiddie rides in Fun Fair. (Courtesy of Suzanne Emery.)

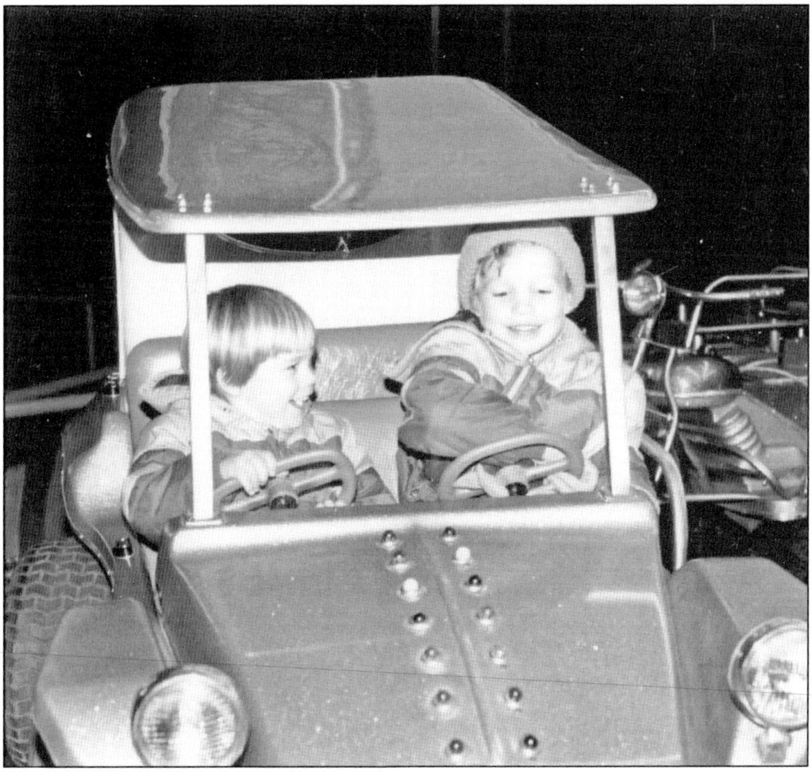

Brothers Geoffrey Emery and Turner Emery are shown riding the kiddie cars. The Emery boys grew up, completed college, and are both married. Geoffrey Emery is currently the owner of his own landscape company, while older brother Turner is an oral surgeon who became a father to a daughter, Mary McClure Lomax Emery, in 2008. (Courtesy of Suzanne Emery.)

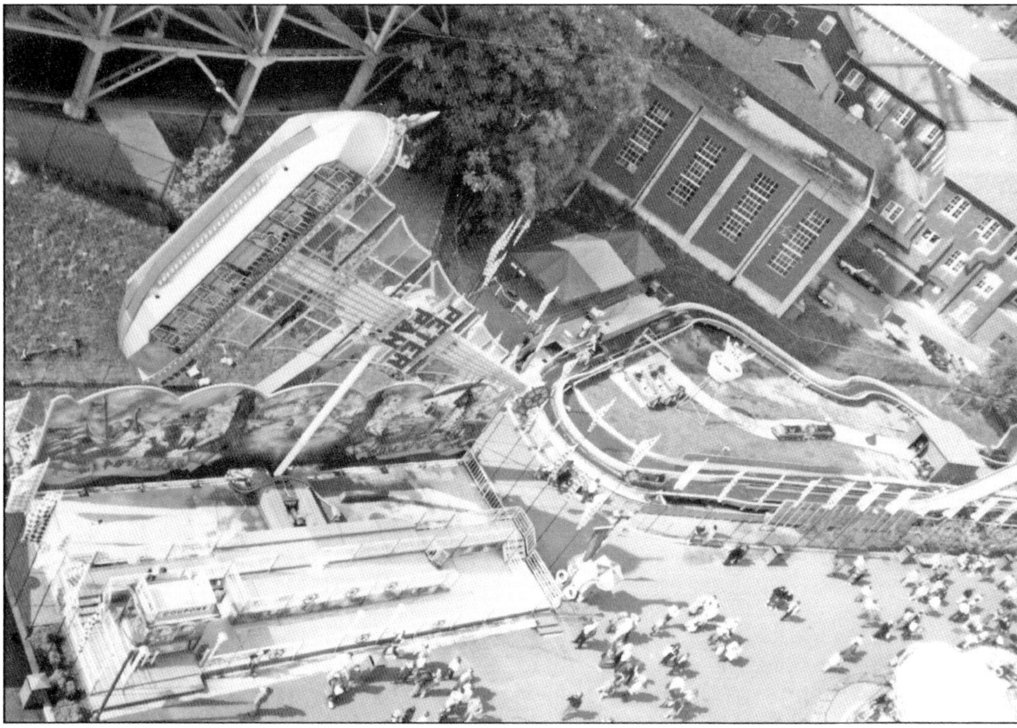

A ride called the Pirate was installed next to the log flume. It operated like a large pendulum. (Courtesy of the Prather family.)

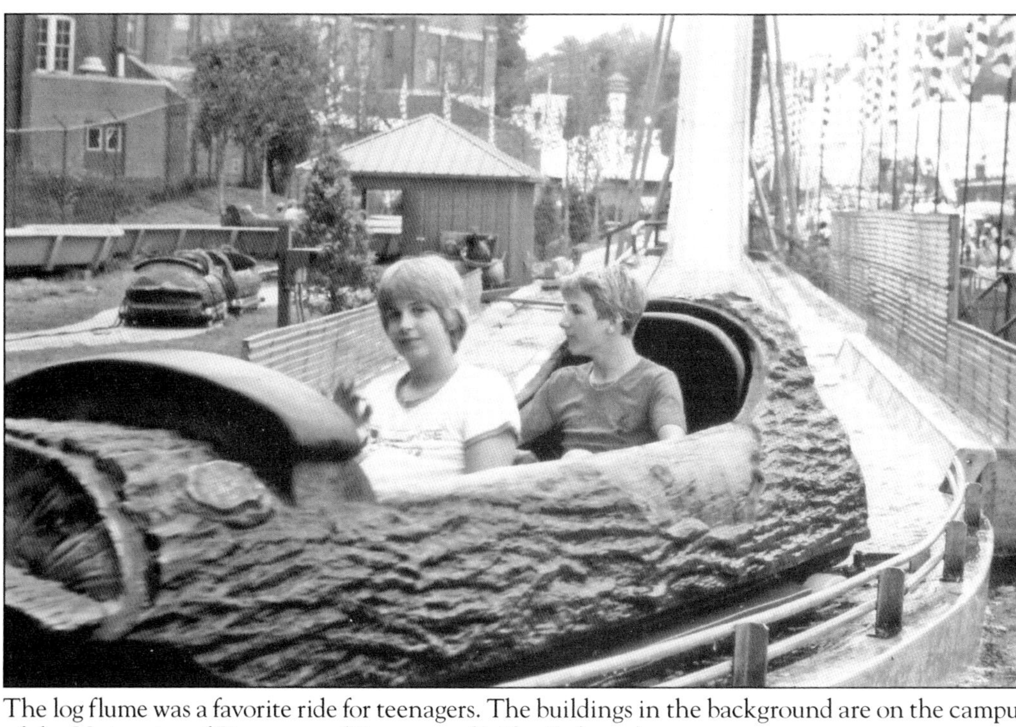

The log flume was a favorite ride for teenagers. The buildings in the background are on the campus of the University of Tennessee. (Courtesy of Miles Roberts.)

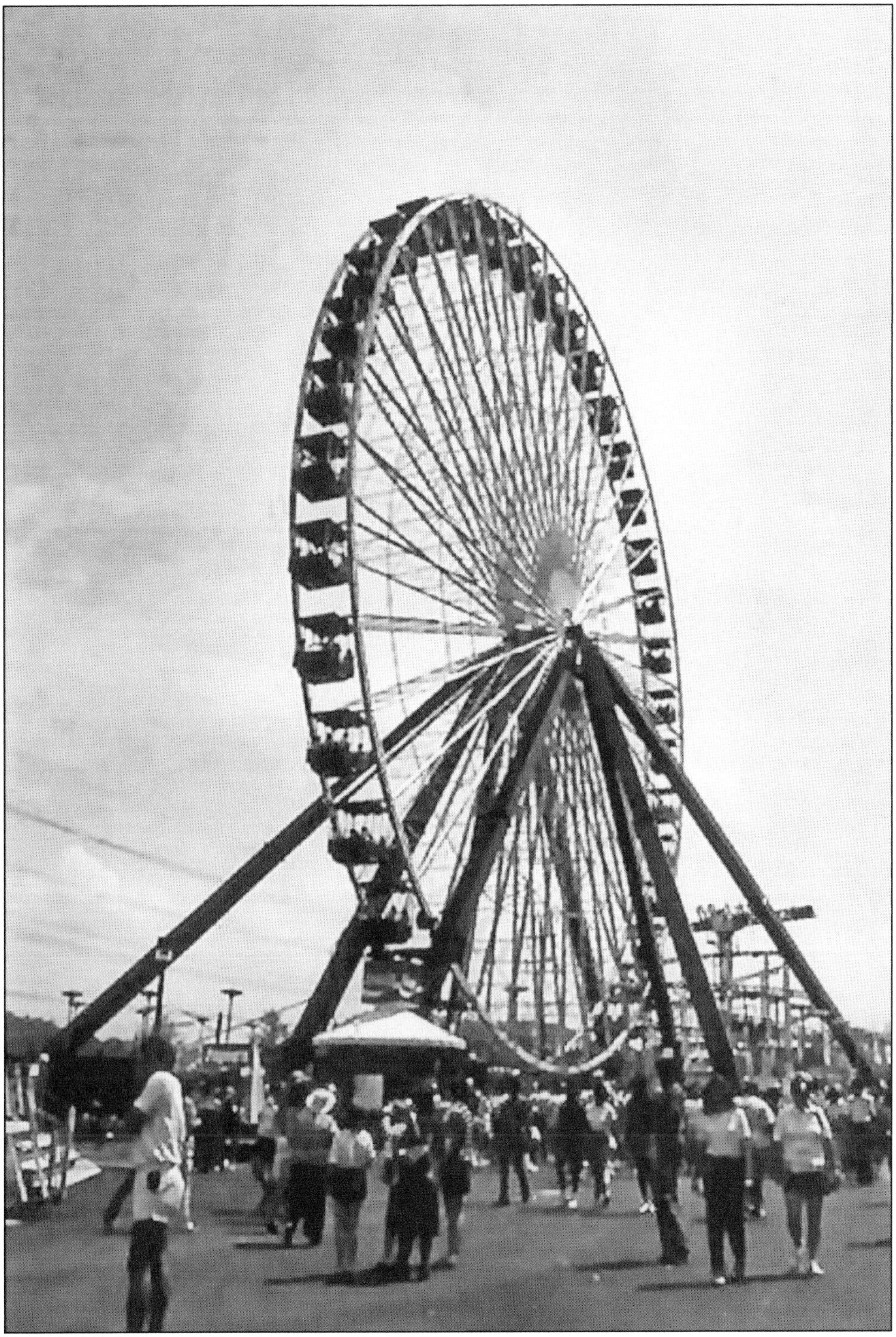

Riders on the Ferris wheel could view Neyland Stadium, the site for the football game played between the University of Tennessee and the University of Alabama on October 16, 1982. The game was won 35-28 in an upset victory by the University of Tennessee. (Courtesy of the Prater family.)

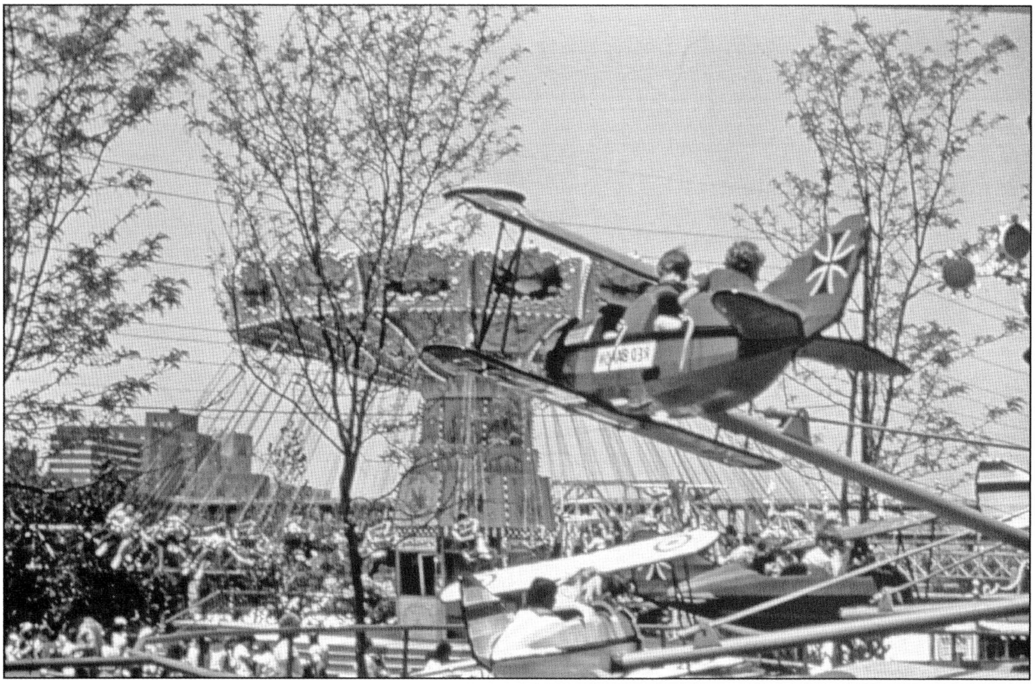

Photographer Miles Roberts caught the uplifting feelings of the fairgoers in this colorful photograph of the kiddie airplane ride. (Courtesy Miles Roberts.)

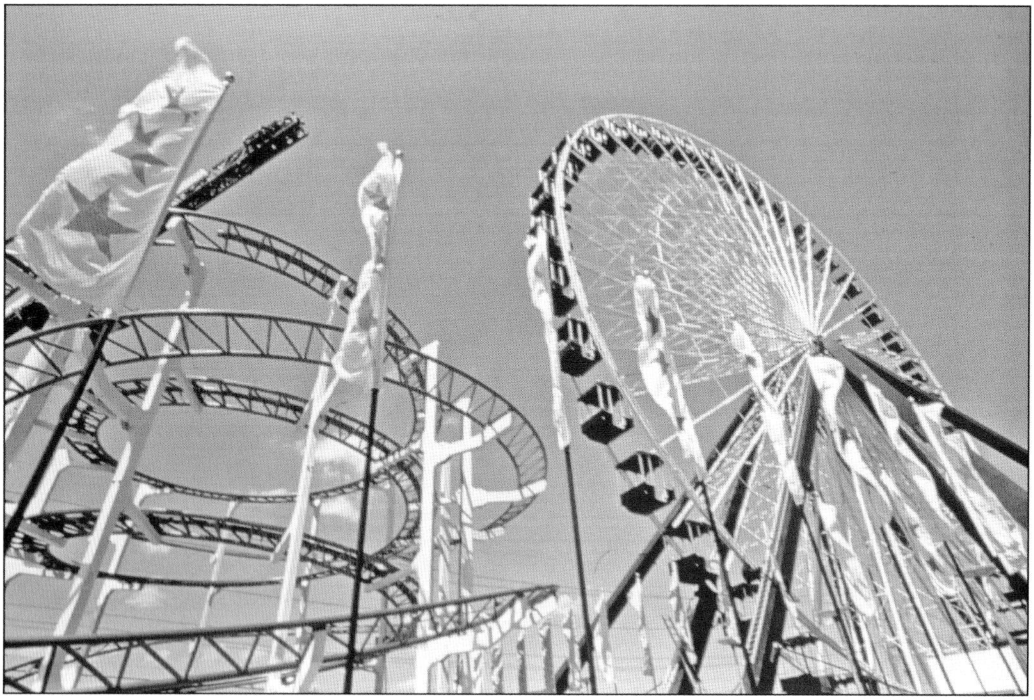

Photographer Miles Roberts was able to show the energy that seemed to flow throughout the Energy Expo with this photograph, which contains both the roller coaster and the Ferris wheel. (Courtesy Miles Roberts.)

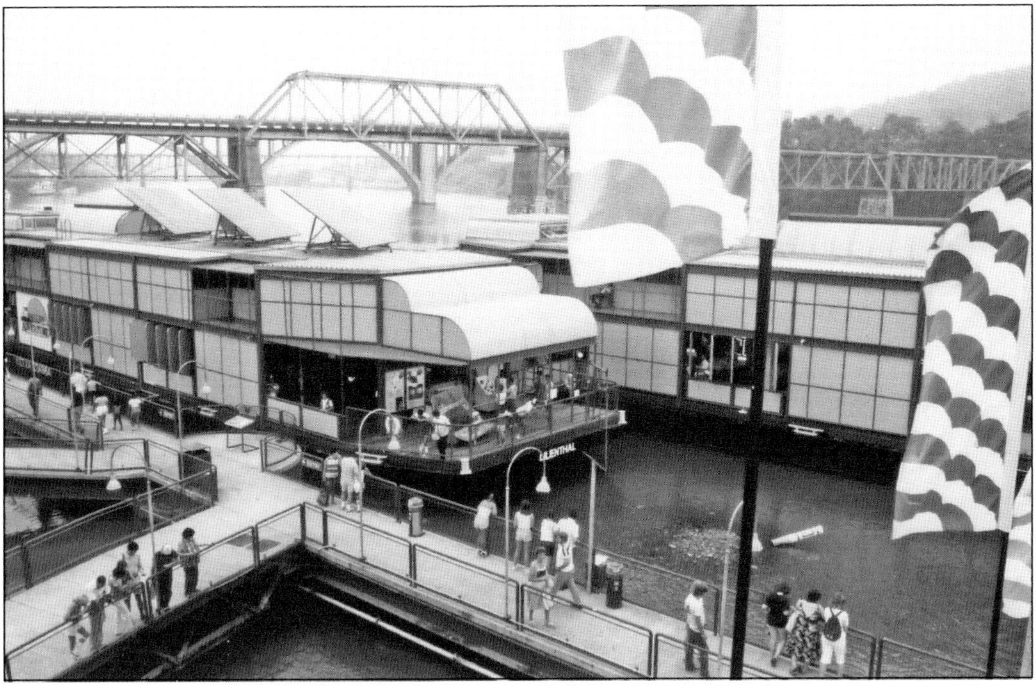

Fun Fair stretched out across Neyland Drive to include a ride on a showboat barge. Colorful flags waved on the shores of the Tennessee River. (Courtesy of Charlie Brookes.)

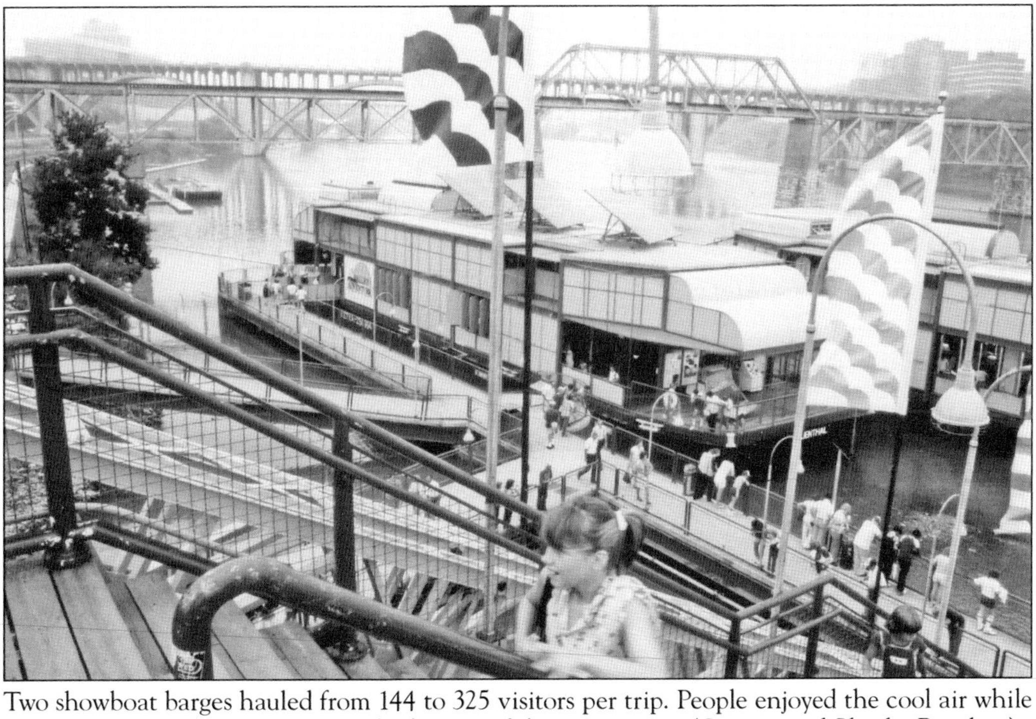

Two showboat barges hauled from 144 to 325 visitors per trip. People enjoyed the cool air while gliding along the river looking at the beauty of the mountains. (Courtesy of Charlie Brookes.)

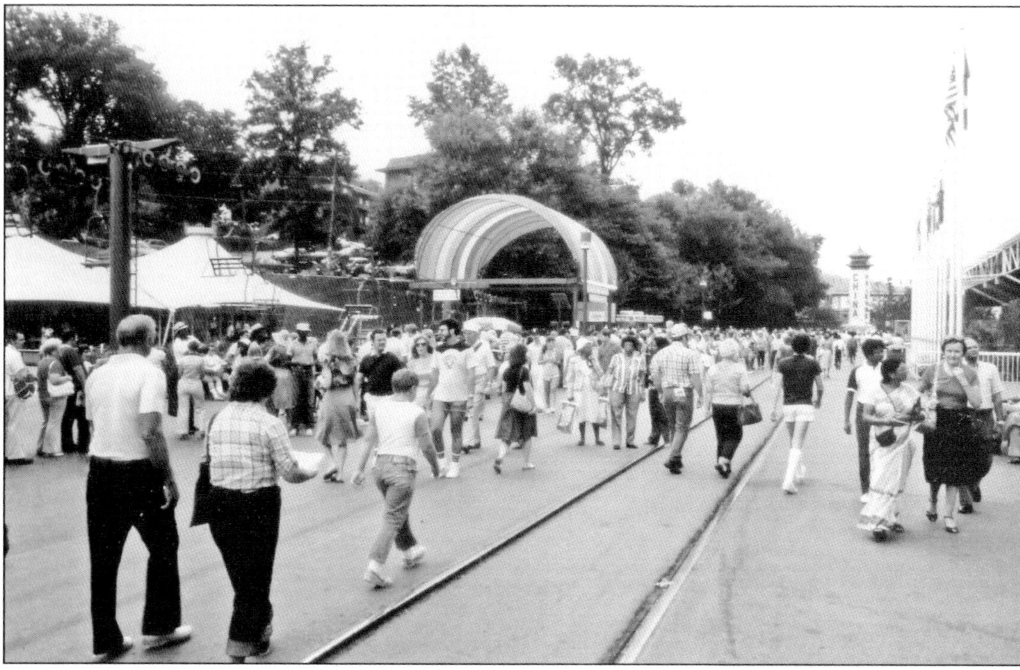

Visitors hurry towards the Chinese Pavilion and also to the Fun Fair. (Courtesy of Charlie Brookes.)

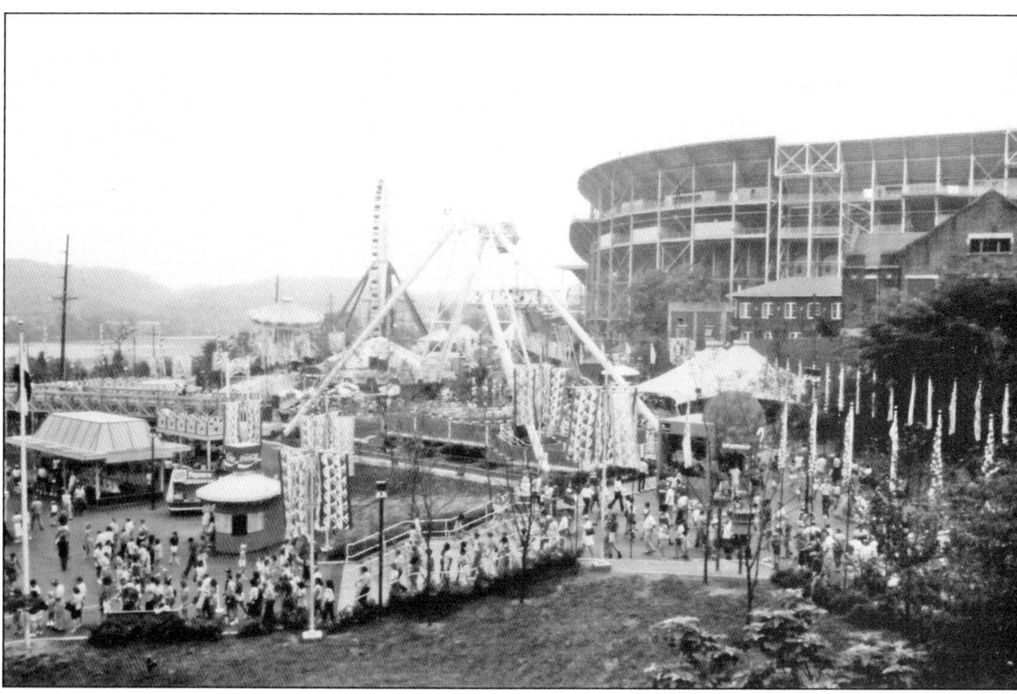

Neyland Stadium provided a point of reference for visitors who were looking for the amusement rides in the Fun Fair section of the fair. (Courtesy of Miles Roberts.)

Six

The Tennessee Amphitheatre

History never looks like history when you are living through it.

—John W. Gardner

The Tennessee Amphitheatre is an oddly shaped structure with three large "tent-like" canopies made from peaked fiberglass. The $2.8-million structure was built alongside the fair's artificial lake, Waters of the World, and was one of the few newly constructed buildings intended to remain on the site permanently. It sits within 200 feet of the Sunsphere, the only other permanent building remaining on the site.

Horst Berger designed the Tennessee Amphitheatre in 1981. He was a part of the McCarty Bullock Holsaple, architects of Knoxville, and Geiger Berger, engineers of New York. Berger is known internationally for his lightweight tensile structures. The 1982 World's Fair Guide Book described the Tennessee Amphitheatre as "The translucence of the fiber glass fabric and the open-sided design provide a striking outdoor feeling, while the twin 76-foot peaks of the main audience structure create a dramatic visual effect that can be seen throughout the fairgrounds. An added benefit of the open-sided design is that it extends audience viewing beyond the actual enclosure. There is covered seating for 1,443 spectators with enough room around the perimeter of the amphitheatre for up to 1,000 more. As the stage is visible from across the fairgrounds the actual audience size could increase to nearly 6,000. The theater is capable of creating a 'black box' effect by enclosing the rear of the stage with a large curtain. To provide acoustical excellence, the saddle-shaped stage creates a band shell which directs sound toward the audience."

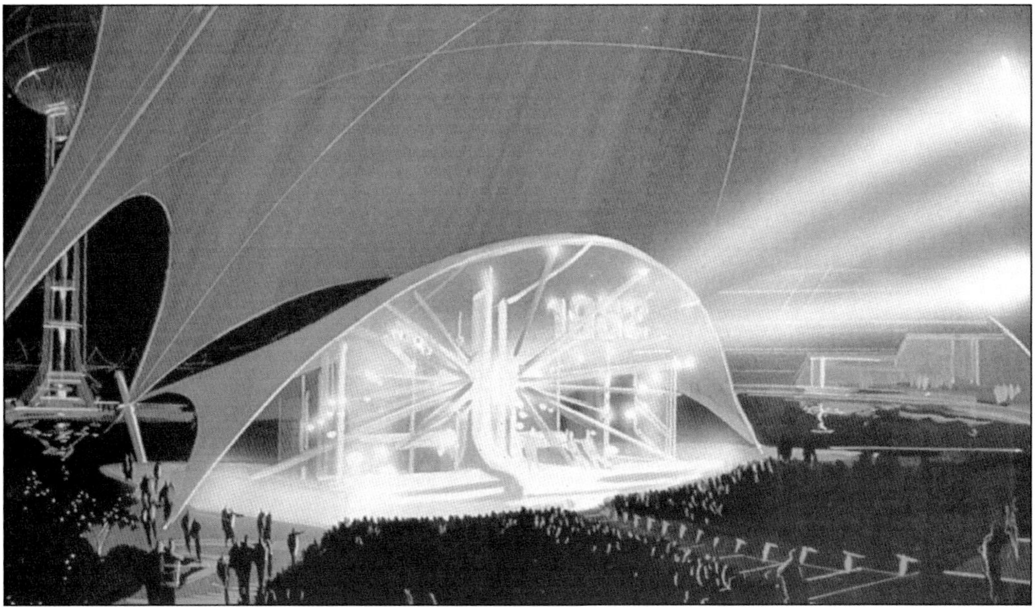

This postcard is an artist's idea of what the Tennessee Amphitheatre would look like. The actual theater was pared down in size. Although the lighting was an amazing spectacle, it was not as brilliant as shown in this rendition. (Courtesy of KIEE.)

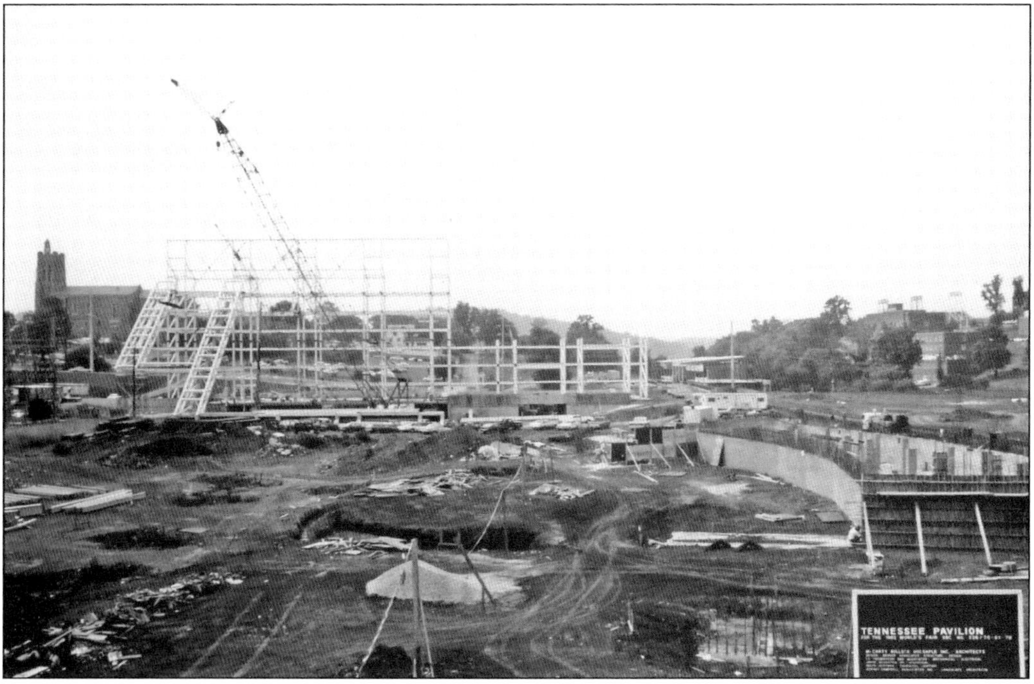

The fair site in 1981 looked like one big dirty brown spot. No one could be sure the fair would be ready to open on schedule. "We went a lot on faith," explained Jesse Barr. (Courtesy of Charlie Brookes.)

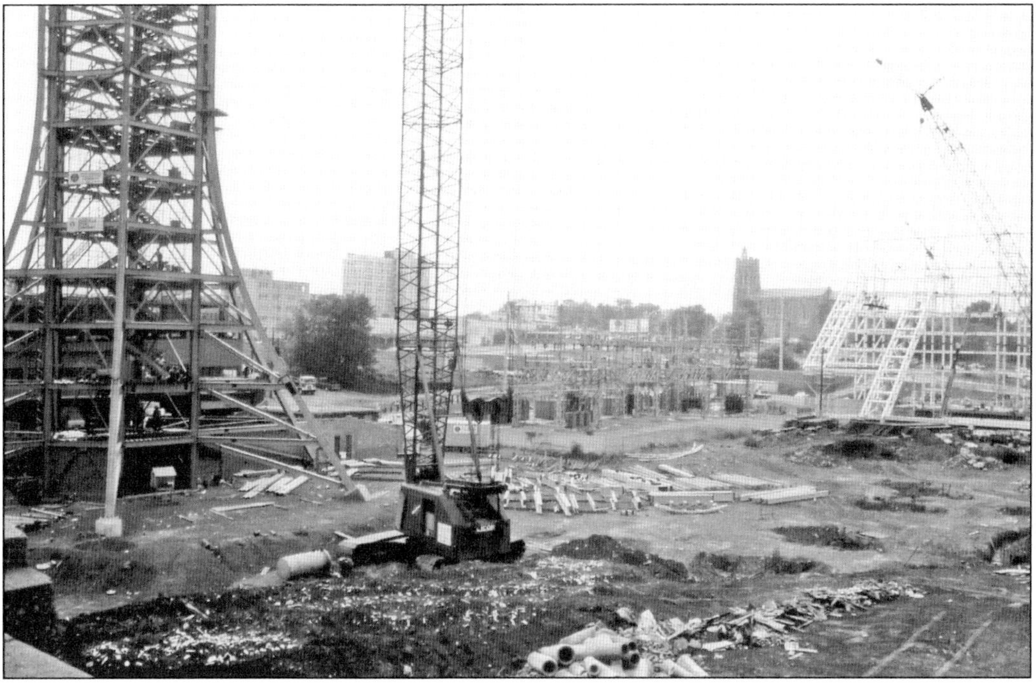

The Tennessee Amphitheatre, the Sunsphere, and the United States Pavilion are the three buildings constructed as permanent structures for Expo '82. (Courtesy of Charlie Brookes.)

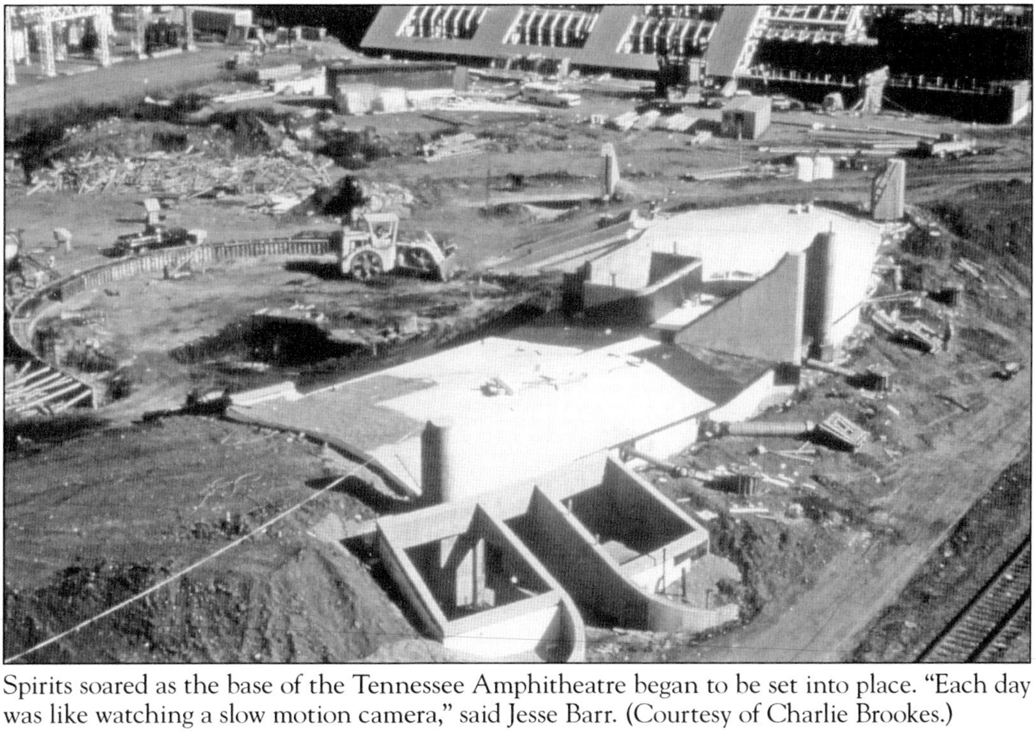

Spirits soared as the base of the Tennessee Amphitheatre began to be set into place. "Each day was like watching a slow motion camera," said Jesse Barr. (Courtesy of Charlie Brookes.)

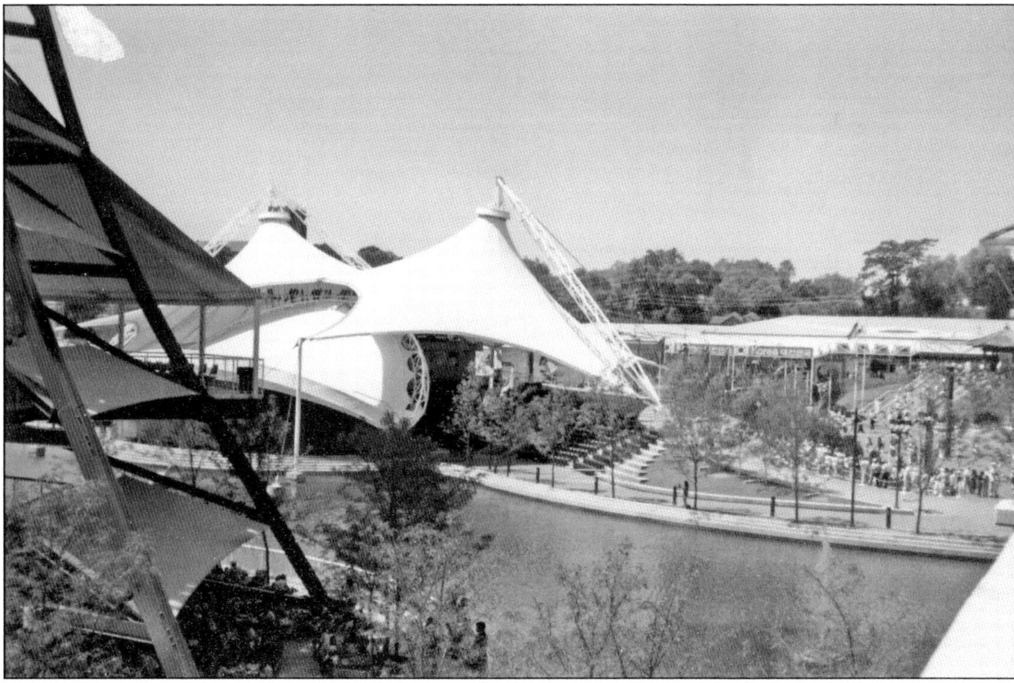

The Tennessee Amphitheatre, seen in 1982, was considered an engineering marvel. The tent-like canopy could be rolled and unrolled much like a widow awning. Canoes or paddleboats were for rent on the artificial lake named Waters of the World. (Courtesy of Mike Prather.)

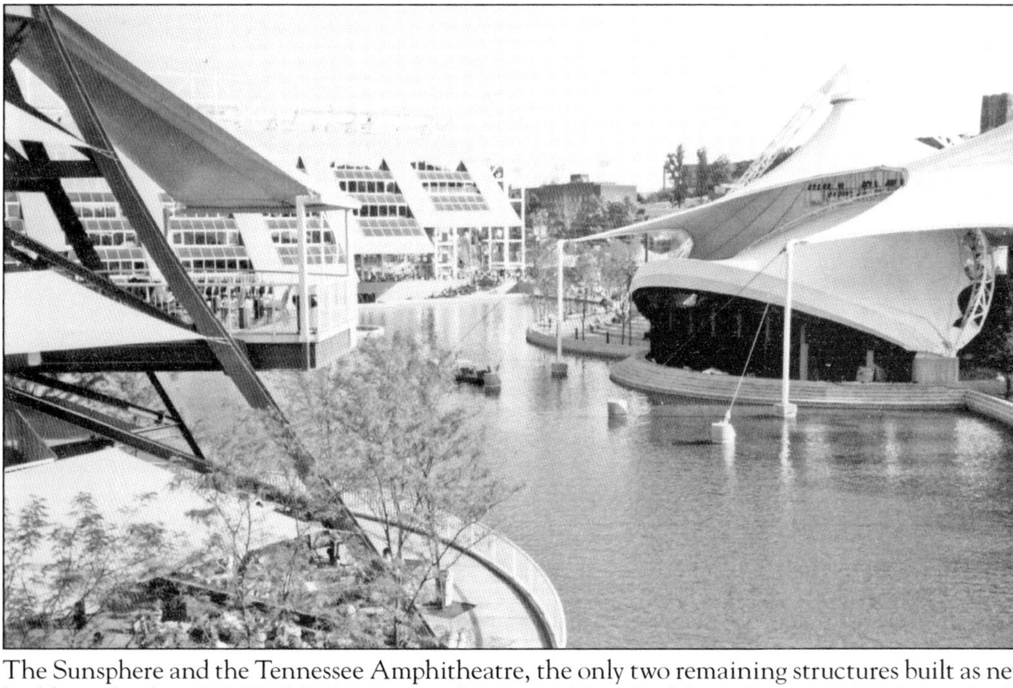

The Sunsphere and the Tennessee Amphitheatre, the only two remaining structures built as new buildings for the 1982 World's Fair, rest within several hundred feet of one another. In 1982, the Sunsphere also sported yellow, tent-like canopies, which helped visitors get out of the hot sun. (Courtesy of Mike Prather.)

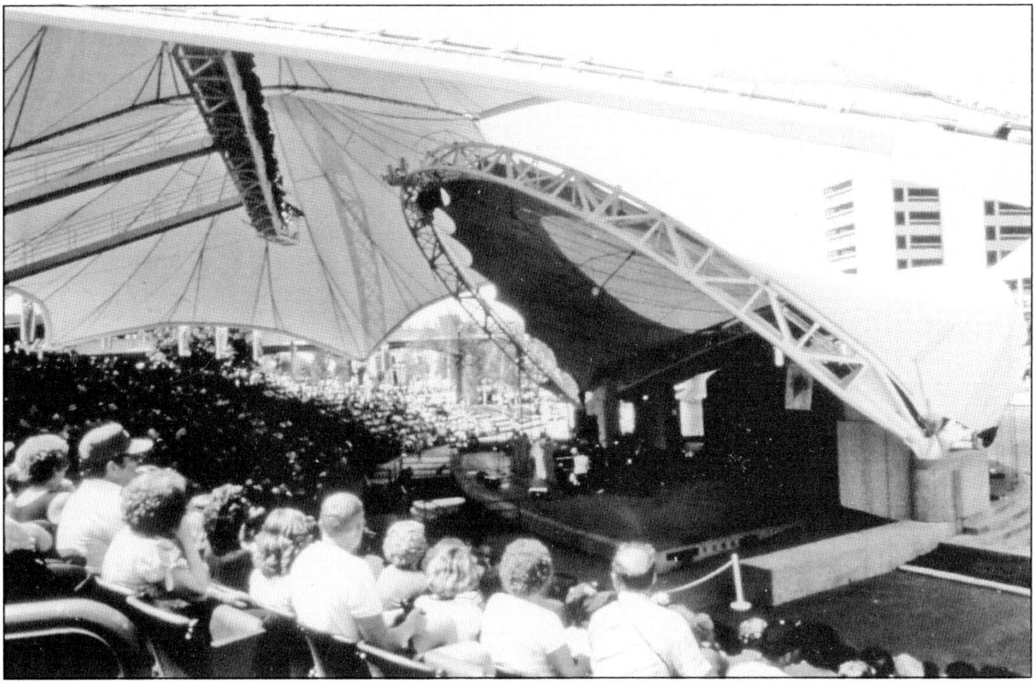

The Tennessee Amphitheatre was the venue for entertaining the throngs of visitors who daily crowded into the 1,443 seats. Another 1,000 visitors could see the stage while standing nearby. (Courtesy of Charlie Brookes.)

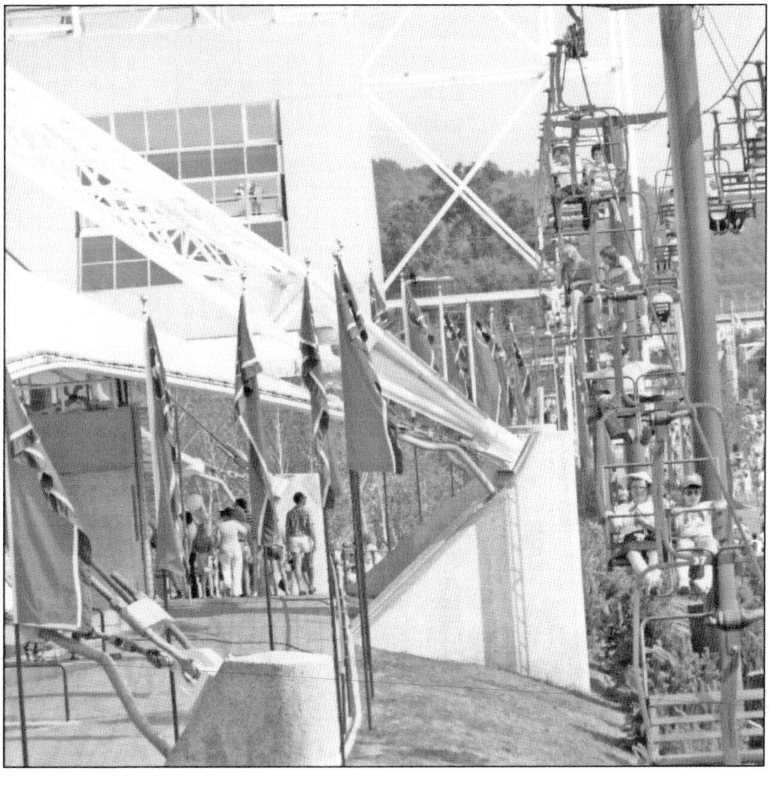

Rows of the Tennessee state flag flew around the Tennessee Amphitheatre. The tent-like structure contained a concrete base on which the fiberglass tents were stretched. (Courtesy of Charlie Brookes.)

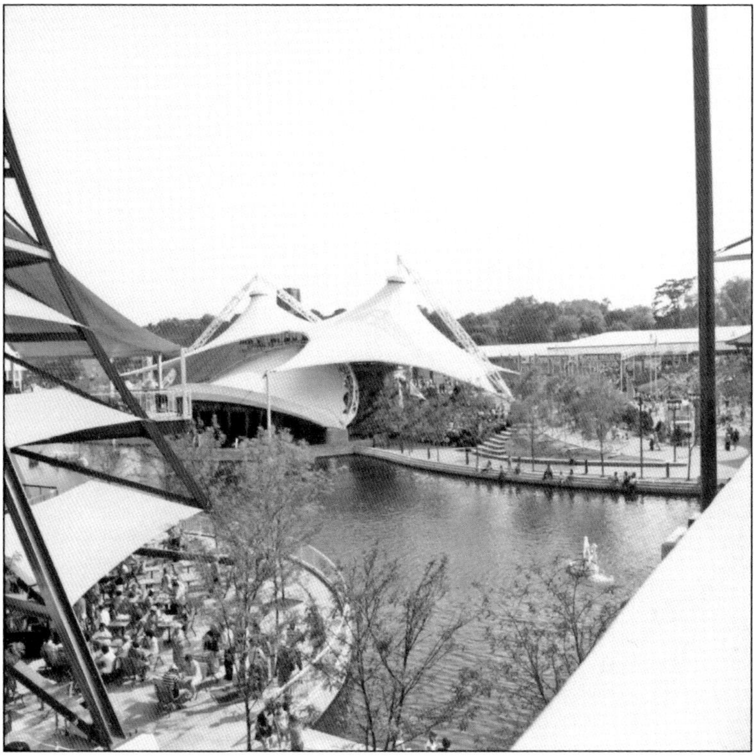

The Tennessee Amphitheatre's three tent-like awnings were called "visionary," providing interest as well as a permanent structure to be used after the fair closed. (Courtesy of KIEE.)

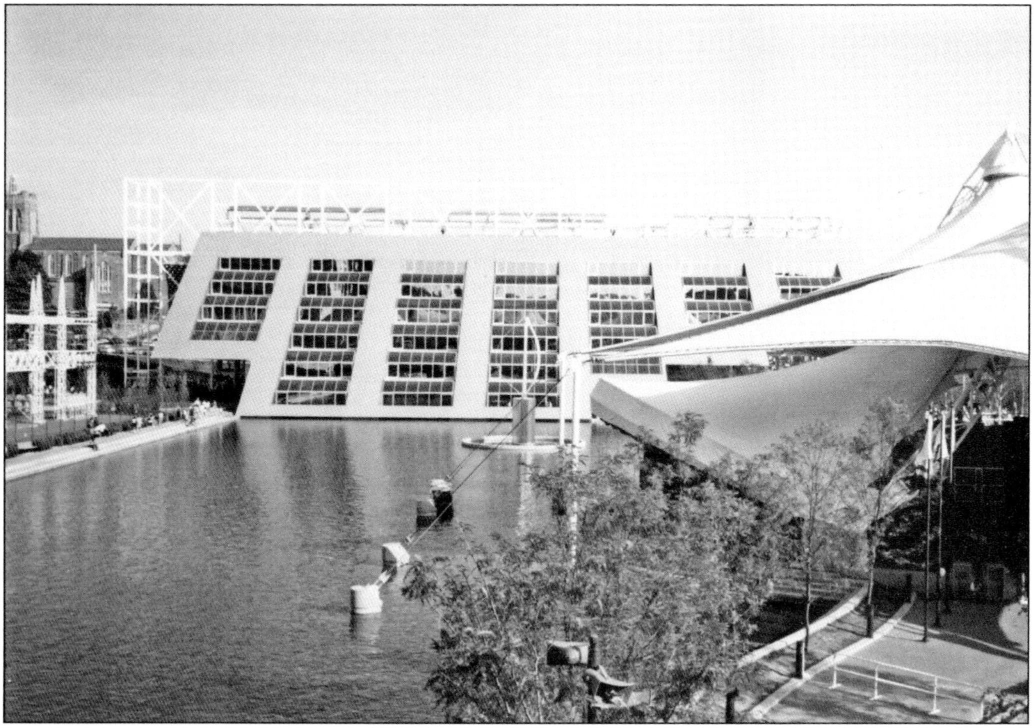

The Tennessee Amphitheatre was built near the United States Pavilion and was used as a place for people to rest from the heat as well as a performance theater. (Courtesy of the Prather family.)

Seven

The Sunsphere

If you keep getting no for the answer, you are talking to the wrong people.

—William Denton, architect

The Sunsphere consists of a 192-foot steel tower that serves as the base for the 74-foot spherical ball containing 360 windows. The windows were sprinkled with 24-carat gold flakes so they would twinkle and glow in the bright sun. Three elevators run up and down the tower while the golden ball contains five floors of space, used as a restaurant, a meeting space for a catering business, office space, and an observation deck, which is open and free to the public.

The Sunsphere was the theme structure for the 1982 World's Fair and was patterned after similar towers used in previous World's Fairs, such as the Space Needle in Seattle, Washington, and the two towers built for the 1964 World's Fair in Queens, New York.

The first drawings of the building made by architect Hubert Bebb (1903–1984) proposed a giant sphere on the ground, which could be used after the fair as a restaurant; however, Jake Butcher wanted the theme structure to "tower over the fairgrounds so guests could ride up the glass elevators and look out over the total site."

In 1979, William Denton was asked to think of something about energy because the theme for the fair was "Energy Turns the World." Denton knew the sun is the source of all energy, and he named his tower the Sunsphere.

Builders began working on the Sunsphere in December 1981 by breaking ground and digging in the earth. William Denton, who was the president and lead architect for Community Tectonics, did much of the day-to-day work on the structure with help from Don Shell, another architect who worked for Community Tectonics.

The Sunsphere was the only spherical structure with a golden ball on its top until 2002, when the new city of Astana, Kazakhstan, built Bayeterk, a 314-foot tower that could be a twin for the Sunsphere.

The Sunsphere was purchased by the City of Knoxville in 1984 for $750,000 from a private group of individuals. It has been called a very expensive birdhouse since it is a popular perch for pigeons and starlings. The temporary structure built at the base of the building was removed in 1984 when Hardee's Restaurants pulled out of the location as a result of lack of business.

The Sunsphere has engineering very much like that of a common floor lamp. There is a wheel of concrete under the building heavier than the tower and golden ball. It would take a wind of over 110 miles per hour to bring the building down. The golden windows would blow off before the steel tower would fall.

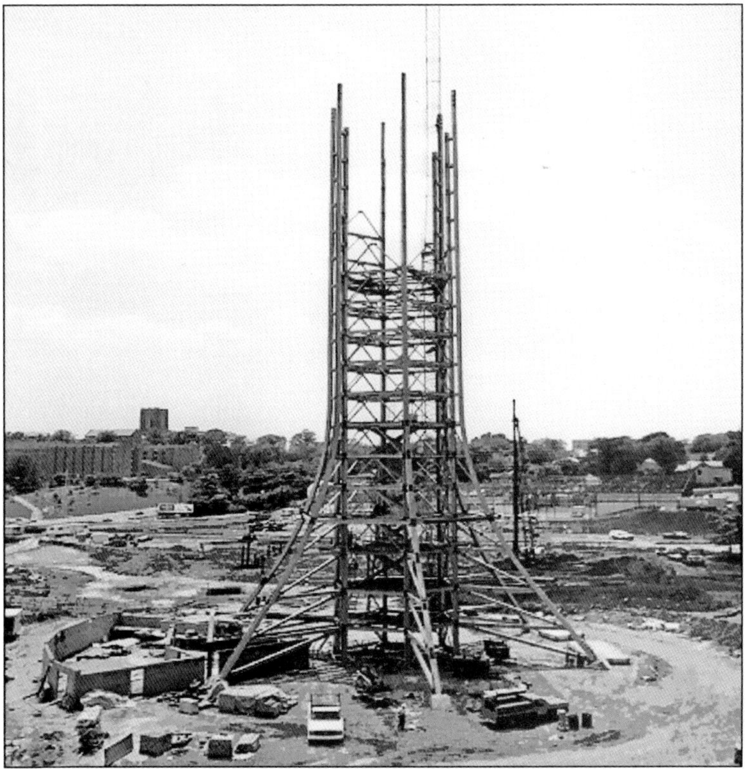

The Sunsphere, designed and constructed by Community Tectonics and Rentenbach's Engineering, came together like the pieces in a giant erector set. (Courtesy of Community Tectonics.)

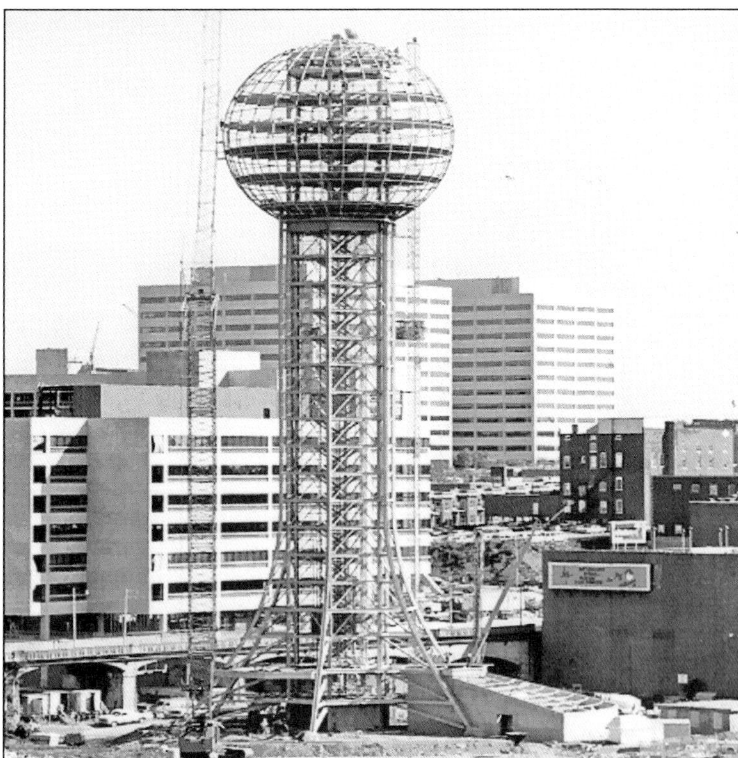

Local citizens were thrilled to watch the unusual building as it came together. No one had ever seen a building quite like the Sunsphere. (Courtesy of Community Tectonics.)

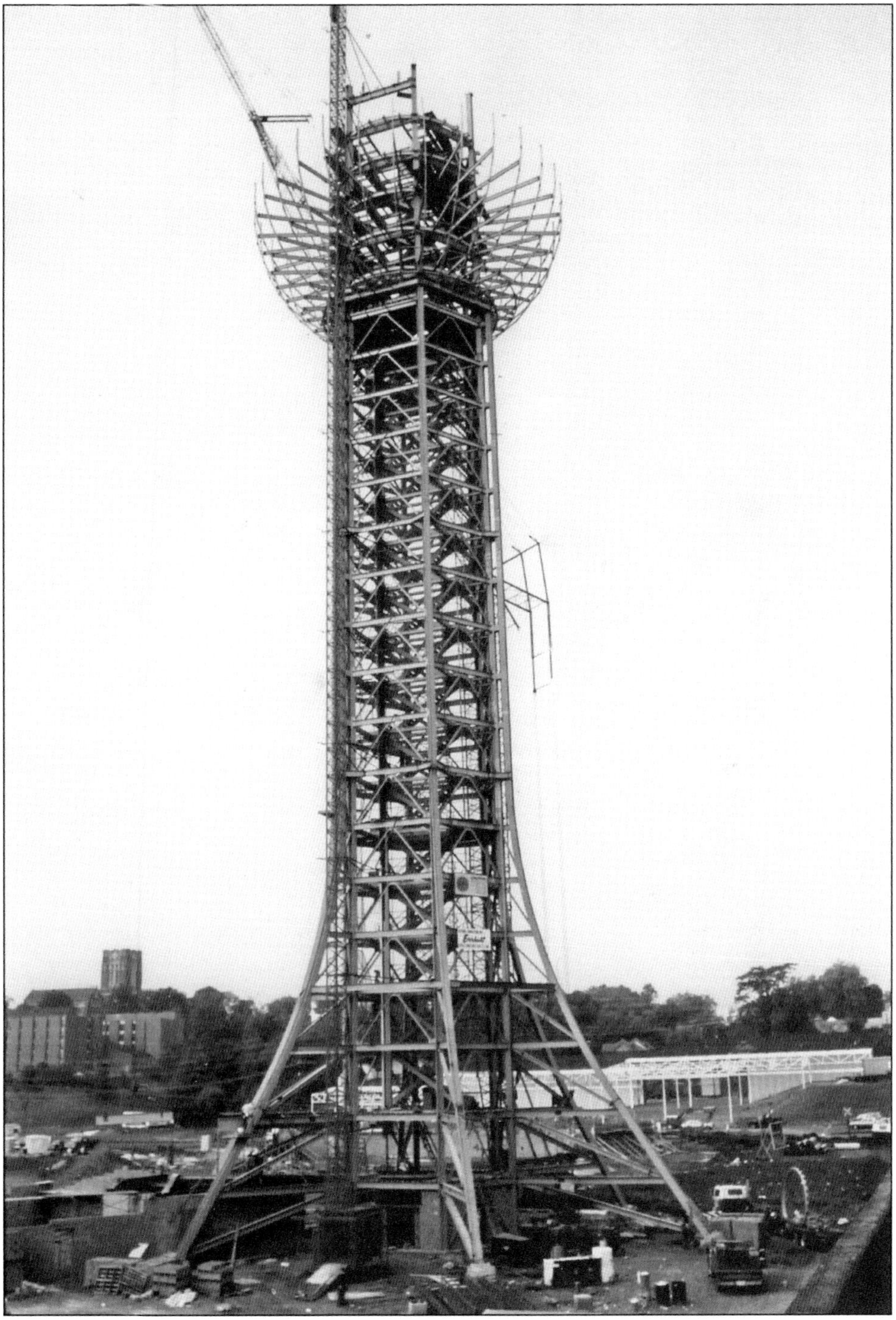

The skyline of Knoxville, Tennessee, was changed forever once the 266-foot tower was set into place. In order to get permission from the Knoxville Community Development Corporation, the architect, William Denton, had to convince the panel the Sunsphere was a building that had five floors instead of 26, which it appeared to have because of its height. Once he was able to do this, his company got permission to build the unusual building. (Courtesy of Community Tectonics.)

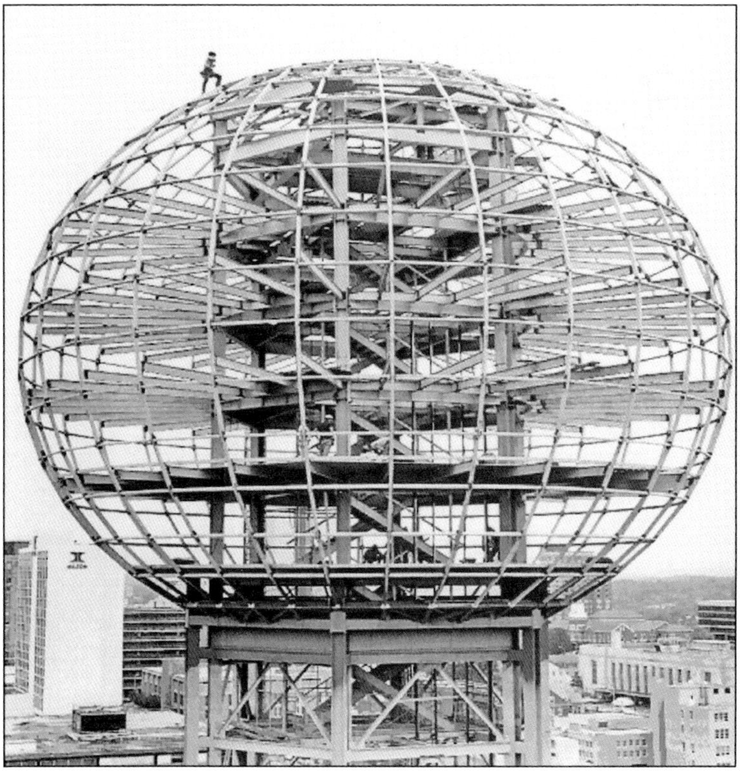

As the final steel girder went into place, this photograph of a construction worker standing on top of the first spherical building ever built in the United States was sent around the world. Financier Jesse Barr was instrumental in getting an Urban Development Action Grant, the source of the first $1.2 million spent on the Sunsphere. (Courtesy of Community Tectonics.)

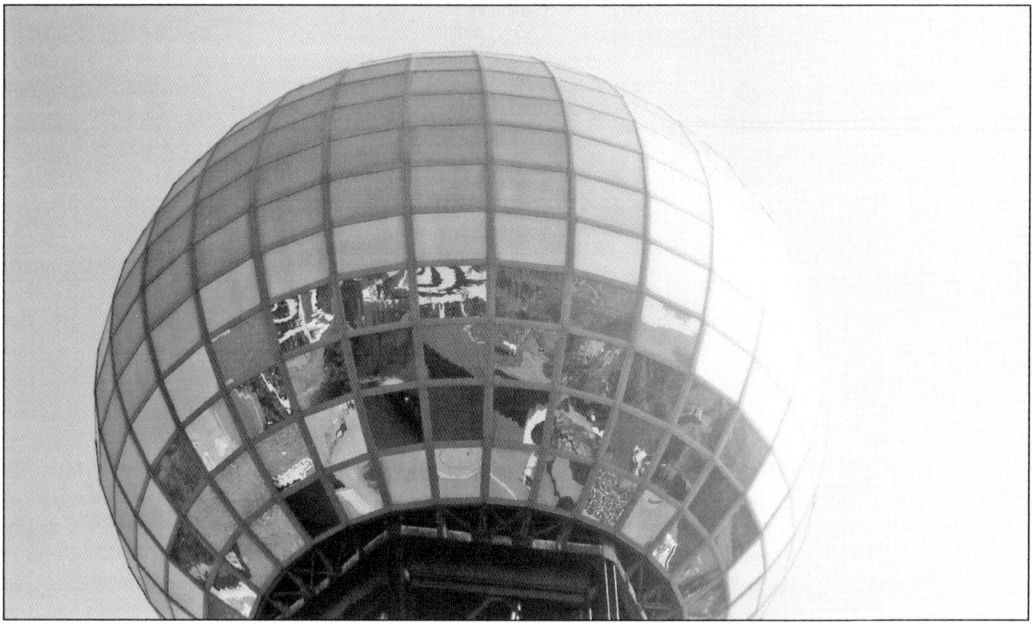

Each of the 360 golden windows cost $1,000. In May 1982, a gunshot rang out and struck a golden glass windowpane of the Sunsphere. Although no one was ever arrested for the incident, it seemed to express the frustration of the local citizens, who were already hearing rumors of cost overruns and mounting debts surrounding the construction of the Sunsphere. It has been determined the final cost to build the Sunsphere was $6.6 million. (Photograph by Barrett Buie.)

The Sunsphere's base became a popular place for visitors to sit and rest as picnic tables were provided by Hardee's Restaurant, which sold fast food from a temporary structure on the left side of the building's base. The brightly colored yellow canopies provided a festive feel to the tower and relief from the hot sun. Sun Oil Corporation provided a tunnel-like structure at the base of the Sunsphere to be used as a kind of museum about the sun for visitors to pass through as they waited to ride the elevator. (Courtesy of the Prather family.)

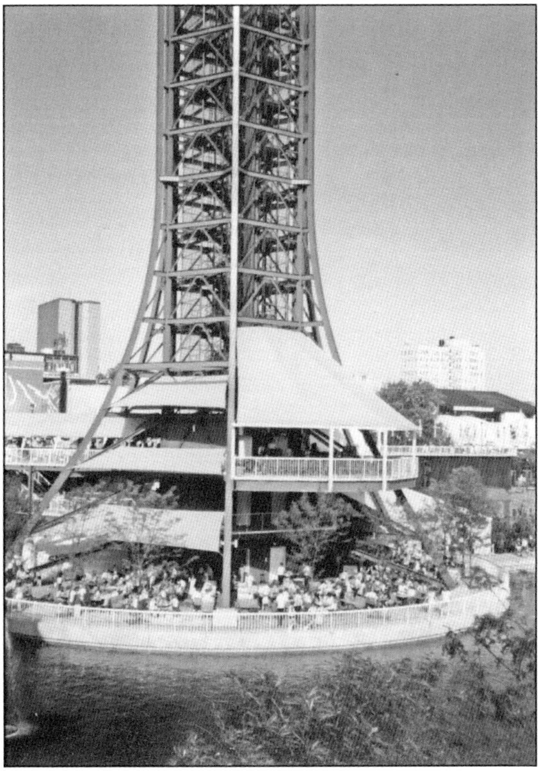

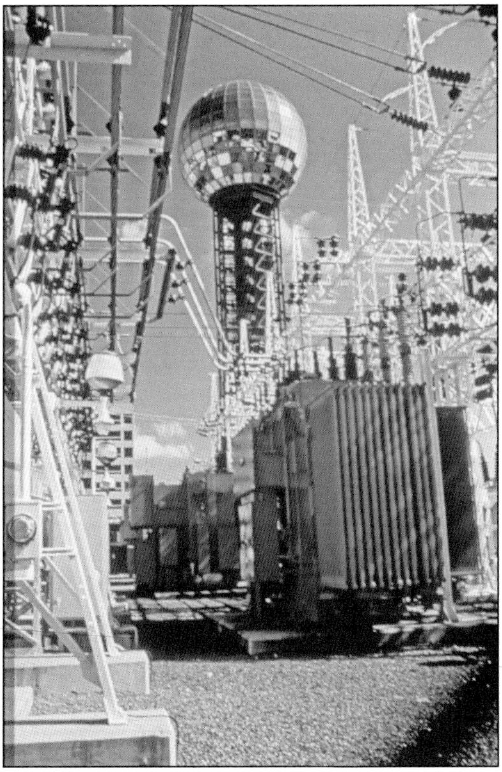

Ironically, the fair that had energy as its theme was powered by a massive power plant located in the center of the fairgrounds. (Courtesy of Randy Tyree.)

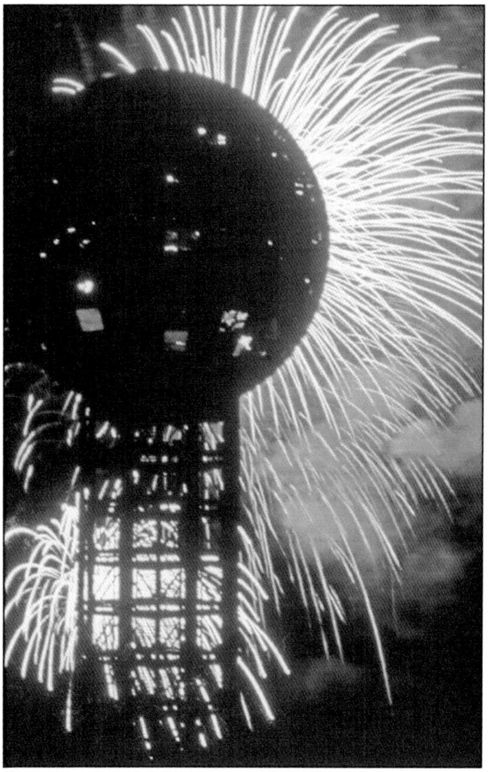

The Sunsphere at night provided a marvelous opportunity for photographers. (Courtesy of Charlie Brookes.)

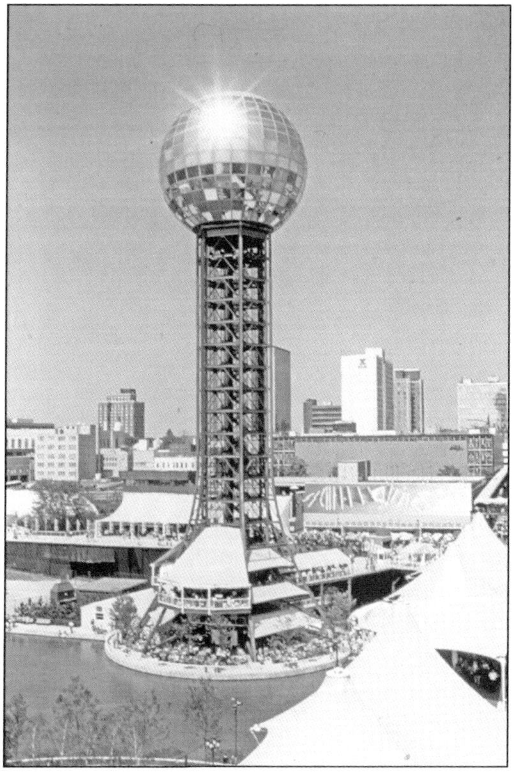

The Sunsphere and the fairgrounds were caught in all their glory in 1982. There are three elevators running up and down the 192-foot tower and five floors inside the golden ball. (Courtesy of Charlie Brookes.)

Eight

THE PROBLEMS

If you're going through hell, keep going.

—Winston Churchill

It would not be historically accurate to offer only the positive side of the fair. As far back as 1975, there was organized opposition to the fair from the group Citizens Against the Fair, organized by Joe Dodd, professor at the University of Tennessee. They held rallies, spoke before city council, wrote letters to the editors of local newspapers, and hosted protests. They were against the fair because "of the ever-increasing allocations of pork-barrel funds that strain our pocketbooks and fatten the wealthy while the nation's serious social and economic problems are ignored," said Dodd, their leader.

Dodd's book *Expose: The Real Story Behind the Knoxville World's Fair*, published in 1982, remains available at Amazon.com in 2008. The introduction says, "The 1982 World's Fair is a case history in political wheeling and dealing, a story that shows how the rich and influential can create a dream for themselves that may turn out to be a nightmare for the city and the state."

After the fair, Dodd wrote, "The fair did open on schedule. It ran its six month course with a high degree of organizational efficiency. The ups were there. And so were the downs. Basically, the fair as an entertainment event was fairly well received, with most of the visitors enjoying themselves. Knoxville International Energy Exposition, the Expo Corporation, said it reached the projected attendance of 11 millions visits. It was able, KIEE reported, to pay off an up-front $33 million loan and end up in the black. But, the fair's impact on Knoxville's economy was far more mixed. To be sure, the times were good for many. On the site itself, activity was brisk with near perfect weather over the six months. Rides were taken; beer was consumed; Petros were eaten. To the chagrin of many others, however, the fair was a world class bust. In spite of widespread expectations to the contrary, the fair was played out largely on-site with off-site economic activities dramatically less than expected."

The major problems that occurred before the fair were as follows: 1. the refusal of the city to allow the issue of the fair to come before the voters for a referendum; 2. eviction of renters by greedy landlords; 3. the creation of Knox Visit, which held a monopoly on hotels/motel rooms; and 4. the way construction contracts were handed out to family and friends of Jake Butcher.

During the fair, the main problems were the following: 1. lack of adequate restrooms and drinking fountains; 2. difficulties visitors had renting motel/hotel space; 3. the quality of the available rental spaces; 4. price gouging for rental rates, food, and parking; 5. organized groups of pickpockets; 6. the heat; 7. lackluster exhibits; and 8. the fair's negative effect on off-site economic activities.

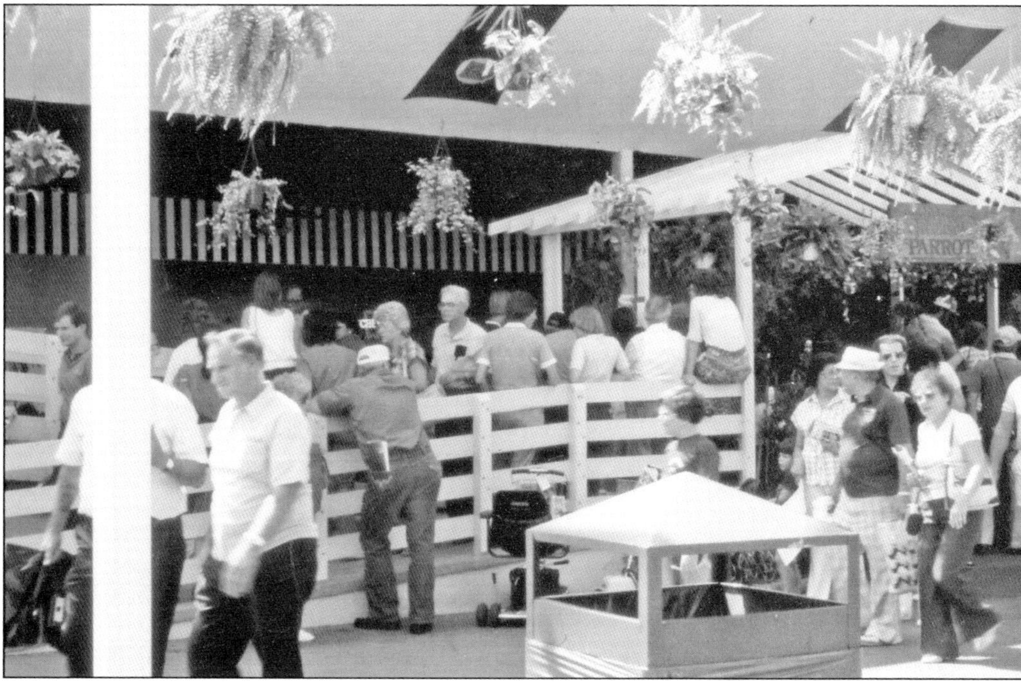

Visitors, who waited in long lines for over two hours in the hot sun, expected to be dazzled. (Courtesy of Miles Roberts.)

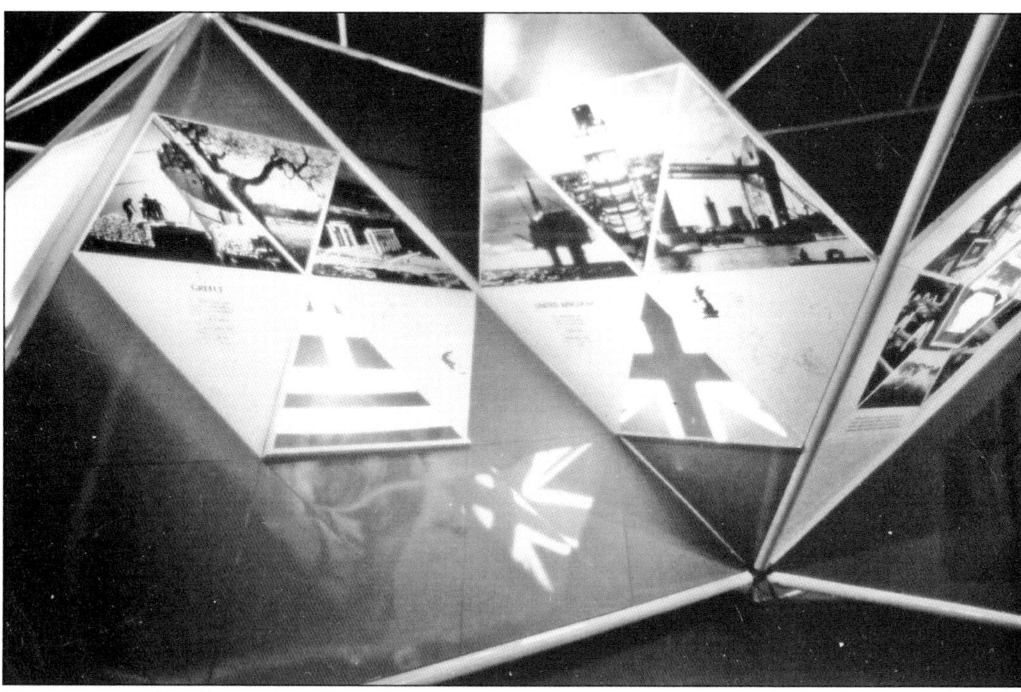

Visitors were often disappointed with lackluster displays of nothing more than posters, photographs, and flags. (Courtesy of Miles Roberts.)

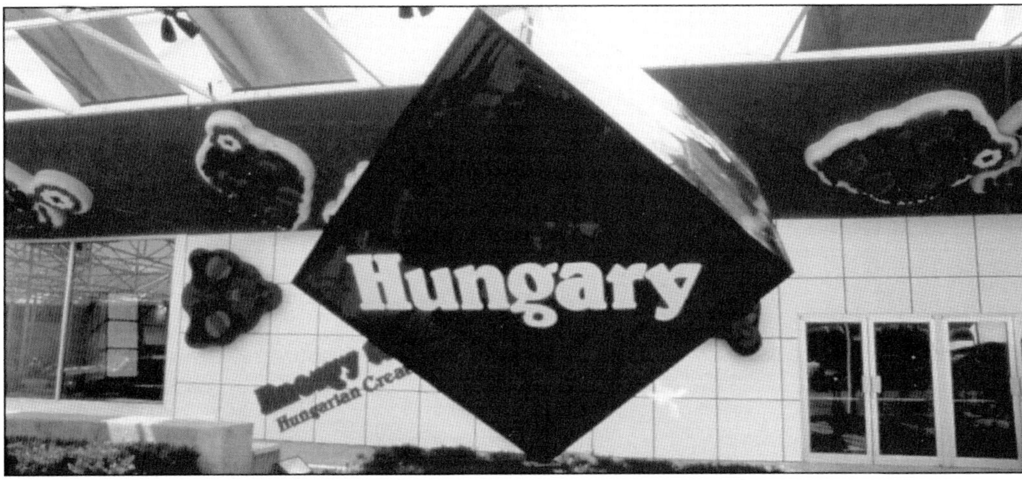

Fairgoers who were disappointed by lackluster exhibits in many pavilions were not disappointed by the pavilion from the Republic of Hungary, which was cheerfully decorated with the red, green, and white of the country's flag. As one of the landlocked European countries bordered by seven other countries, Hungary proudly offered visitors four sections of displays. One showed biographical data about famous artists, scientists, and warriors who distinguished themselves throughout the history of their country. Another section displayed a mock up thermal power station and a model of Thorex surface mining. The third section showed energy-saving ideas used in agriculture, while the fourth section contained a restaurant that served authentic Hungarian foods. (Courtesy of Charlie Brookes.)

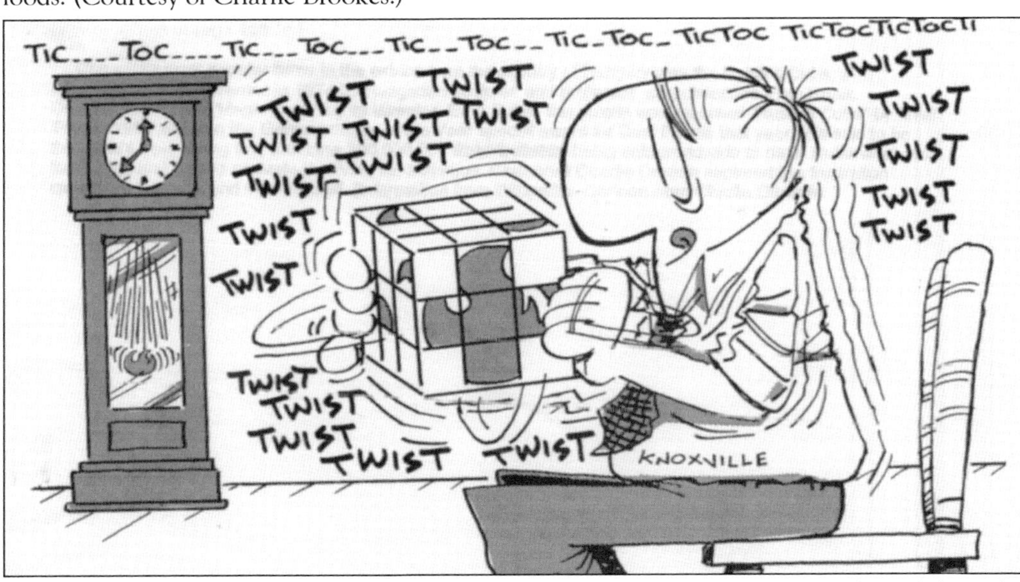

One of the most popular items in the exhibit from the country of Hungary was the Rubik's Cube, a mechanical puzzle invented in 1974 by Hungarian sculptor and professor of architecture Erno Rubik. Originally called the "Magic Cube" by its inventor, this puzzle was renamed Rubik's Cube by Ideal Toys in 1980 and won the German Game of the Year special award for Best Puzzle that year. It is said to be the world's best-selling toy, with over 300 million sold worldwide to date. Rubik attended the 1982 fair and hosted contests involving his invention. Cartoonist Charlie Daniels captured the frustration caused by the cube and the fair itself. (Courtesy of Charlie Daniels; information from Official 1982 World's Fair Guidebook.)

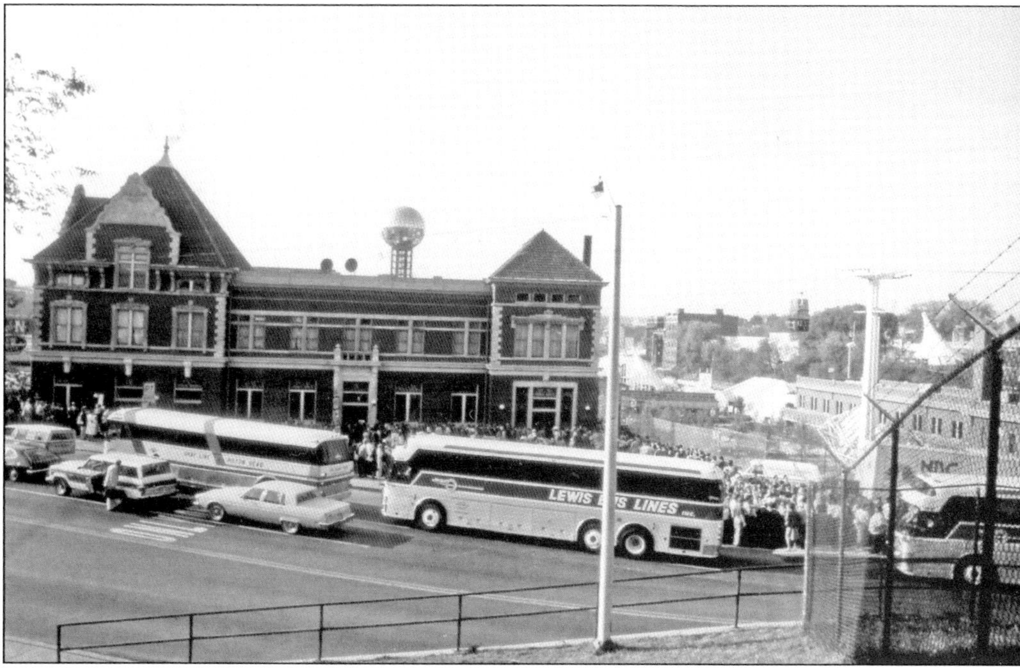

A pre-fair transportation study determined that most visitors to the fair would arrive by car. However, most people arrived by bus because of the inability to make reservations for local rooms. Hotel and motel owners in surrounding areas quickly responded to the need for lodging by providing tour buses and fair tickets. "When we saw all those buses lining the streets every morning, we knew we were in big trouble," said Jesse Barr. (Courtesy of Charlie Brookes.)

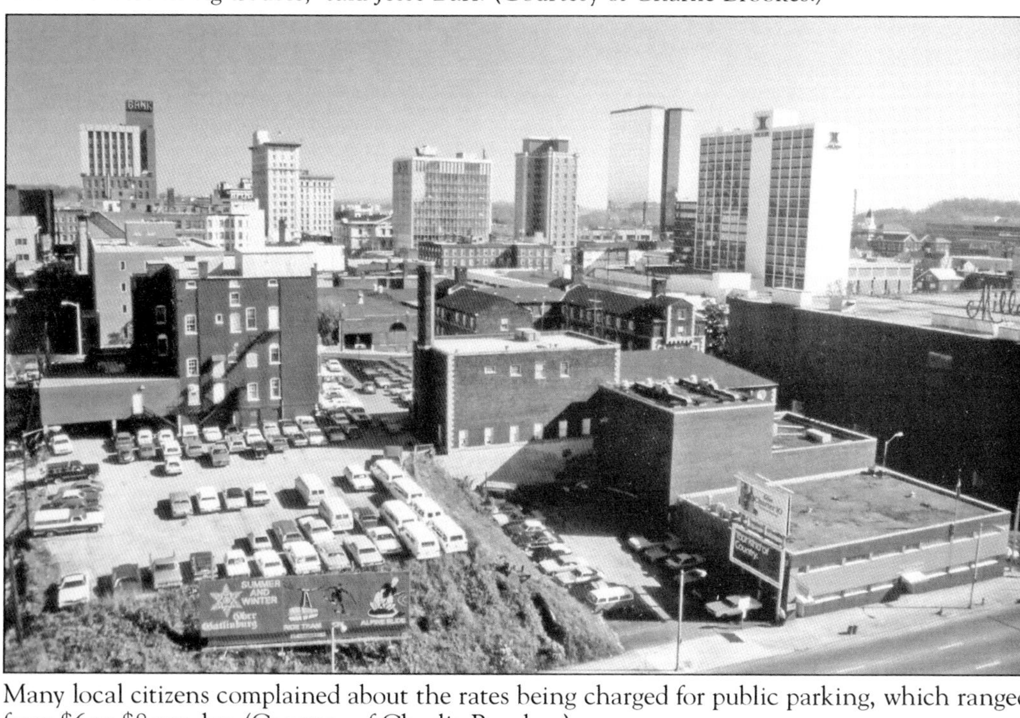

Many local citizens complained about the rates being charged for public parking, which ranged from $6 to $8 per day. (Courtesy of Charlie Brookes.)

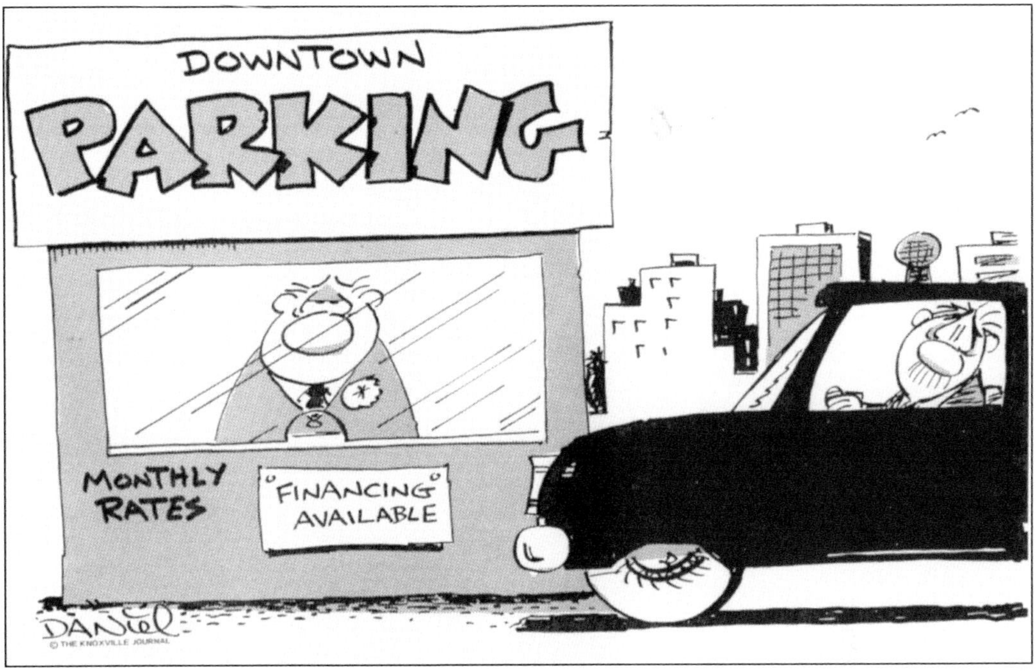

Cartoonist Charlie Daniels captured the issues of high prices for parking and the greed that took over in the business community. (Used by permission of the artist.)

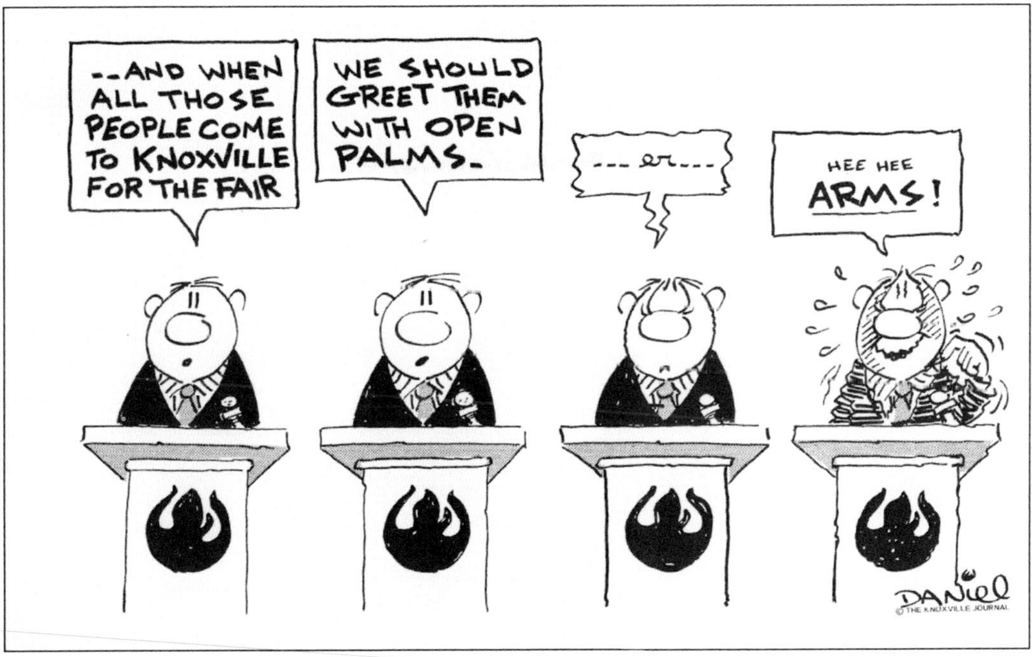

Rumors began before the fair about price gouging, landlords evicting longtime residents, millions of dollars in loan money being used by insiders, and other ways in which KIEE appeared to be preparing to make money off the visitors to the fair. All of these led cartoonist Charlie Daniels to sum up the feelings of the local citizens. (Used by permission of the artist.)

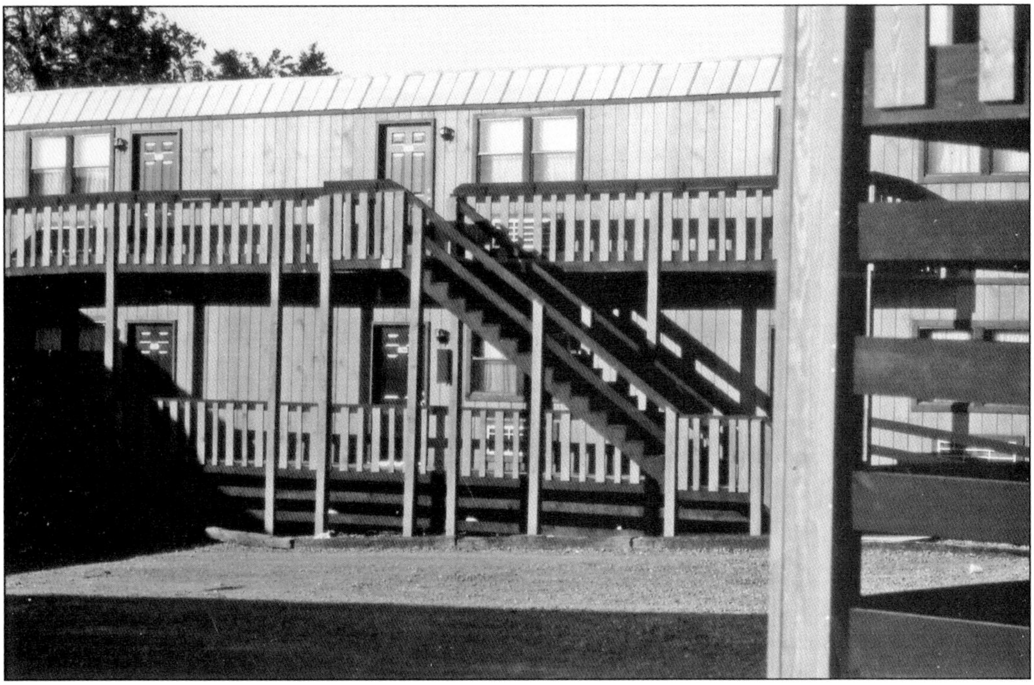

Use of temporary structures that looked a lot like mobile homes became an issue as citizens complained about the "hillbilly hotels." (Courtesy of Charlie Brookes.)

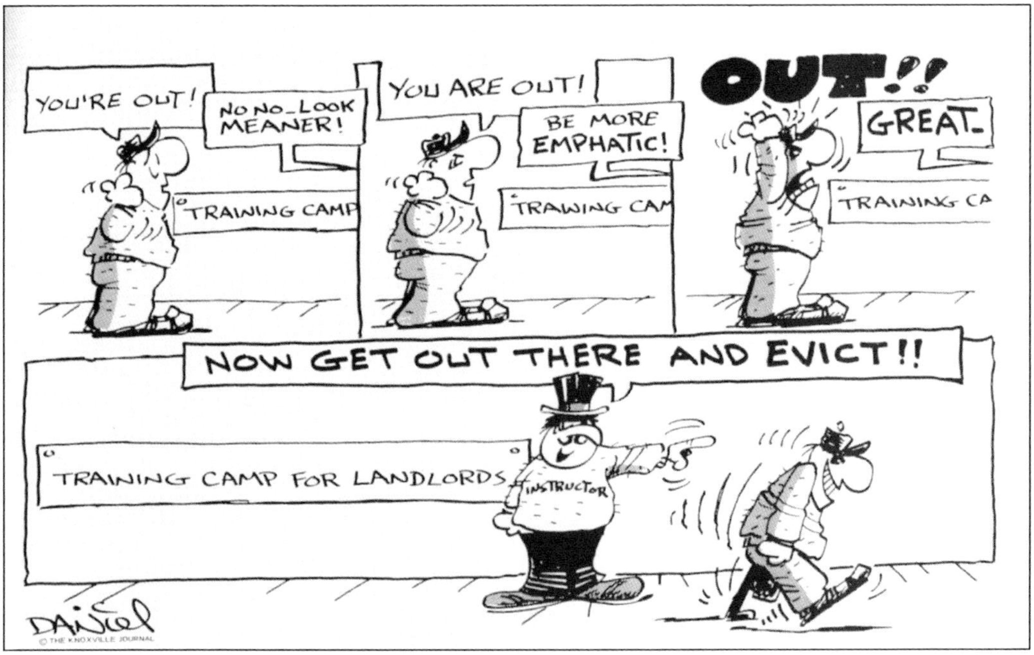

Cartoonist Charlie Daniels expressed the feelings of the public with his cartoon about the harshness of the landlords who evicted their longtime renters in order to gouge fairgoers. (Used by permission of the artist.)

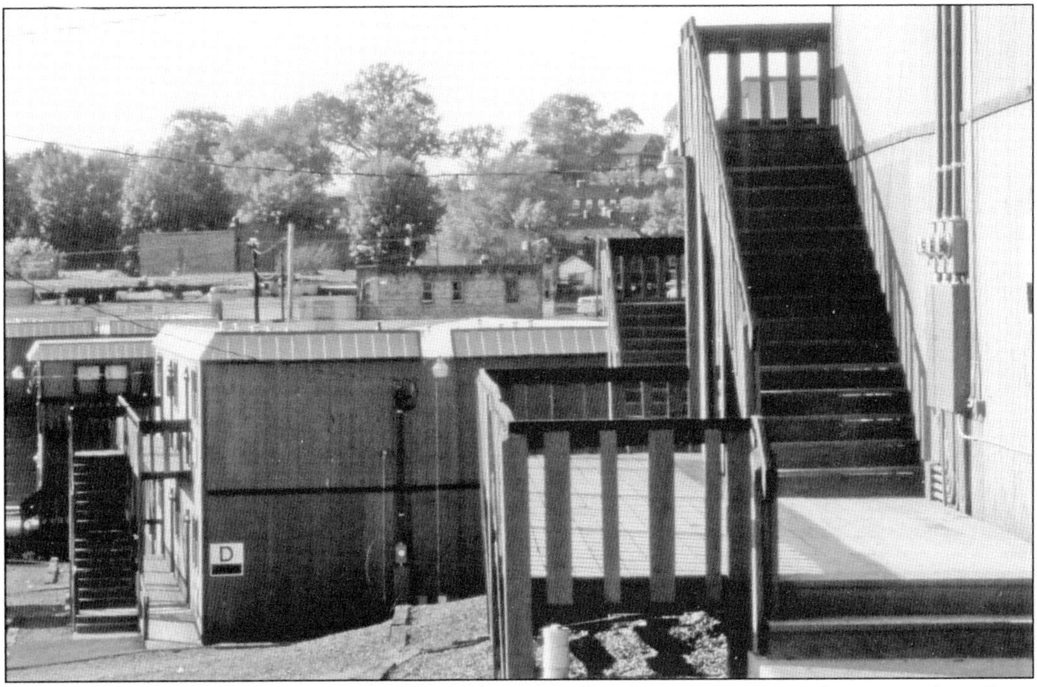

Some 3,500 people sued the 1982 World's Fair because of inadequate accommodations, such as these mobile homes stacked on top of each other and called a motel. (Courtesy of Charlie Brookes.)

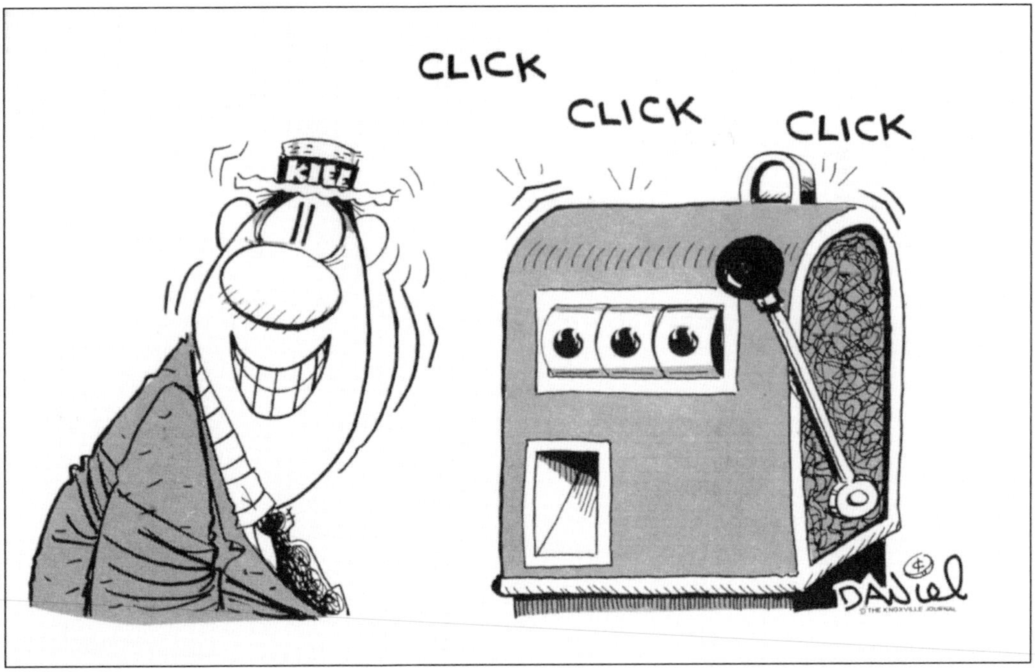

Knoxville International Energy Exposition became known as a greedy group. (Used by permission of the artist.)

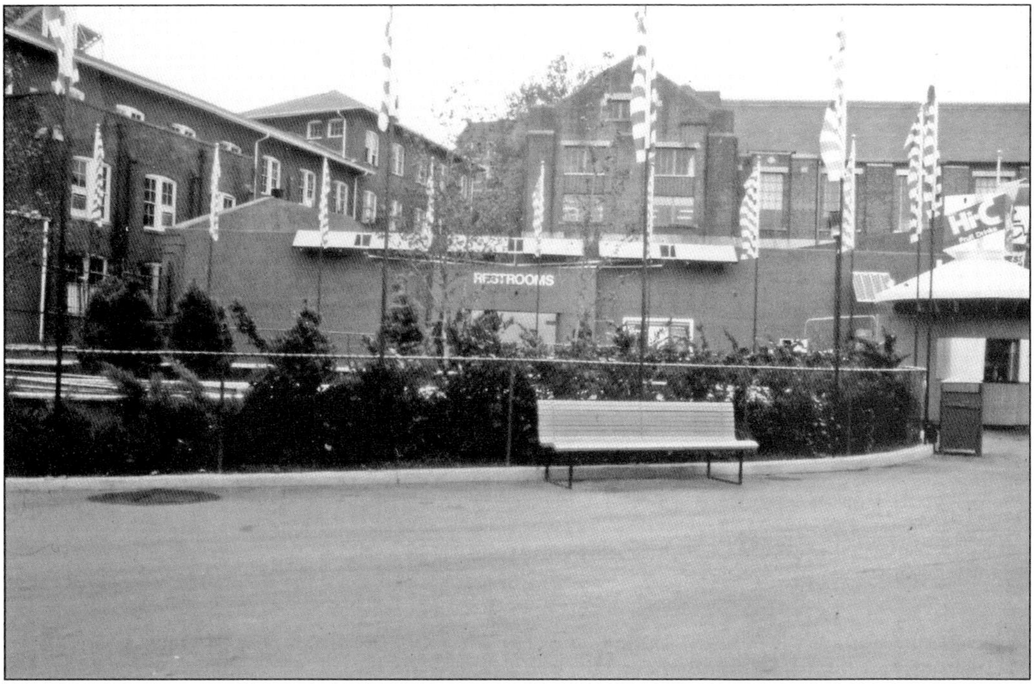

Visitors mainly complained about the lack of restrooms and their locations. Only one was provided near the Fun Fair section of the fair. (Courtesy of Miles Roberts.)

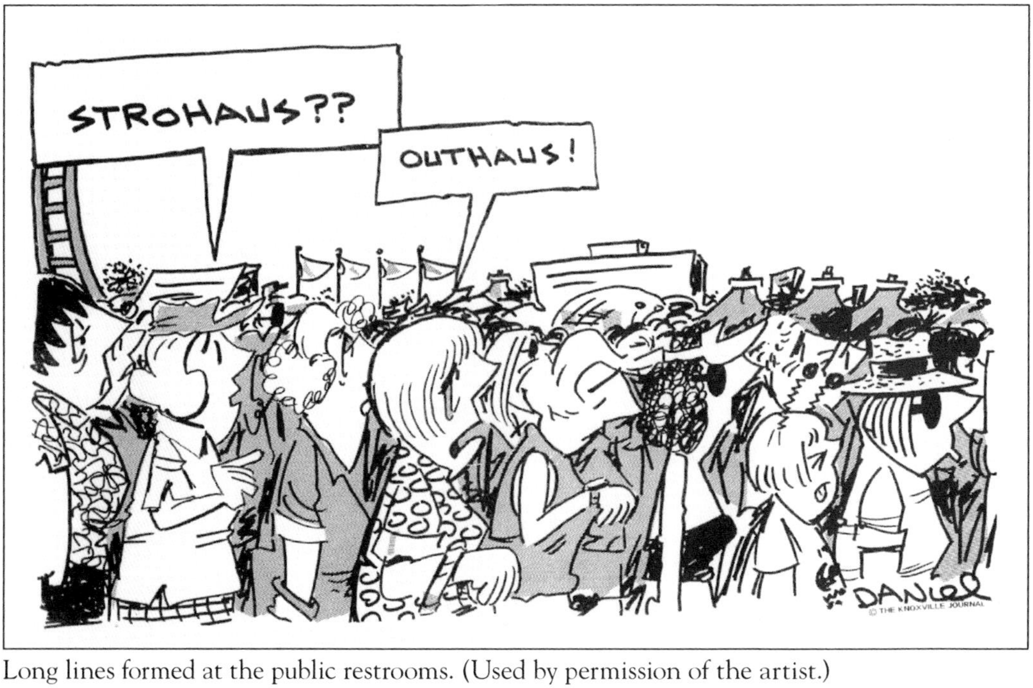

Long lines formed at the public restrooms. (Used by permission of the artist.)

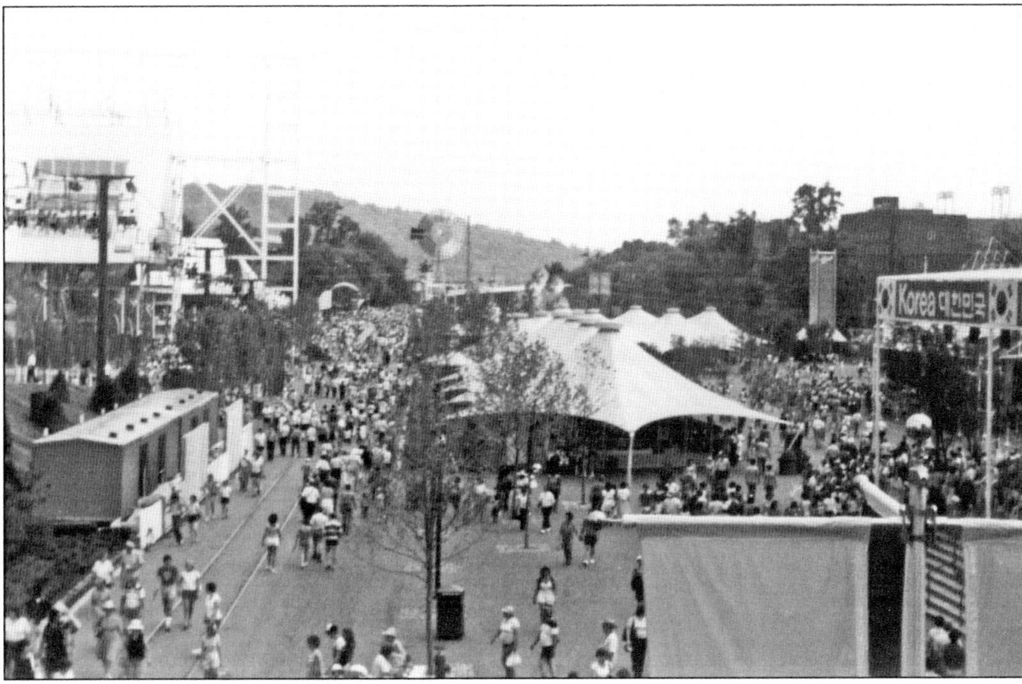

Portable restrooms, installed on the lower fairgrounds by the end of July, helped to alleviate the restroom deficiency. The structures were quickly nicknamed "Jake's Outhouses." (Courtesy of the Prather family.)

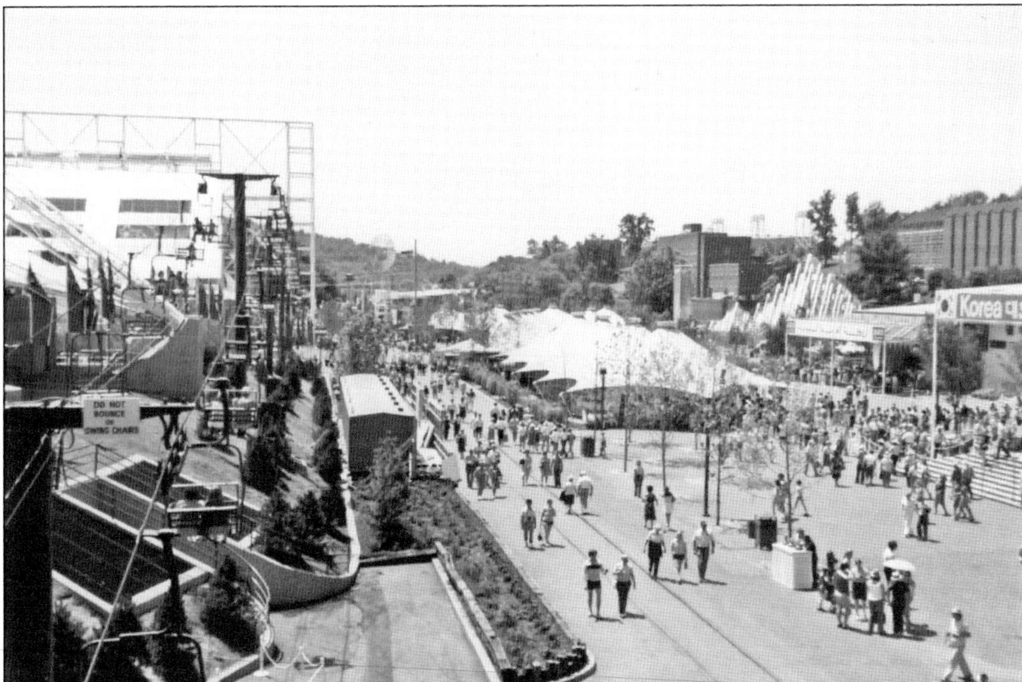

Crowds began to thin as rumors about high prices for souvenirs, lack of adequate restrooms and drinking fountains, and lackluster exhibits spread. (Courtesy of the Prather family.)

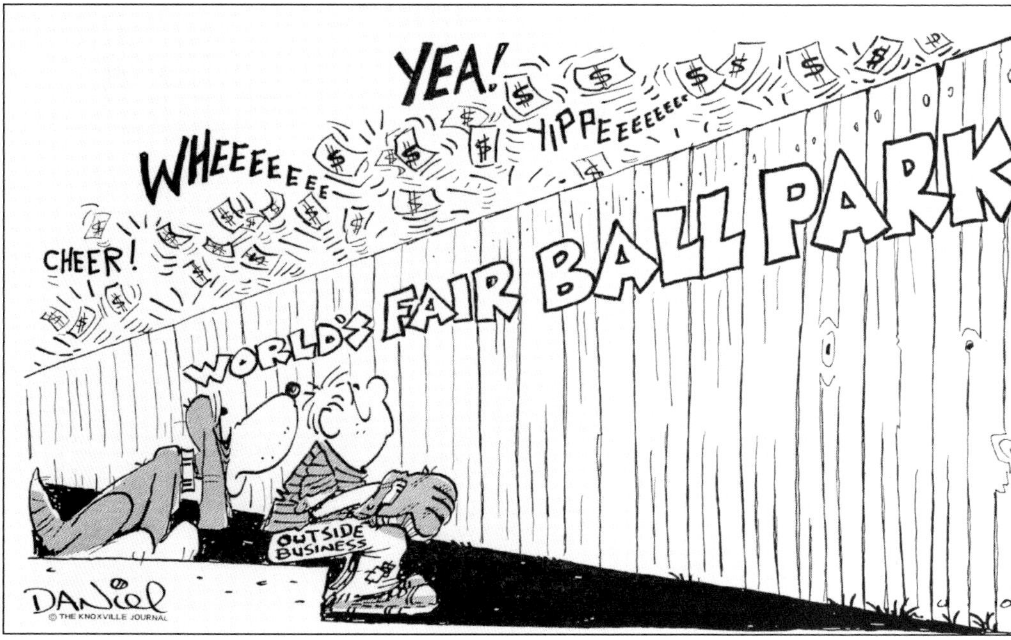

"The only businesses that made any money were those lucky enough to be inside the fairgrounds," explained Don Ault. (Used by permission of the artist.)

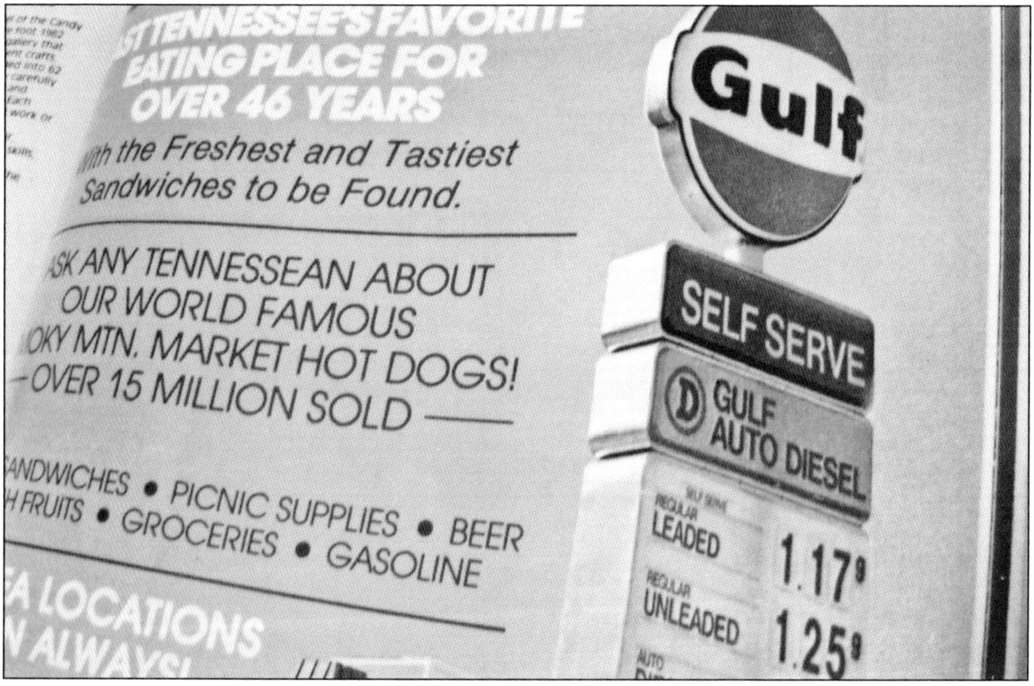

Gas prices per gallon in 1982 were $1.17/9 for leaded and $1.25/9 for unleaded. The Gulf Corporation changed its name to BP for British Petroleum. (Courtesy of KIEE.)

Nine

Entertainment

I studied the lives of great men and famous women, and I found that the men and women who got to the top were those who did the jobs they had in hand with energy and enthusiasm.

—Harry Truman

All entertainment was organized under an "umbrella" named World Festival of Entertainment. Hundreds of musicians, cloggers, square dancers, pop singers, mimes, gospel quartets, jugglers, puppets, jazz bands, and clowns entertained around the clock. There were also symphonies, theaters, operas, ballets, celebrity performances, and championship sports scheduled inside the fairgrounds while others were booked into surrounding venues. There was always something going on, and much of it was included in the price of the ticket to the fair.

The Stokely Folklife Festival featured traditional music, dance, crafts, exhibits, and films as various performers took to the stage daily. Special concerts were held on Wednesday evenings and Sundays with music from such entertainers as Ava Barber, Roberta Peters, Chet Atkins, Peter Nero along with the Knoxville Symphony Orchestra, and regional symphony orchestras and bands.

Guests gathered to watch the daily parades. Led by the Anheuser-Busch Budweiser Beer Wagon with eight Clydesdale horses, the parades included the 1982 World's Fair Marching Band, parade units, a train, high school bands from all across the country, and more.

Over 200 world-famous entertainers performed at the fair, including June Carter Cash and Johnny Cash, Red Skelton, Victor Borge, Jimmie Walker, Helen Cornelius, Bob Hope, Lynn Anderson, Rudolf Nureyev, Glenn Campbell, Jerry Lee Lewis, Ricky Skaggs, Bill Monroe and the Bluegrass Boys, Dinah Shore, Roberta Peters, Porter Wagoner, Leontyne Price, Leonard Rose, Isaac Stern, and Jiri Belohiavek.

Some of the sporting events scheduled for the fair were as follows: the Avon Women's 10K Road Race, Team Murray World Cup BMX Motocross Races, the Athletic Congress Championships, the 1982 World's Fair Baseball Championships, the Marathon Canoe and Kayak Invitational, an International Basketball Tournament, an exhibition game between the New England Patriots and the Pittsburgh Steelers, the National Slow-pitch Conference Championship, the PGA Cup Matches, and the U.S. National Team vs. USSR Swimming Competition.

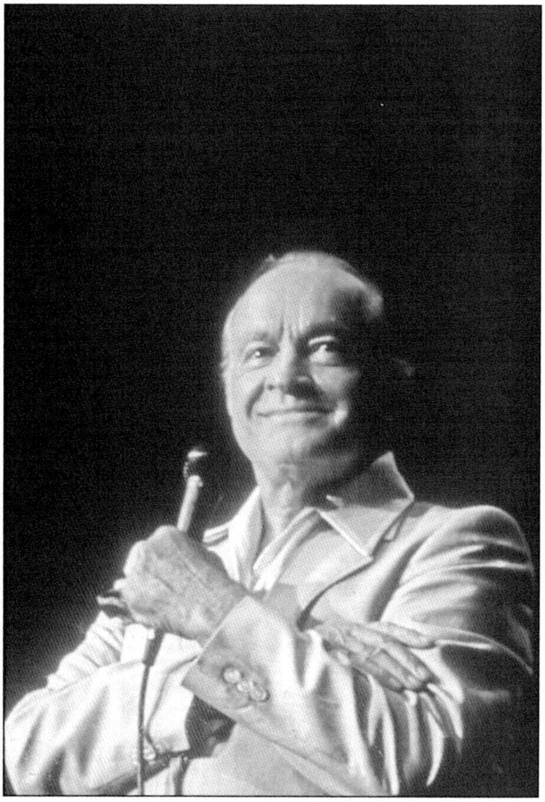

Perhaps the best known entertainer to appear at the 1982 World's Fair was Bob Hope (May 29, 1903–July 27, 2003). Hope appeared on NBC television for 60 years; he was most noted for entertaining the U.S. military troops stationed overseas during each Thanksgiving and Christmas season, beginning in 1948, by leading USO tours. Hope, known for his "one-liner" joke style, thrilled the fairgoers with lines such as: "I planted a garden at my house. I put in seeds, watered them every day, and before long up came a yard full of rabbits." (Courtesy of KIEE.)

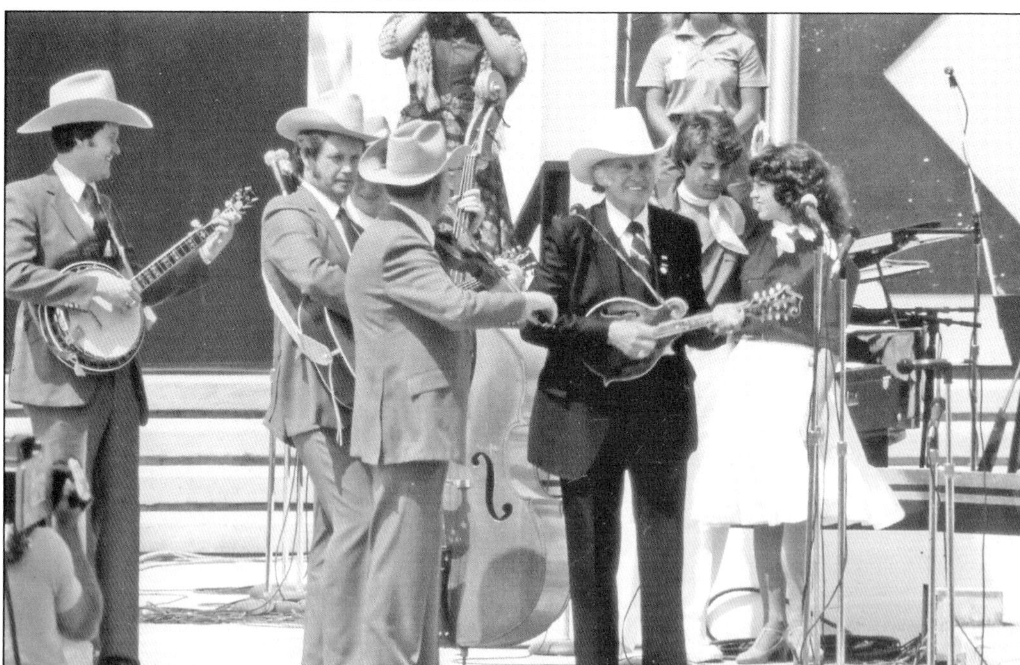

The performance of Bill Monroe (September 13, 1911–September 9, 1996), often called "the father of bluegrass music," is remembered as one of the highlights of the 1982 fair. (Courtesy of KIEE.)

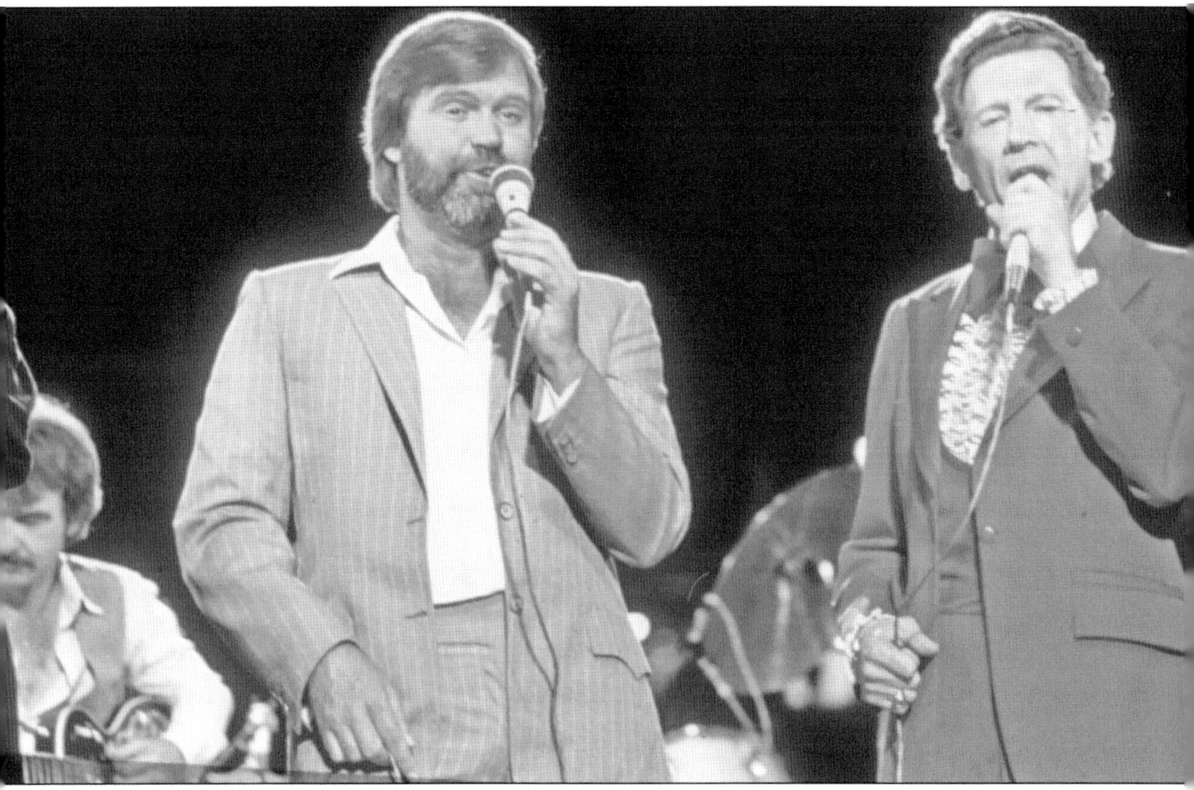

Glen Travis Campbell (born April 22, 1936, in Delight, Arkansas) is a Grammy-winning, Dove Award–winning American country pop singer, guitarist, and occasional actor. He is best known for a series of hit songs he recorded in the 1960s and 1970s, as well as for hosting a television show called *The Glen Campbell Goodtime Hour* on CBS. Some of his most memorable hit songs are "Gentle on My Mind," "By the Time I Get to Phoenix," and "Wichita Lineman." Campbell's largest-selling single was "Rhinestone Cowboy," which sold over two million copies in a matter of months in 1974–1975. Jerry Lee Lewis, perhaps one of the best piano players in the modern music scene, was born to the poor family of Elmo and Mamie Lewis in Ferriday, Louisiana, on September 29, 1935. He began playing piano in his youth with his two cousins, Mickey Gilley and Jimmy Swaggart. His parents mortgaged their farm to buy him a piano. Lewis developed his own style of music, mixing rhythm and blues, boogie woogie, gospel, and country music. Lewis's big hit at the time was "Thirty Years Old and Holding." The audience gave the two singers a standing ovation. (Courtesy of Charlie Brookes.)

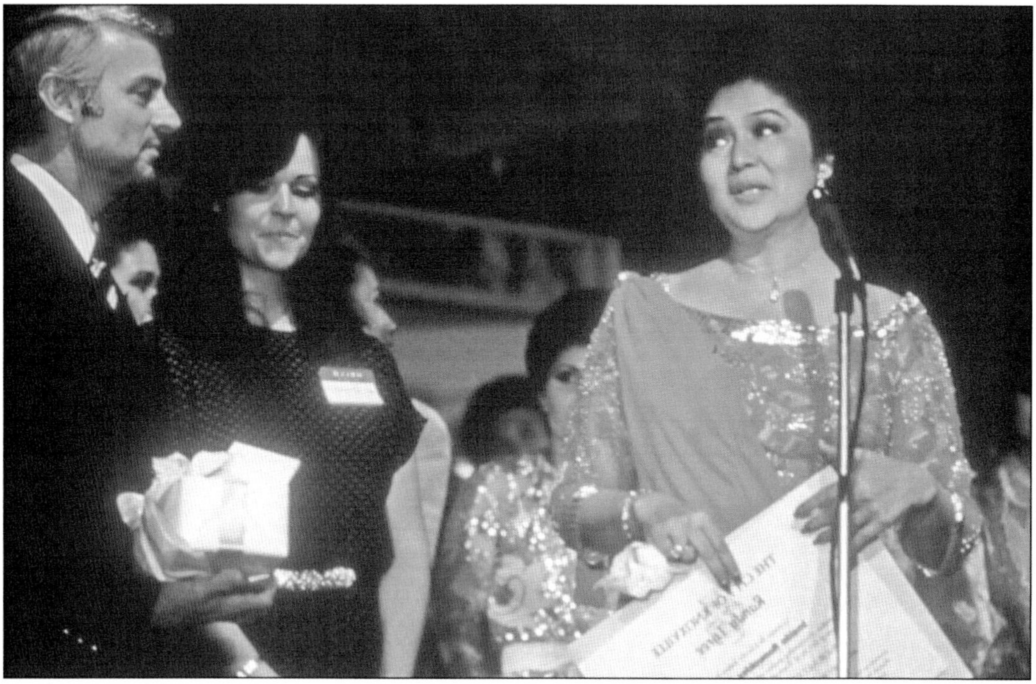

Madame Imelda Marcos, First Lady of the Philippines, visited the World's Fair on two separate occasions. Shown here on her first visit in May, she was given a key to the city by Mayor Randy Tyree and his wife Mary Pat, as she dedicated the Philippine Pavilion. (Courtesy of KIEE.)

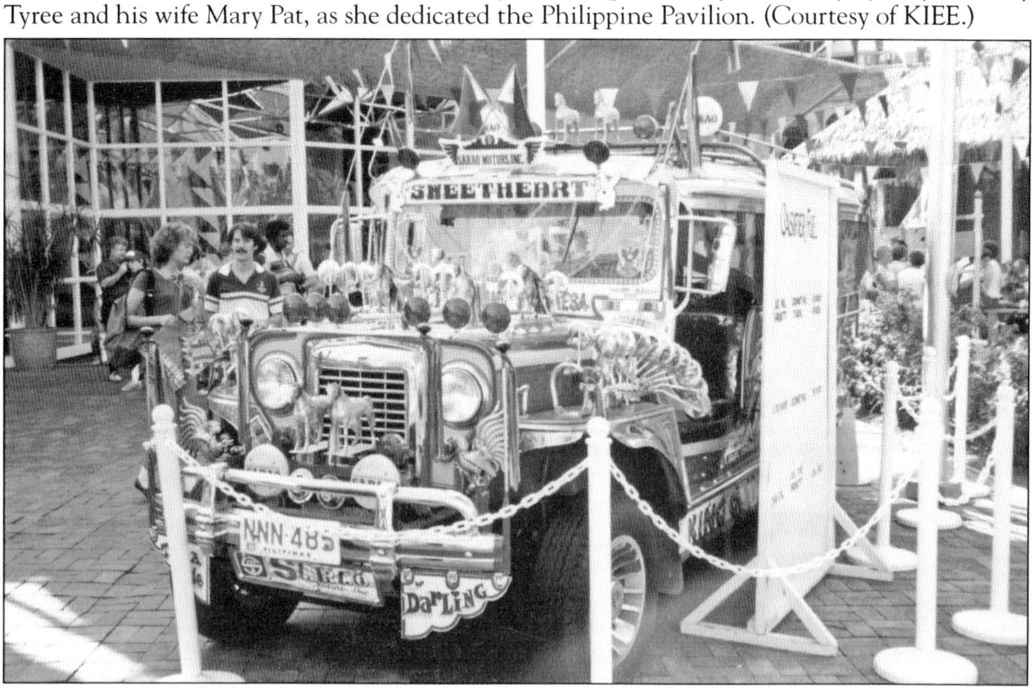

On her second visit to the fair, the First Lady was accompanied by her husband, His Excellency Ferdinand Marcos, the president of the Republic of the Philippines at the time. An overly ornate jeep on display outside the Philippine Pavilion was said to be a personal car for the president and First Lady of the Philippines. (Courtesy of the Prather family.)

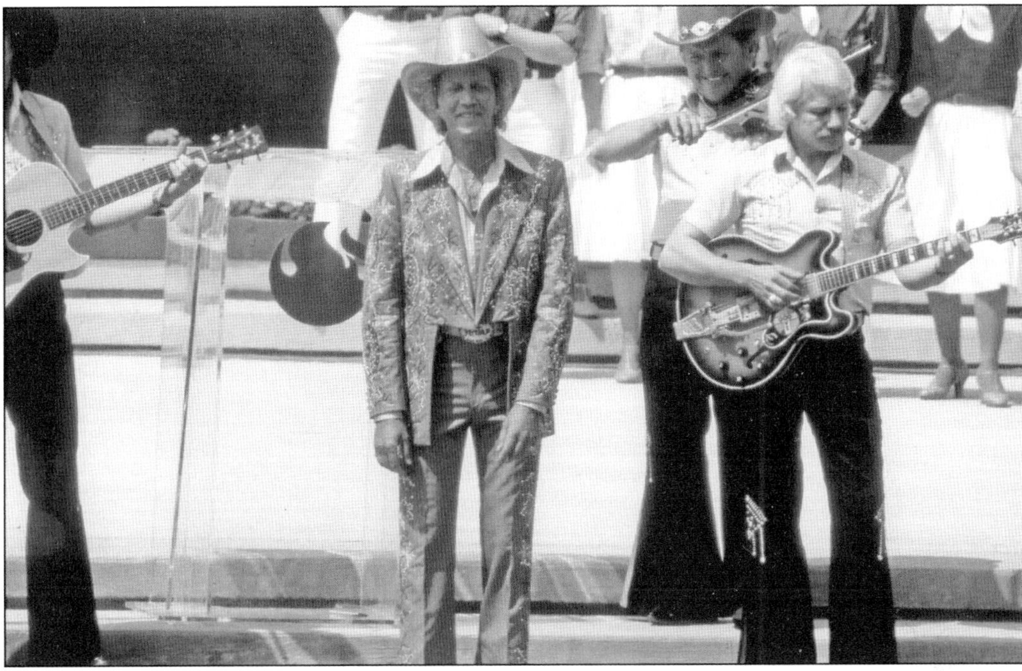

Country music star Porter Wagoner and his band performed during the opening day ceremonies. Wagoner was wearing a lilac-colored, rhinestone-studded suit and a pink shirt. He was definitely a crowd favorite. (Courtesy of Charlie Brookes.)

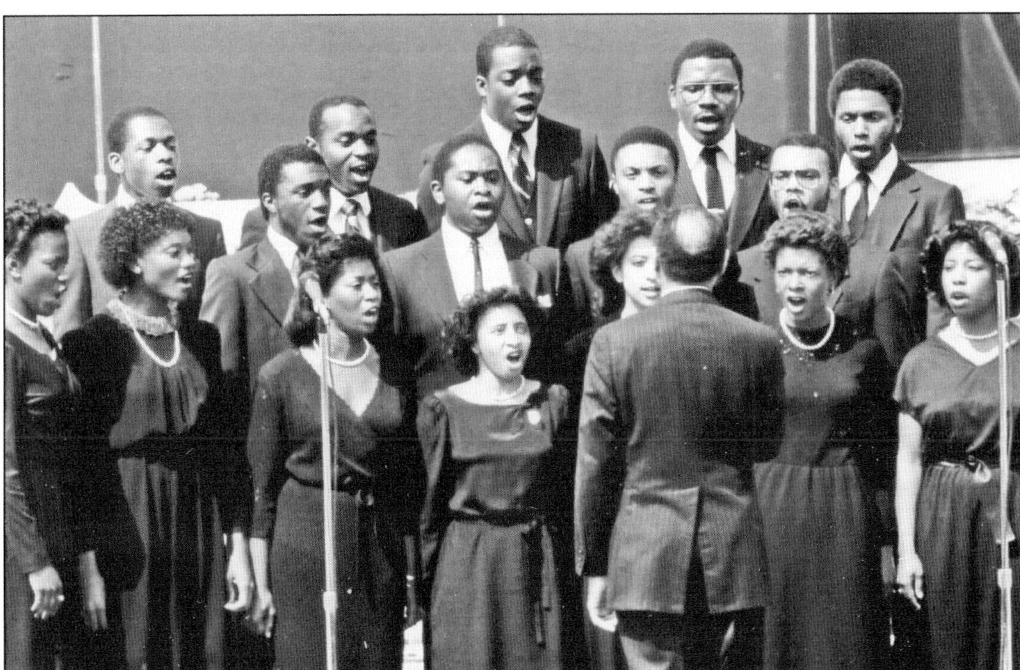

The Fisk Jubilee Singers, an African American a cappella ensemble, traveled from Nashville, Tennessee, to Knoxville to performed "Negro spirituals" at the opening ceremonies. (Courtesy of Charlie Brookes.)

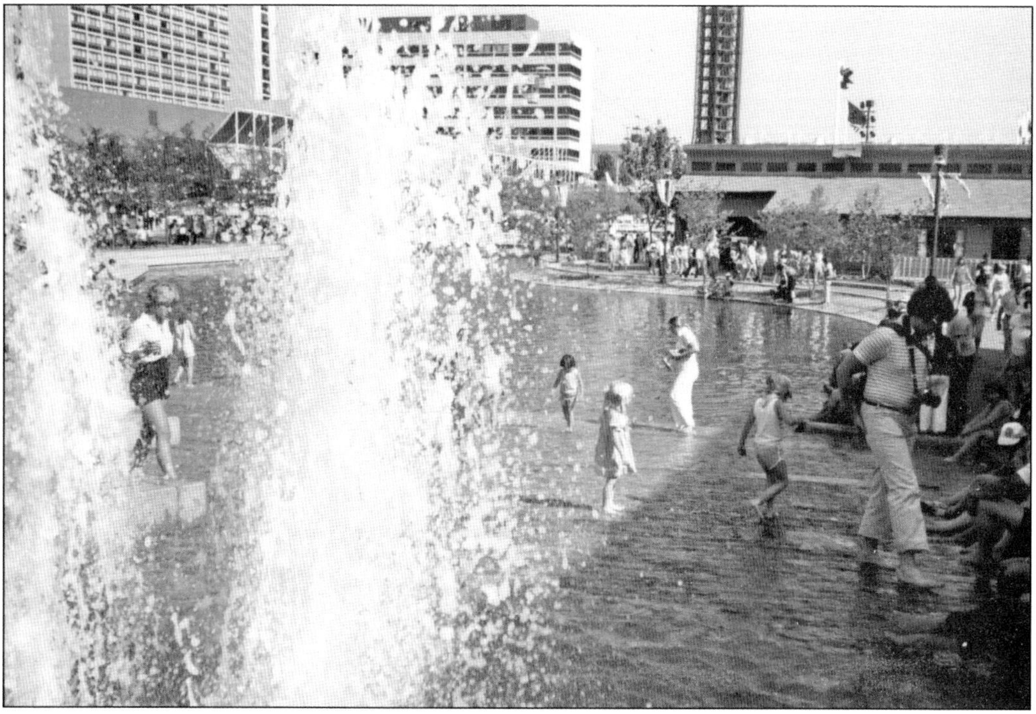

Fairgoers enjoyed splashing in cool waters from the fountains located in the middle of the fairgrounds. These same fountains are in use today and are extremely popular with children. (Courtesy of the Prather family.)

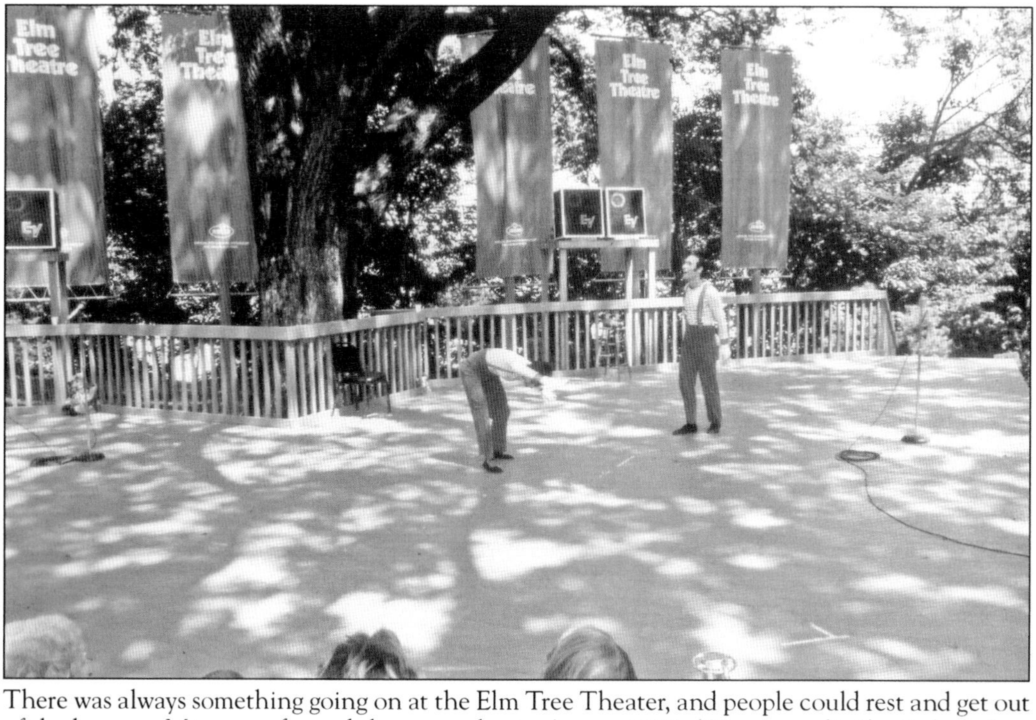

There was always something going on at the Elm Tree Theater, and people could rest and get out of the hot sun. Mimes performed there one day in August 1982. (Courtesy of Miles Roberts.)

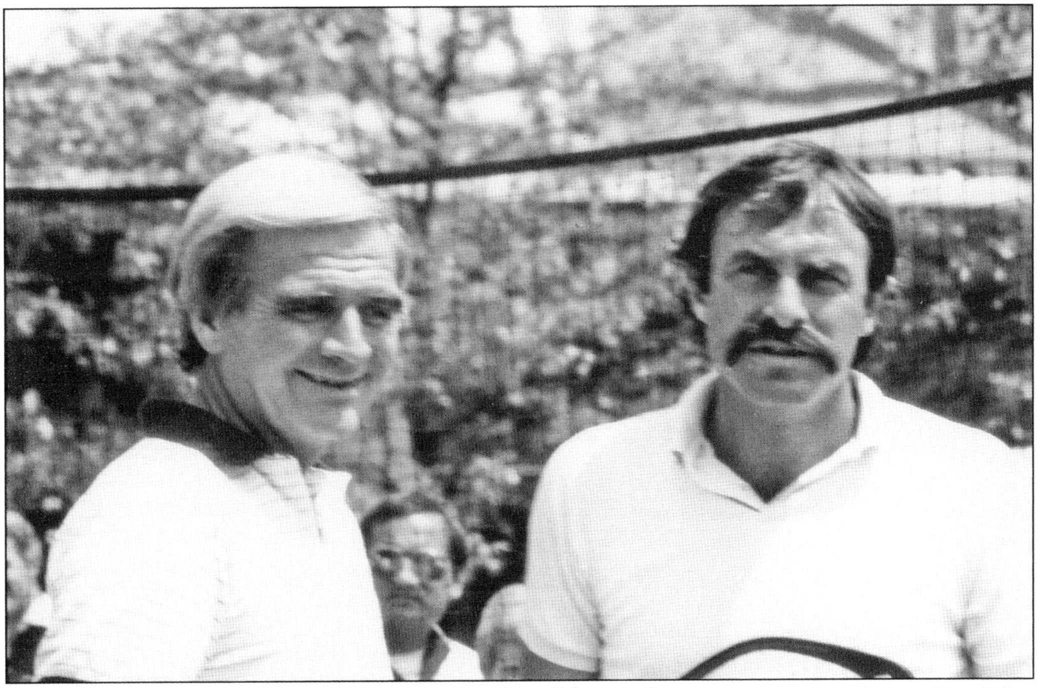

S. H. Roberts, president of KIEE, enjoyed a day of fun with tennis sensation Australian John Newcomb. Newcomb, known for his lightning-fast serves and good looks, was a crowd favorite. (Courtesy of Charles Brookes.)

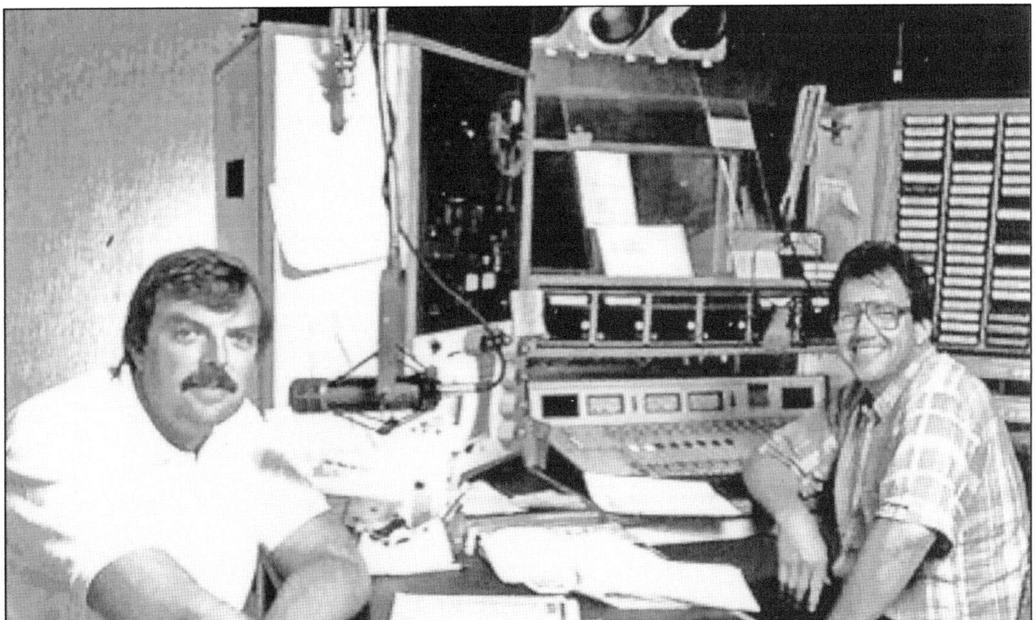

WIVK radio talk show hosts Walker Johnson and Curtis Parham, from the *CP and Walker Show*, broadcast from the fairgrounds for six months. "We had a ball," explained Johnson. "We met everyone from Willie Nelson to Bob Hope. It was a blast." (Courtesy of Walker Johnson.)

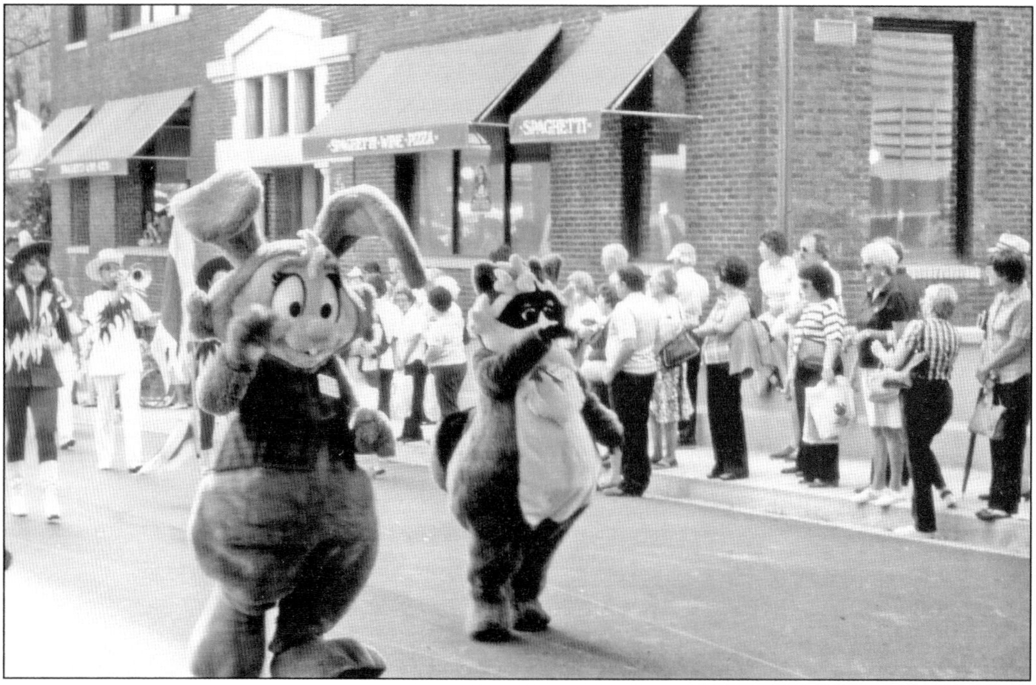

Life-size theme characters marched in the two parades held daily and also strolled through the fairgrounds waving at children and posing for pictures. (Courtesy of Charlie Brookes.)

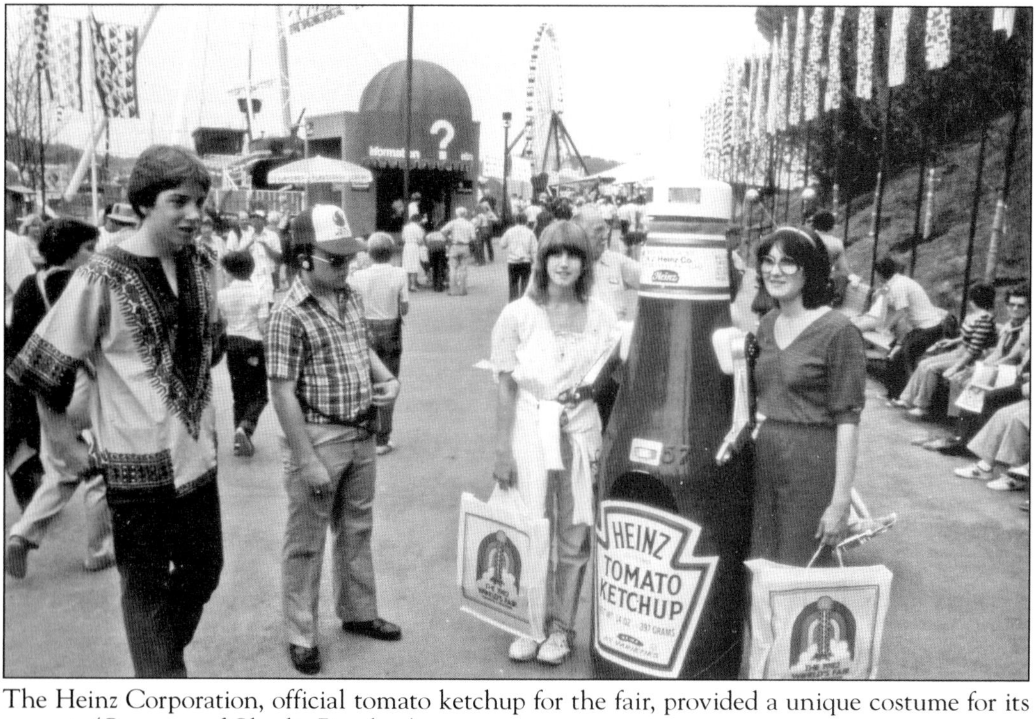

The Heinz Corporation, official tomato ketchup for the fair, provided a unique costume for its mascot. (Courtesy of Charlie Brookes.)

Ten

After the Fair

There is a time for everything, . . . a time to tear down and a time to build, . . . a time to scatter stones and a time to gather them, . . . a time to keep and a time to throw away.

—Ecclesiastes 3: 1–6

In the 26 years since the 1982 World's Fair, Knoxville, Tennessee, has seen many changes. The population has grown; new schools, hospitals, and businesses have been built; and the University of Tennessee has grown in numbers of students while enjoying an ever-expanding campus, as construction of new buildings is a continual process.

The individuals who were the leaders in the Knoxville International Energy Exposition of 1982 slipped back into private life, and some of them have passed away.

C. H. Butcher Jr., former financial magnate who went to prison for bank fraud after his banks collapsed in 1983, died Tuesday, May 1, 2002, at age 64 in a hospital in Georgia, apparently following a fall at his home.

Jake Butcher was arrested in 1983, went to trial, was found guilty of bank fraud, and spent nearly seven years in federal prison. In 2008, Jake Butcher is said to live in Georgia where he works in the used car business or possibly at a truck stop.

Former mayor Randy Tyree practiced law in Knoxville and worked in a variety of other statewide positions. He most recently ran for the office of Knox County sheriff as the Democrat nominee but lost to his Republican challenger, Jimmy Jones.

Jesse Barr also went to prison for bank fraud. After his release, he moved to Oak Ridge, Tennessee, where he lives happily with his wife. He works for a truck dealership.

Immediately after the fair, all individuals, corporations, and countries who kept space at the fair were handed a letter that assigned them a day and time on which they could return to the fair site and remove their exhibits. A few months later, there was a huge sale of "all things World's Fair." Picnic tables, souvenirs, food, uniforms, containers, park benches, posters, staplers, extension cords, and thousands of items were auctioned off for pennies on the dollar. Buildings were torn down and sold as lumber while even nails and tools were sold.

Money from all sales was applied towards the city's debt for the fair. Although it has been suggested the city made $57 from the fair, the debt for the bonds taken out to pay for the fair was paid off in May 2007.

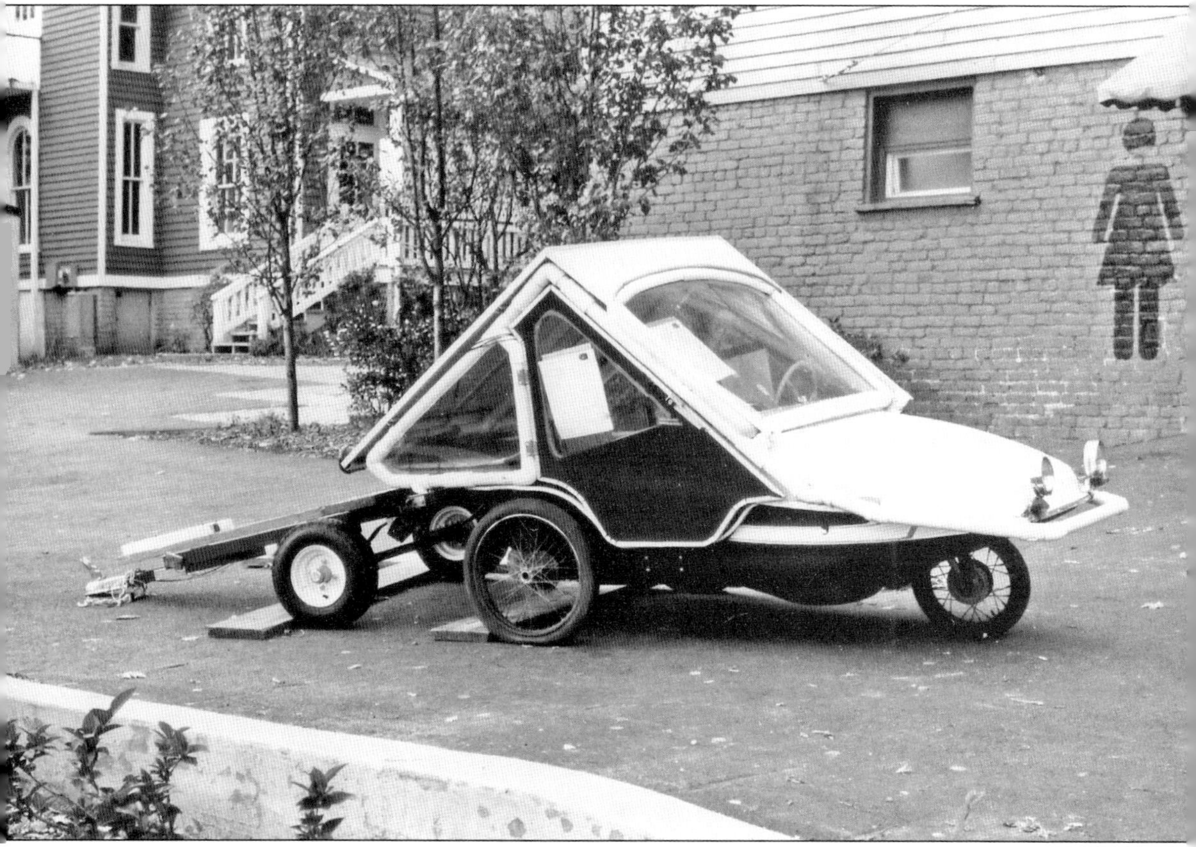

The odd car, which was used to pull floats for the nightly parade, was designed to be an example of transportation for the future. The car was powered by a solar panel located on the back, and seated two people. It was made of lightweight materials such as bicycle tires. After the fair, it was sold at public auction, as were most of the items used in the fair. (Courtesy of Miles Roberts.)

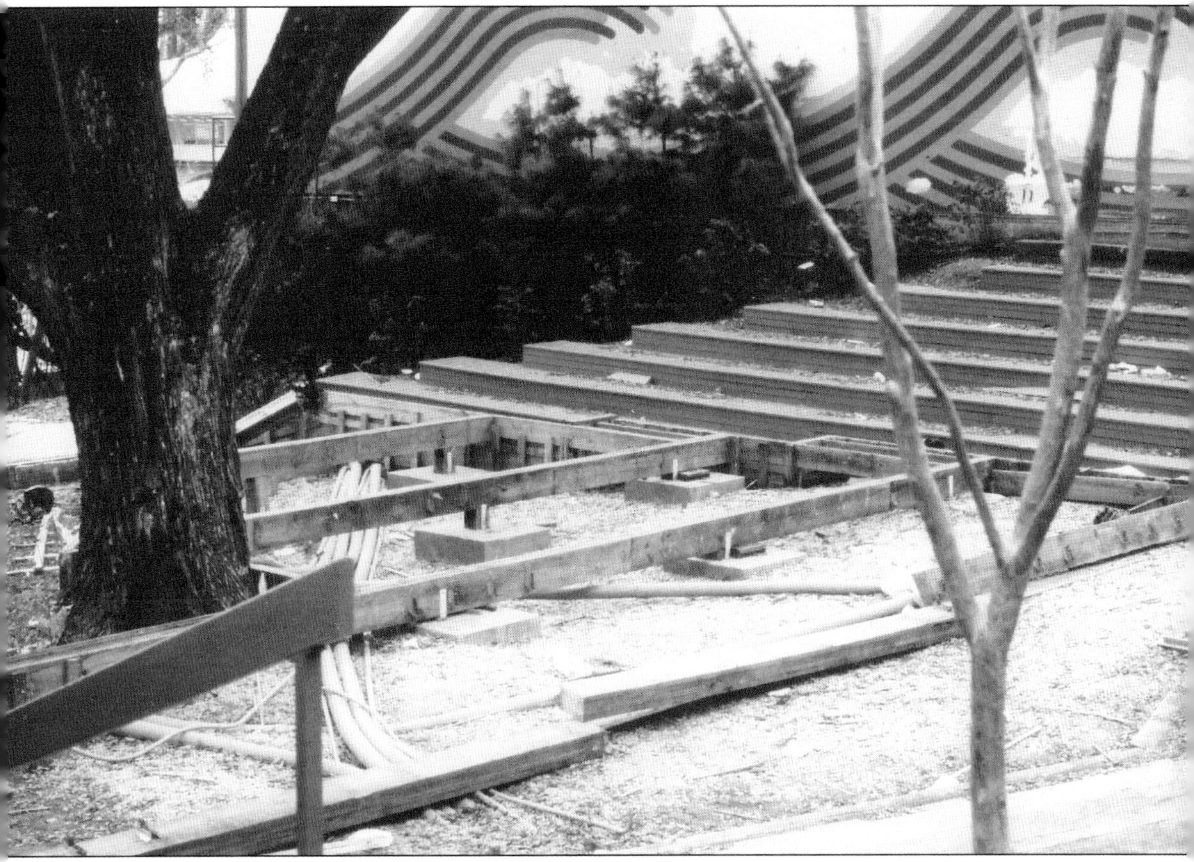

The architects and landscapers who planned the fair were sensitive to the beauty and shade provided by a huge elm tree located on the fairgrounds. They decided to build an outdoor theater under the massive tree and created the Elm Tree Theatre, which was used by a variety of entertainers. When not in use for shows, the theater was used for seating by visitors looking for a place to rest and get out of the hot sun. After the fair, the Elm Tree Theater was dismantled and the lumber was sold in a public auction. Several years later, the elm tree was hit by lightning and split in half. It had to be chopped up and removed. (Courtesy of Charlie Brookes.)

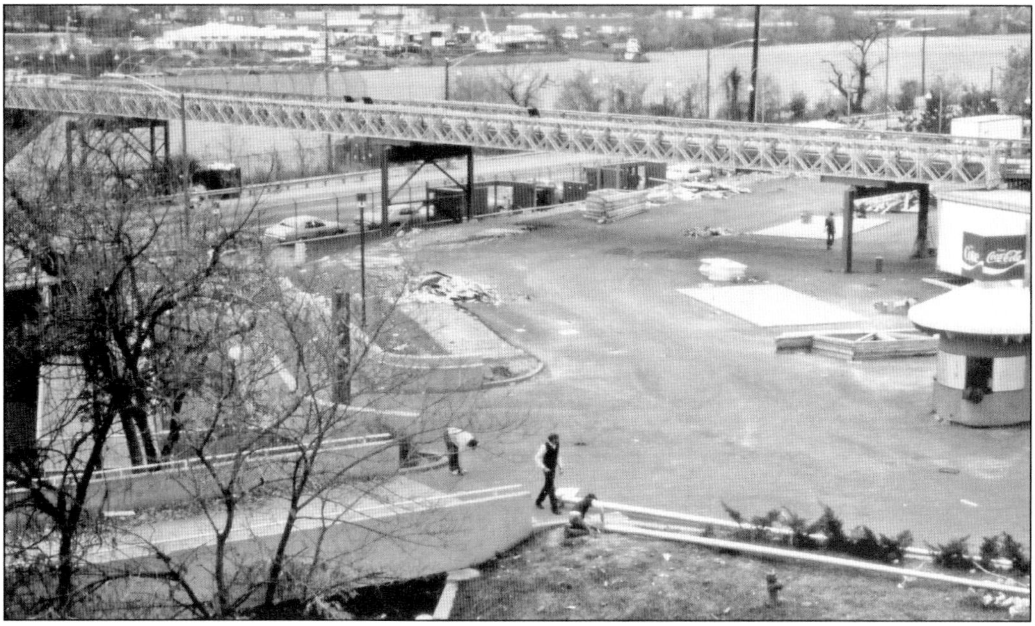

The fairgrounds, once a busy site full of visitors, became a desolate area as buildings and rides were quickly dismantled. The "bucket ride" was sold and reassembled near the Knoxville Zoo for use at a local park. After many years of use, it wore out, became unsafe, and was sent to the scrap heap. The amusement rides were sold or returned to their rental companies. The "largest Ferris Wheel in the world" was taken down and moved on to the next venue. (Courtesy of Miles Roberts.)

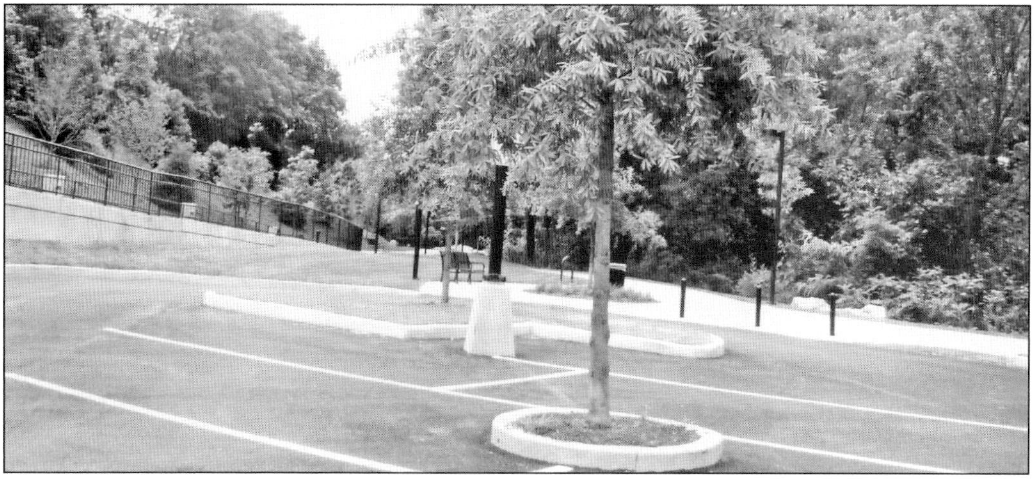

The section of the fairgrounds located across Cumberland Avenue at Eleventh Street, home to the pavilions of Canada and Australia, was turned into a greenway and parking lot. The largest part of the 70-acre fair site is now called World's Fair Park and used as a public park and greenway. Plants, benches, and a walking and bike trail have been added over the years. It is now possible to walk or bicycle on concrete sidewalks from the former fairgrounds, beginning near Clinch Avenue to Neyland Drive at the edge of the campus of the University of Tennessee, through a calm and peaceful setting surrounded by flowers, trees, birds, and squirrels. The bubbling waterfalls, installed in 1982, continue to rise up from the concrete and are extremely popular for children who play in the splashing sprays. There are also several large parking lots on the fair site. (Photograph by Martha Rose Woodward.)

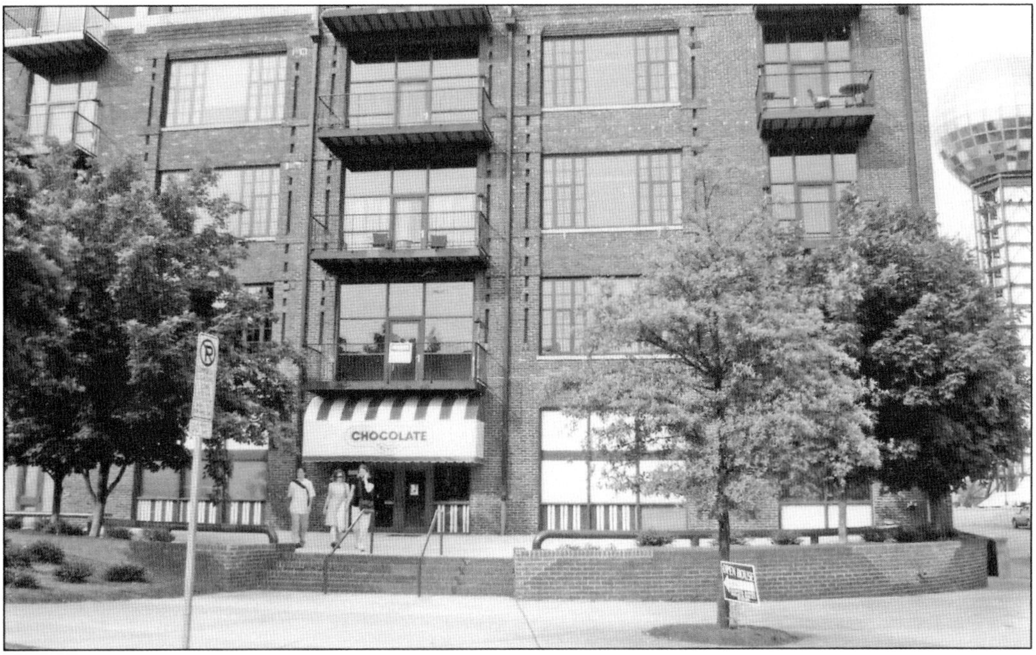

The Candy Factory was sold by the City of Knoxville in a reverse eminent domain case in 2005. It has been converted into upscale condos, which sell for as much as $300,000 each. The Chocolate Candy Company remains on the lower floor and is said to have brisk sales. (Photograph by Martha Rose Woodward.)

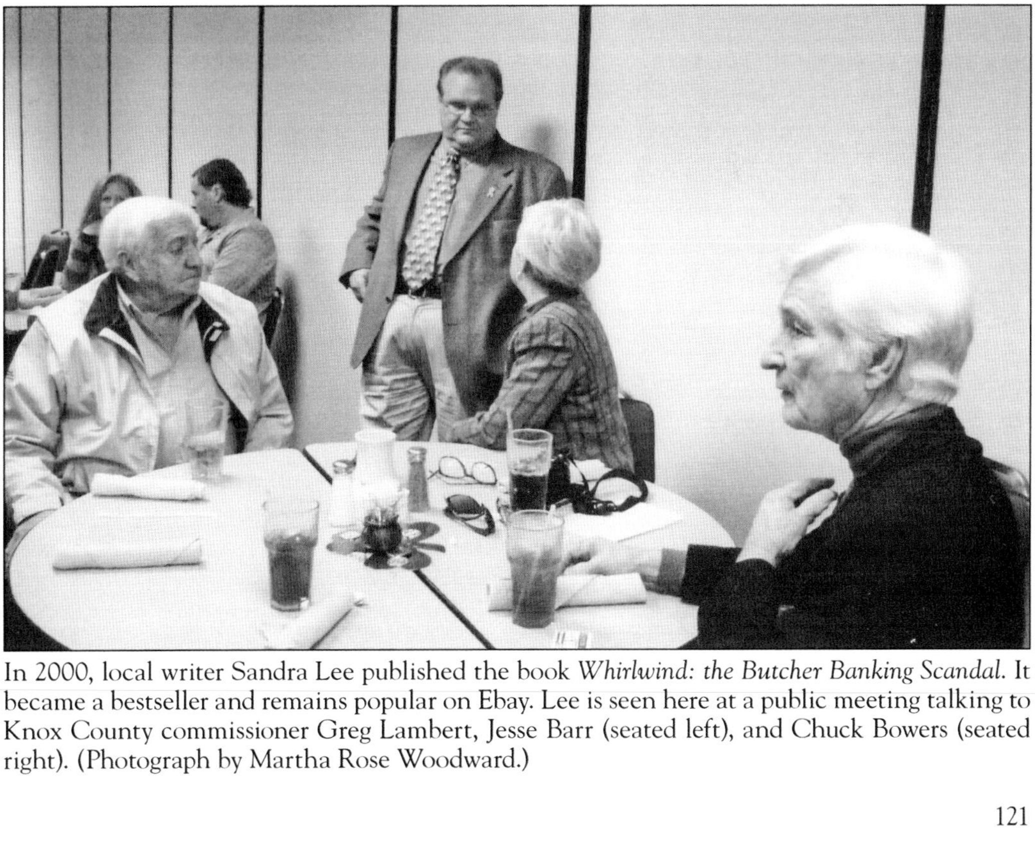

In 2000, local writer Sandra Lee published the book *Whirlwind: the Butcher Banking Scandal.* It became a bestseller and remains popular on Ebay. Lee is seen here at a public meeting talking to Knox County commissioner Greg Lambert, Jesse Barr (seated left), and Chuck Bowers (seated right). (Photograph by Martha Rose Woodward.)

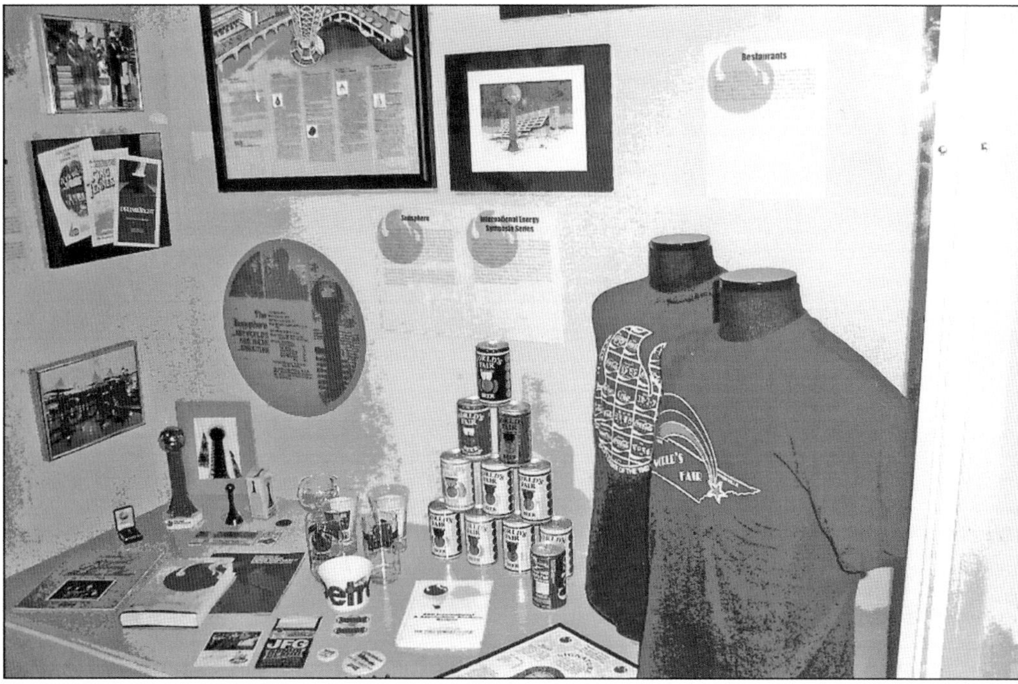

In the summer of 2007, the East Tennessee Historical Society sponsored an exhibit in celebration of the 25th anniversary of the 1982 World's Fair. It was well received by the locals who remember the fair as a time of fun. (Photograph by Martha Rose Woodward.)

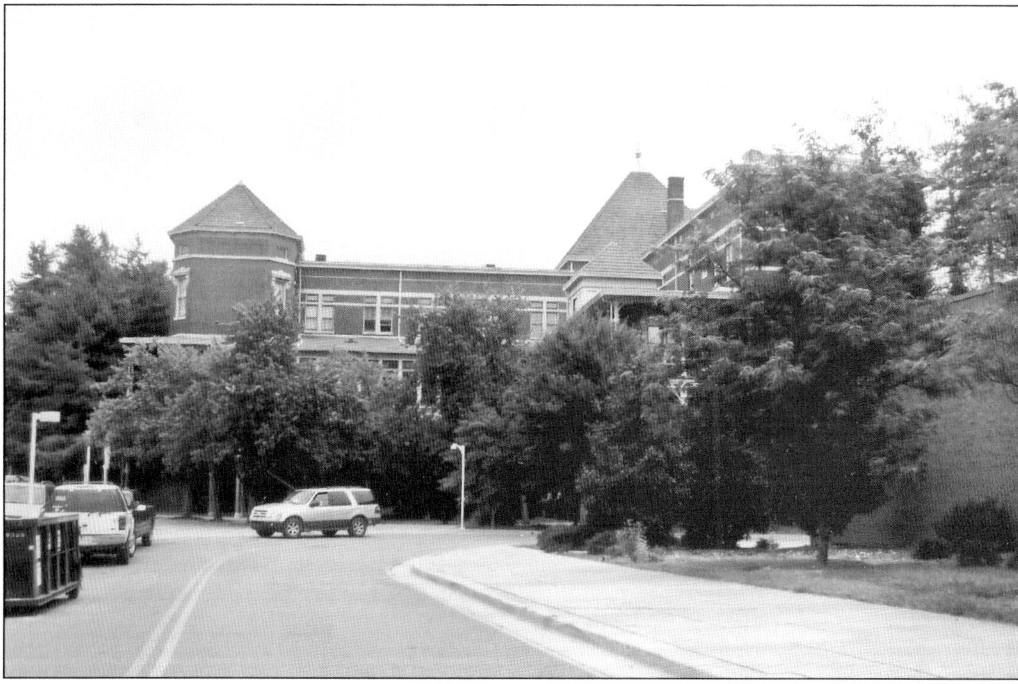

The L&N Railroad Station continues to be well-kept and used for office space and to house a restaurant. It is currently privately owned and is said to be for rent. (Photograph by Martha Rose Woodward.)

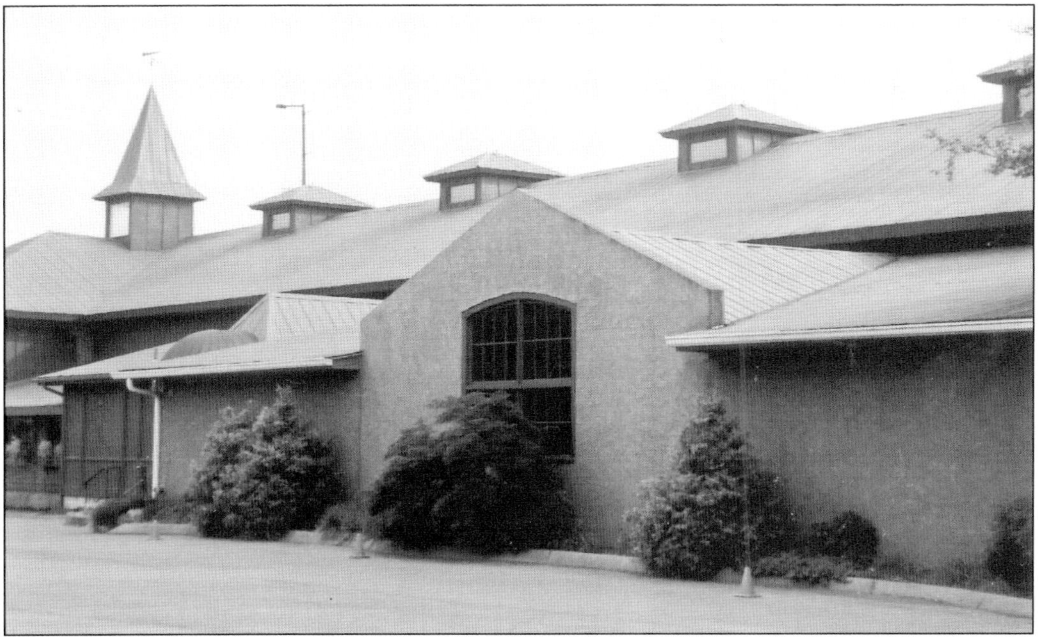

The Foundry is kept in good repair and is frequently used as meeting space. It is owned by Mary Ann Green. (Photograph by Martha Rose Woodward.)

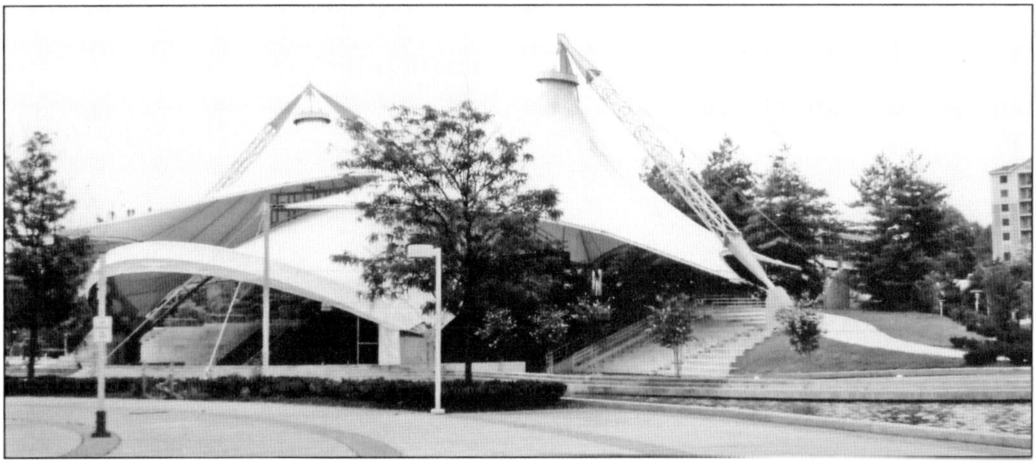

Most of the artificial lake named Waters of the World in 1982, near the Tennessee Amphitheater, has been turned into a sidewalk and walkway. It is no longer possible to rent canoes or paddleboats from this site. As years passed by, no good use could be found for the United States Pavilion. Bruce Schulman, a local historian who closely followed the fair, wrote about the United States Pavilion, "On April 4, 1991, the United States Pavilion was demolished after the city spent millions of dollars trying to find a way to put the odd building to good use. The six-story cantilevered building, which was one of the few permanent buildings on the fair site, had 5000 square feet of solar panels on its roof, enough to supply the energy required for its own ventilation system. The pavilion was built from a $20.8 million Congressional allotment for Federal representation in the exposition. The 86,409 square foot building featured exhibits on the past, present, and future of American energy. There were many proposals for the re-use of the pavilion after the fair, but the building remained deserted and fell into disrepair." (Photograph by Martha Rose Woodward; courtesy of Bruce Schulman.)

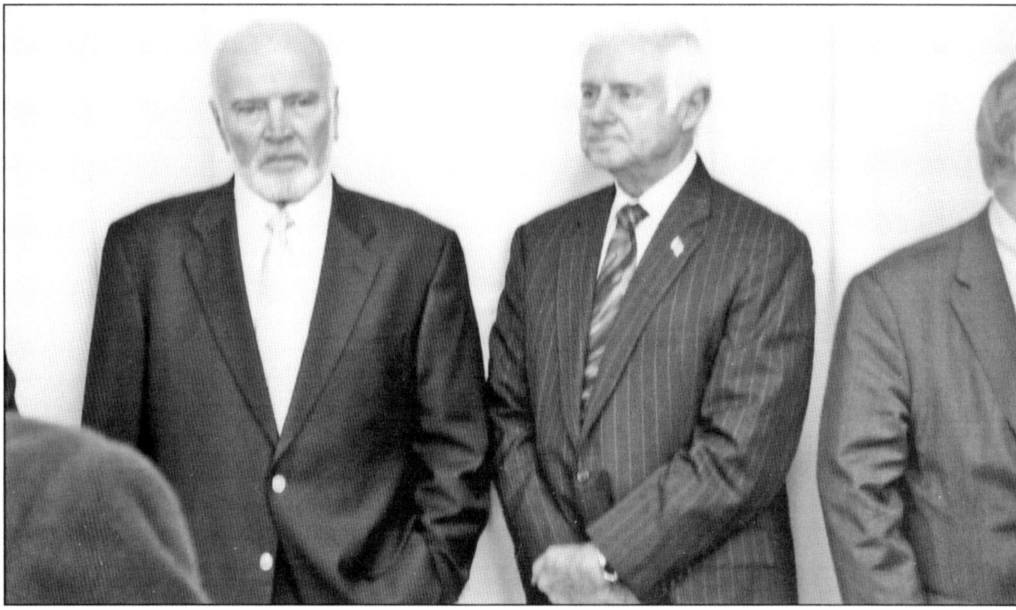

In May 2008, former mayors Kyle Testerman (left) and Randy Tyree (right) spent a pleasant morning sharing memories before they were honored by the City of Knoxville during an unveiling of their portraits, to be hung in a special gallery in the City County Building. In 1992, Tyree was asked to write a summary about the 1982 World's Fair for its 10th anniversary. He wrote, "The World's Fair was an appropriate answer to two major problems, urban renewal and jobs. The principal debt that remains is only a debt of gratitude. The overall downtown area did benefit greatly from the fair. Three new hotels, the Convention/Trade Center, the restoration and development of the City Hall complex, and the Summitt Hill Projects gave Knoxville a much needed economic boost as well as enhancing the aesthetics of the area greatly." (Photograph by Martha Rose Woodward; courtesy of *Knox-News Sentinel.*)

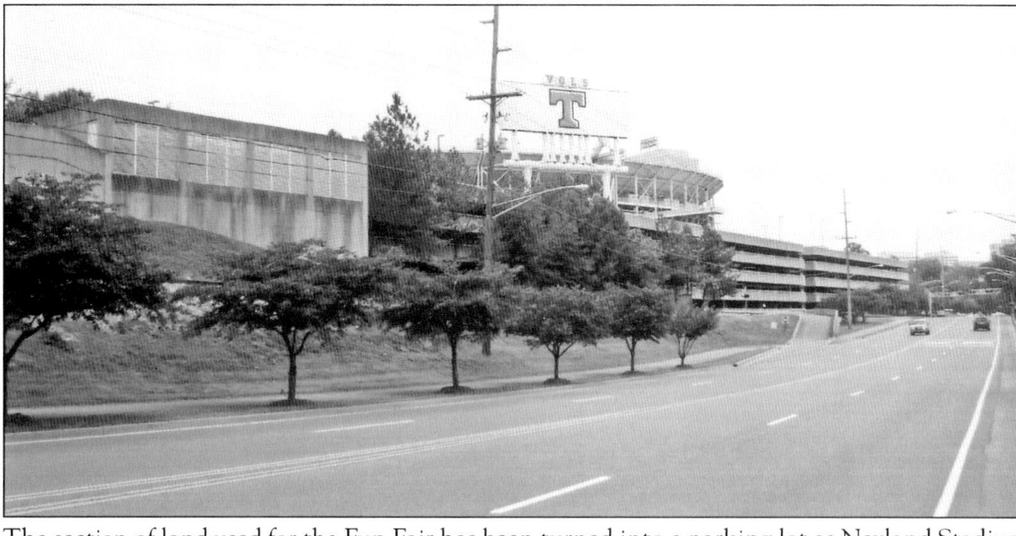

The section of land used for the Fun Fair has been turned into a parking lot as Neyland Stadium has grown in size. Knoxvillians were thrilled in 1998 when the football Vols won 13 and lost 0 games. Coach Phillip Fulmer and quarterback Tee Martin led the team as they won the National Football Championship Game in January 1999. (Photograph by Martha Rose Woodward.)

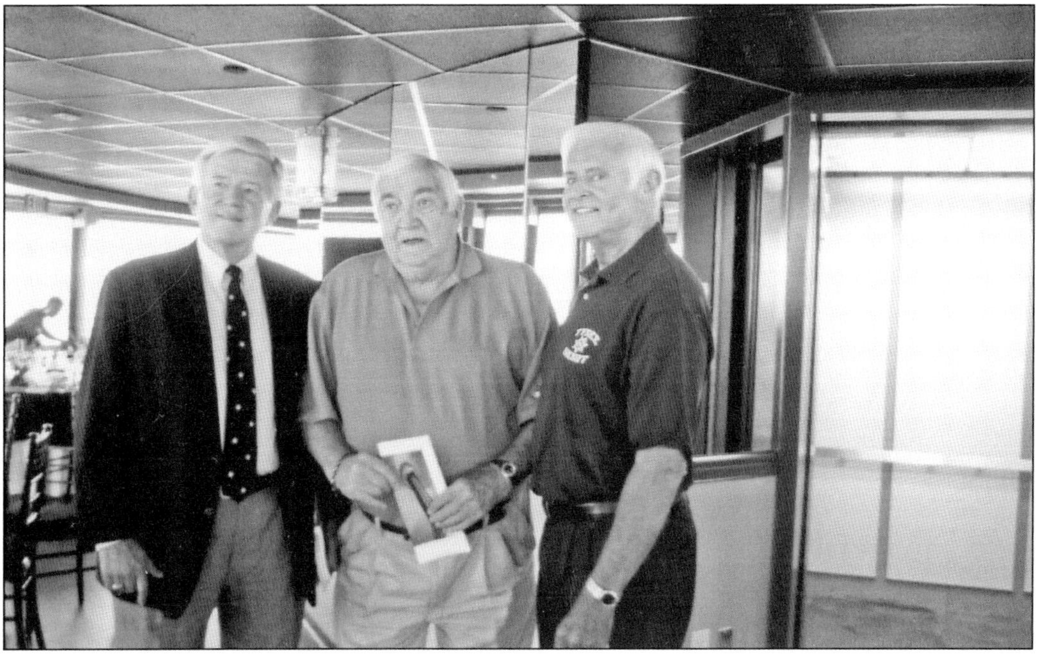

Architect William Denton (left) was invited back to the Sunsphere in July 2008 to give a historic lecture he titled, "The Challenges of Creating a Theme Structure." Jesse Barr (center) and Randy Tyree (right) were on hand for the event, held on the sixth floor of the building, which would not exist if it were not for the tenacity of the three men honored on that day. (Courtesy of Carolyn Buttram.)

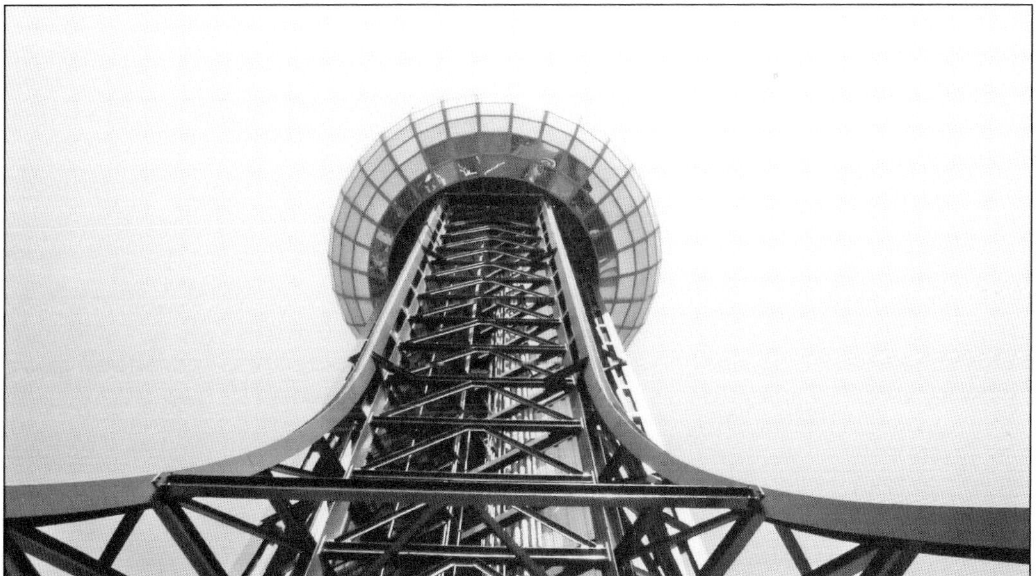

In June 2007, the Sunsphere had been closed to the public for nearly eight years. The community truly wanted the building reopened. In 2006, approximately $1 million was appropriated through the sale of the Candy Factory and three Victorian homes on the fair site. The money was spent on renovations for the Sunsphere. As of the writing of this book in August 2008, one floor of the Sunsphere is open free to the public as an observation deck. (Photograph by Barrett Buie.)

›unsphere architect speaks about project's adversiti

JEREMY Z. YOUNG
ung@TheKnoxvilleJournal.com

An East Tennessee archi- ːt, Bill Denton had the ›portunity, and the over- ıelming task, of design- g Knoxville's most ıown landmark: The nsphere.

He spoke about the sign and construction of is magnificent circular ucture during a lun- eon July 28 hosted by ıoxville World's Fair storian and author ırtha Woodward.

At the time, Denton was ›rking for the ›rristown architectural m, Community ːtonics.

Thinking of a concept Knoxville's Energy po, Denton said, "Since sun is the chief source energy, why not refer- ːe the sun's energy wer."

At first, the sunsphere s to be on the ground. ›wever, relating to the n, plans to hoist the ›rld's first circular struc- e soon came into play.

Denton talked about the difficulty of trying to get someone to provide funding for the structure that could leak, topple over or any number of other possibilities.

"Even though we had investor people," Denton said. "Finding the money was another story.

"We had a lot of fascinating plans that we didn't have the money for," Denton said.

One of those ideas was a rotating restaurant floor that would allow patrons to sit down, have a meal, and complete a revolution of Knoxville's skyline.

"The health department had never heard of a restaurant 200-some feet in the air," Denton said of the proposed restaurant.

Anything larger than a seven-story structure must be made of concrete, zoning regulations state. The planet's first spherical building couldn't be made of concrete.

Somehow, Denton was able to convince the Board

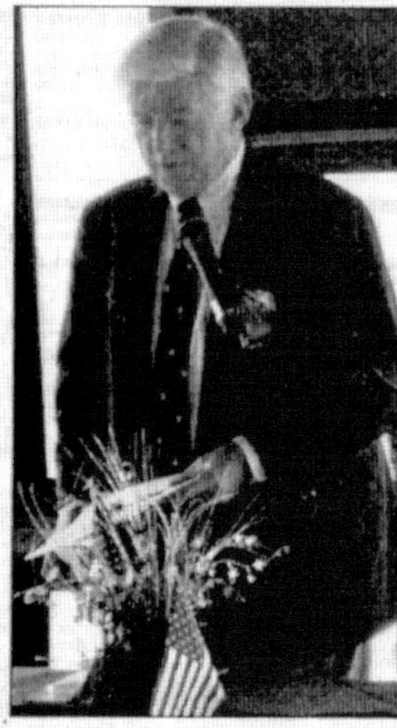

Photo by Jeremy Z. Young

Sunsphere architect Bill Denton came to a luncheon in the structure Jul 28 to talk about the difficulty of building the world's first spherical building.

of Zoning that the Sunsphere was to be a 5-story structure from street level, not ground level, which is highly inconsistent with the actual 260-foot tall structure. Those figures don't make sense for a reason: they don't make sense.

"Thank Jesus," De said. "Without him, r of this would've been sible."

"We had about seve eight problems like tl he said.

Other adversities fa the Sunsphere inclu wet mud core sam over 30 feet deep were taken from the prior to construction.

Denton said Sunsphere is desig much like an old f lamp. The base is larg that if the top shakes, large base can steady structure. He said 30 cubic yards of conc make up the floating l of the Sunsphere.

"One-hundred r winds, an earthquake something like that cc rock the Sunsphere on base like a floor lan Denton said.

Denton reflected bac the construction, rem bering being atop structure during sto and feeling it move.

Twenty-six years after its completion, the Sunsphere was the topic of a historic lecture reported by feature writer Jeremy Young for the *Knoxville Journal* newspaper. Students from Emerald Youth Foundation, staff from the Knox County Sheriff's Office, representatives from the Knoxville Woman's Club, and interested citizens gathered to listen to architect William Denton. The event was sponsored by Knox County commissioners Phil Ballard and Amy Broyles, Sheriff Jimmy Jones, and state senator Tim Burchett. Douglas Young was the master of ceremonies; Barrett Buie provided logistical support and videotaped the event for the television program *Homespun Hobbies*, which airs on Community Television of Knoxville (www.ctvknox.org).

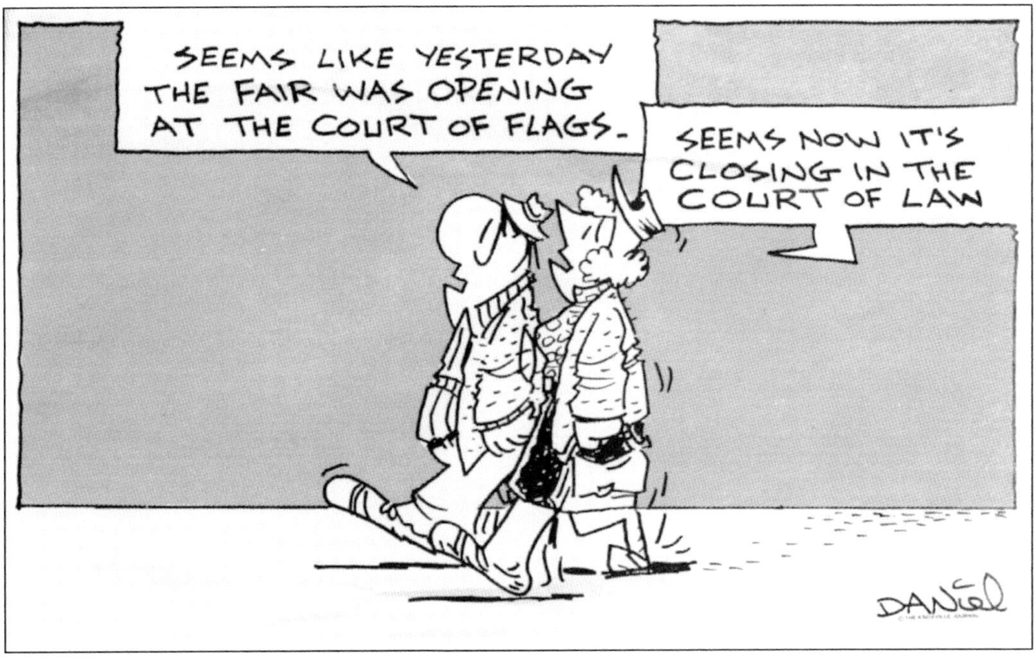

The fair was marred with scandals; however, it was a great event. Local political cartoonist Charles Daniels says it best with his salutes to Expo '82. (Both used by permission of the artist.)

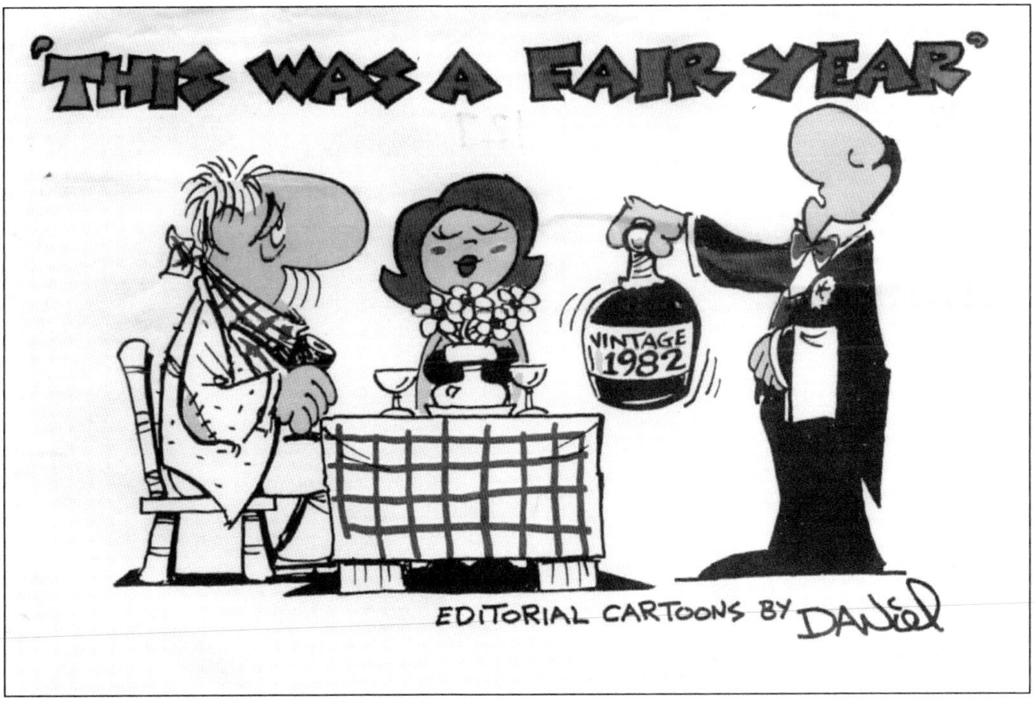